ALLEY-OOP
TO ALIYAH

AFRICAN AMERICAN HOOPSTERS
IN THE HOLY LAND

DAVID A. GOLDSTEIN

Skyhorse Publishing

Skyhorse Publishing books may be purchased in bulk at special discounts for sales promotion, corporate gifts, fund-raising, or educational purposes. Special editions can also be created to specifications. For details, contact the Special Sales Department, Skyhorse Publishing, 307 West 36th Street, 11th Floor, New York, NY 10018 or info@skyhorsepublishing.com.

Skyhorse® and Skyhorse Publishing® are registered trademarks of Skyhorse Publishing, Inc.®, a Delaware corporation.

Visit our website at www.skyhorsepublishing.com.

10 9 8 7 6 5 4 3 2 1

Library of Congress Cataloging-in-Publication Data is available on file.

Cover design by Tom Lau

Cover photo © Seffi Magriso /Euroleague Basketball /Getty Images

Print ISBN: 978-1-5107-2479-2

Ebook ISBN: 978-1-5107-2481-5

Printed in the United States of America

To my family

CONTENTS

PREFACE

THE CONCEPT FOR *ALLEY-OOP TO Aliyah: African American Hoopsters in the Holy Land* originated in the most unlikely of places—an assisted living residence for seniors in Jerusalem. It was May 2007, and my brother and I were visiting my maternal grandparents who had invited some of their friends over to drink coffee, eat dessert, and swap stories about their respective grandkids. The guests—all women well into their eighties—displayed a polite interest in my grandmother's proud description of our careers, but the conversation took a distinct and serendipitous turn when my grandmother mentioned that we were from Toronto.

"Ohhh, Toronto—Anthony Parker!" the octogenarian ladies exclaimed. Parker, an African American basketball player from Illinois, had chosen to sign with the Toronto Raptors following five successful years playing in Israel and they were beyond excited that we were from his new adopted hometown. "*Eizeh motek!*" they exclaimed, Hebrew for "What a sweetie!" They also characterized him as "*be'emet mentsch!*"—Hebrew and Yiddish for "truly an honorable man!"

I was stunned by the reaction. It was not news to me that Maccabi Tel Aviv, Parker's former team, was a European powerhouse and Israel had its own domestic professional league. I also knew that, similar to other international basketball leagues, some of the players in Israel were African American expats. But I had no sense that the current city of residence of a prior Israeli league basketball player would be common knowledge among a group of elderly ladies in a religious neighborhood of Jerusalem. That Anthony Parker, beyond being familiar to these women, was beloved by them, was equally unexpected. If such is the knowledge of, and passion for, an African American basketball player who once lived in Israel in *this* group, what might that reflect for the rest of the country? My curiosity—about basketball in Israel, generally, and the experience and impact of African American players there specifically—was piqued.

By the time I boarded my flight home, I had printouts of enough Israeli basketball articles to keep me busy for the entirety of the twelve-hour trip. And so began what would ultimately become a decade-long process of research and writing, culminating in this book. Intrigued by what I'd discovered and hungry to learn more, I connected with basketball contacts I'd developed in the United States and Canada, and cold-called numerous others. In all, I conducted interviews—detailed, deeply personal, often funny, and always interesting—with more than forty people. I spoke with some individuals repeatedly over the years. At face value, the request was simple: open up to a random outsider you knew nothing about for a project whose outcome was uncertain. The players, and at times their wives and children, allowed me into their lives and entrusted me with their personal narratives—a responsibility and privilege that I have endeavored to treat with the utmost respect and gratitude. My role in all of this was to research, read, and write. The essence of this book, however, is based entirely on a phenomenon that captured my imagination and warmed my heart.

Alley-Oop to Aliyah has come a long way since that afternoon in Jerusalem, and I'm thrilled to share with you the final product. Enjoy!

David A. Goldstein
August 2017

ACKNOWLEDGMENTS

ALLEY-OOP TO ALIYAH: AFRICAN AMERICAN Hoopsters in the Holy Land has been a thoroughly enjoyable team effort. For more than a decade, I have been reaching out to, meeting with, interviewing, and collaborating with dozens of amazing people, many of whom started out as strangers. The response has been overwhelmingly positive, accommodating, helpful—and often moving. To everyone mentioned below and the many others who have helped shape this idea into a reality, I am deeply grateful.

My two editors, Janet Spencer King of Spencer King Author Services and Byron Laursen of Write on the Range, have been fantastic to work with—their revisions and suggestions were invaluable in improving the book's narrative flow. I am grateful to my mentor, colleague, and friend Gord Kirke for all of his support, wisdom, and encouragement. Stephen Selznick provided helpful and practical advice on all intellectual property-related matters. Special thanks to Professor Pam Harkins, who taught me African American studies at Northwestern University and opened my mind to questions, concepts, and issues that shaped this book in many ways.

Once the immense scope of the impact of African American basketball players in Israel came to my attention, I was instantly certain that it merited proper chronicling. As one might expect, it took some special people with forward vision to similarly recognize the value and importance of pursuing this opportunity with me. I am forever indebted to my literary agent, Sam Fleishman of Literary Artists Representatives, for taking a chance on a project that did not check any traditional boxes or fit into a customary book classification. Sam was an unflappable and relentless advocate for *Alley-Oop to Aliyah*, eventually finding the perfect publisher and supporting me with sage guidance and advice throughout the process. Skyhorse Publishing is known for being an author-friendly company that relishes working on an "eclectic and maverick" list of titles. Like Sam, they took a courageous chance on me and on this topic. They have an outstanding reputation and my experience with them supports all the accolades and praise they are receiving. To Ken Samelson, Madeleine Ball, Emmie Twombly, and everyone else at Skyhorse, thank you for seeing in my manuscript a book worth publishing.

When taking on a project of this magnitude, it's wise to stand on the shoulders of giants. My research was aided by the tremendous writing that has already been done on the subject of basketball in Israel and sports in the country more generally. Specifically, the work of the following writers was invaluable: Yarone Arbel, Amir Bogen, Yarin Cohen, Dr. Yair Galily, Allon Sinai, and Alexander Wolff. I am also indebted to the agents, team executives, journalists, and others who connected, introduced, facilitated, and enabled my interviews with more than forty sources. In particular I would like to thank Jim LaBumbard and the Toronto Raptors media relations department, Nitzan Ferraro of Maccabi Tel Aviv, Dan Shoshani of Hapoel Jerusalem, Andrew Wilson of Maccabi Haifa, Daniel Ben Tal, Sean Kennedy, Doug Neustadt, and everyone at Priority Sports, for their cooperation and assistance. For providing instrumental context and unique, candid viewpoints regarding basketball in Israel, I would like to thank Mickey Berkowitz, Tal Brody, Omri Casspi, Amir Gissin, Rabbi Yaakov Gloiberman, Allan Houston, Bernie Lee, Shimon Mizrahi, Makhtar N'Diaye, Simmy Reguer, Jeffrey Rosen, and Shmulik Zysman.

This book could not have been written without the bottomless reservoir of support I received from my parents, Sol and Ruhama, and my older brother, Ben. They read and commented on the manuscript countless times, and they provided enthusiastic encouragement and validation alongside important constructive critique during the lengthy process from conceptualization to publication. Special thanks to Ben for coming up with the title of this book. After years of unsuccessfully trying to think of the ideal title, I turned to Ben, who has a knack for this sort of thing. I literally had not had time to grab a pen and paper to jot down his ideas when he had offered up *Alley-Oop to Aliyah*. But for that efficient brainstorming session, this book may have retained its working title, "Nonfiction book about African American basketball players in Israel"!

Of course, the heart of this book is made up of the words and perspectives of the players themselves—African American hoopsters whose basketball journeys brought them to Israel, of all places. When I, a Jewish, Canadian, non-athlete, came knocking on your door offering to share your story, you welcomed me and trusted me. I deeply and sincerely hope that I have honored that trust and openness. To the following individuals, I cannot thank you enough for sharing your stories, which breathed life and legitimacy into this book. Kudos to you for your collective narration: Gene Banks, Maceo Baston, David Blu, Mark Brisker, Stanley Brundy, Rodney Buford, Will Bynum, Fred Campbell (and his son, Toi), Cory Carr, Alysha Clark, Ramon Clemente, Joe Dawson, Simone Edwards, D'or Fischer, Marcus Fizer, Brandon Hunter, Pooh Jeter, Andrew Kennedy, Sylven Landesberg, Roger Mason Jr., Vidal Massiah, Carl Neverson, Jeremy Pargo (whose image adorns the cover of the book), Anthony Parker, Jia Perkins, Aulcie Perry, Jeron Roberts, Derrick Sharp, Willie Sims, Deon Thomas (and his wife, Dafna, and their daughters, Gabrielle and Liel), Alex Tyus, Chris Watson, and Jitim Young. I hope that the publication of this book is just the first stage of the telling of each of your compelling and unique stories.

Finally, to you the reader, thank you for your interest and for helping me realize my dream of bringing this remarkable story, and the mini-stories of which it is comprised, to a broader audience.

1

IN THE BEGINNING

PICTURE A MAN, AN AFRICAN American, in his mid-sixties. He's tall, *basketball* tall, standing 6-foot-10. He used to play the game—no, not in the NBA, though he was a star in high school and college and after that he bounced around in the minor leagues. Born into a Baptist family in Newark, New Jersey, he remains a man of faith. And it's a good thing he does, having had to battle his way through drug abuse, a prison stint, and, more recently, a troublesome aorta that almost killed him. Like many athletes, he retired in the town where he achieved his greatest sporting glory. From time to time he goes to watch games at the old gym, his slower, more deliberate gait belying the graceful strides and springing leaps with which he once brought the crowd to its feet. The fans still recognize him of course, even the younger ones. They call his name and share stories with him and one another about all the amazing things he could do on a basketball court ... once upon a time.

If this was the whole of the man's story it wouldn't be all that extraordinary. But what you might be surprised to learn is that he didn't retire to New Jersey, where he grew up, or Florida, where he went to college. Instead it was Israel, where the fans calling out his name and swapping tales of his hardwood prowess speak to him not in English, but in Hebrew. What's more, this African American man of faith is not a Christian or a Muslim, but a Jew who wears a *kippah* (the traditional Jewish head covering) during his prayers.

This man is Aulcie Perry, an instrumental figure in an epic sports story that yielded a defining moment for the State of Israel. As a player he was also at the forefront of a sea change in Israeli basketball. Since the 1970s, when Perry first chased his hoop dreams across the Atlantic Ocean, the sport has drawn hundreds of African American players to the Holy Land. Their stories and the history of how, when, and why these men ended up playing in Israel is an unlikely and fascinating convergence of race, religion, nationality, politics, and sport.

The Bond of Sports

In Israel, basketball *matters*. Sure it's just a game, but it represents so much more than that, perhaps reflecting the demographic makeup of the state. Many have observed that in countries in which there are large numbers of immigrants from all over the world, achievements in sports take on an added resonance. Israel, founded in 1948 with the specific goal of welcoming and being inhabited by Jews from around the globe, is just such a country. You might assume that its "Jewishness" makes the people of Israel homogenous, but it is quite the opposite. The country's tiny population (about eight million people total, approximately six million of them Jewish) is made up of some seventy different nationalities. As Irish economist David McWilliams describes it, "Israel … is a monotheistic melting pot of a diaspora that brought back with it the culture, language, and customs of the four corners of the earth."

Sports, then, provide a unique commonality in Israel. No matter where citizens are from, or when or how they arrived in the country, an Israeli sports team can be the rare symbol which represents *all* of them. However, in the mid-1970s, both the State of Israel and its sports, best embodied by the iconic basketball team Maccabi Tel Aviv, were very much finding their way. The country was still reeling from the aftereffects of the Yom Kippur War of October 1973. Prior to the war, Israelis had been lulled into a sense of security, what one writer referred to as "almost manic self-confidence" based on the feeling that their military might in the preceding twenty-five years had somehow inoculated them against hostile incursions by their neighbors. The multinational surprise attack on Judaism's holiest day of the year swiftly changed all that. More than 2,600 Israeli soldiers were killed in eighteen days of fighting, and the loss of equipment and the decline in production and exports amounted to the equivalent of Israel's gross national product for an entire year. While it was just one of several wars the country experienced over a span of three decades, the Yom Kippur War uniquely shook Israel's confidence and rattled its hard-earned sense of security.

Maccabi Tel Aviv had long dominated domestic Israeli basketball, but it simply could not gain any traction in Europe. Indeed, the team had never even advanced past the first round of FIBA European Cup (now known as Euroleague) competition. At a time when the country of Israel desperately needed a positive event its citizens could rally around, Maccabi hoped to provide it, but to do so it needed help. Maccabi had been recruiting Jewish American players including its captain, Tal Brody, since the early 1960s, but these players weren't enough to transform it into an elite European team. It took the seemingly inauspicious arrival of Perry, who had the height at 6-foot-10 but a lithe physique that hardly suggested he was the game-changing big man Maccabi so desperately needed. Perry also didn't have much of a track record to speak of, playing his college ball at Bethune-Cookman College, an historically Black school in Daytona Beach, Florida—not exactly an NCAA powerhouse—before spending a few years in the American Basketball Association and the Eastern Professional Basketball League. He made a momentary splash, signing with the New York Knicks of the NBA, but was cut in training camp in 1975. Perry was beginning to consider giving up the game, but his luck, along with Israeli basketball, would change via a summer league game he played in New York City's famous Rucker Park, where NBA superstars and streetball legends alike honed their craft. Maccabi's manager, Shmuel Maharovsky, spotted Perry there and decided to offer him a tryout.

Perry was reluctant, not even sure where Israel was, but he decided to give it a try for a few months. However, Maccabi was still debating whether to sign Perry or another prospective American candidate. That's when the late Ralph Klein, Maccabi's legendary coach and a big believer in the importance of team chemistry, took notice of a small gesture that ended up changing the course of sports in Israel. During a team meeting over coffee at a hotel, a waitress brought out a tray of cake for the team. Perry took one small slice and passed the plate along, while the other contract contender grabbed as many pieces as his hand would hold. Klein watched this and concluded that the type of person who wanted all the cake at the table would likely demand all the shots on the basketball court. Klein chose to bring Perry into the Maccabi fold.

Perry signed for two months, fully expecting only to work on his game and quickly try again for the NBA. But once he made the 6,000-mile trip from Newark to Tel Aviv, his mind-set changed dramatically. "I felt completely at home as soon as I landed in Israel," he said, adding that he was treated so warmly by the Israelis and his teammates, he couldn't imagine that he had almost refused to come. But as much joy as Perry felt living in Israel, his focus was on what he could do to transform a good team into a great one. Maccabi Tel Aviv had many talented players, such as Lou Silver, Mickey Berkowitz, Motti Aroesti, and Brody, Israelis and Jewish Americans alike. But Perry boasted both an incredible basketball IQ and a remarkably diverse skillset: impressive shooting range, great agility for his height, and a knack for making the right pass. (One teammate later described him as "the prototype for a Kevin Garnett," a recently retired fifteen-time NBA All-Star and one of the best and most versatile big men ever.) But it was Perry's uncanny knack for sparking the fast break with a blocked shot and his equally impressive talent for converting in transition that formed the basis for Maccabi's developing identity as a fast, free-wheeling run-and-gun team.

Maccabi sharpshooter Jim Boatwright recalled Perry's immediate impact. "We used to go over to Amsterdam for a preseason tournament," he said, "and we would lose at the bottom of the pool system. Aulcie joined us, and lo and behold, we won the whole thing."

Although Maccabi Tel Aviv started with a surge in 1977, the team was still being taken lightly when entering Champions Cup competition. But after a successful early round of pool play, Maccabi was within striking distance of a finals appearance. Standing in its way were the Russians—the dominant CSKA Moscow team. To advance to the finals, Maccabi would need to beat CSKA in both games of a home-and-home series.

Play was complicated by international politics. Following the 1967 Six-Day War, the USSR had formally broken off diplomatic relations with Israel. This meant that CSKA refused to play the initial game in Tel Aviv, thus forfeiting it. Furthermore, CSKA refused to host the Israeli squad in Moscow, forcing FIBA to find a neutral site for the game. Consequently, on the night of February 17, 1977, all eyes in Israel, and many in Moscow, ended up focused on the small town of Virton, Belgium, where 650 spectators packed into a 500-capacity arena.

It was no mere basketball game and was not anticipated as such. The game between CSKA and Maccabi had particular significance for the Israelis as media buildup reached a peak on the day of the game. Israel's lone television station at the time would be televising the game, making it a national "must-see" event. CSKA is a Russian abbreviation for "Central Sports Club of the Army"—the club was under the direct management of the Soviet military, and during the Cold War it was perceived as representing the entire Soviet bloc. Headlines in Israel's daily papers touted the battle between the East and the West, a fight between David and Goliath. Here was David, with its then-four million inhabitants, representing the entire Western world against the Soviet Goliath of more than 290 million people. The East-West conflict had even more significance for Israelis because of the dire situation of Jews living in the USSR. It was reported that Maccabi coach Klein told his players prior to the game that, "We are fighting for our country as well as for thousands of Jews who cannot immigrate to Israel because of Soviet policy. Let's beat the Soviet Bear!"

And beat the Bear they did, handily defeating the heavily favored Russian squad, 91–79. The game remains etched in the collective memory of the Israeli people to this day, a national identity-consolidating event that goes far beyond the game itself to the country's sport history, self-image, and international reputation. The majority of Israel's population, even those who knew nothing about basketball, watched the game and reveled in its result. It made no difference that Maccabi's starting five consisted of four players who were born in the United States, including Perry, the lone African American. *Israel* had won the game, and if anyone needed more evidence, the celebration that followed would provide it.

Pilots from Israel's national airline, El Al, competed among themselves—like crisply clad, stripe-shouldered rebounders jostling for inside position—over the right to fly the Maccabi players back to Israel. Only the most senior pilots won the honor. But the others, not to be left out, volunteered as flight attendants just to be on the plane bringing the national heroes home, a highly deferential gesture made all the more memorable when considering the hyper-alpha-male bravado customarily associated with Israeli pilots. At Ben Gurion International Airport in Tel Aviv, employees worked double shifts to be among the tens of thousands of people who waited for the Maccabi players to arrive. Five-hundred police officers could not stop the joyous crowd from effectively kidnapping the players to celebrate in the center of the city, where 100,000 people stood with signs welcoming the "hunters of the Russian Bear."

Tel Aviv's mayor Shlomo Lahat prepared an event the likes of which the city had never seen. Five bands were specially invited to celebrate with the crowd eagerly waiting in the city center. The city center pool was filled with equal parts people, water, and champagne. Even doves and hawks were united in their adulation for the team and its victory—Prime Minister Yitzhak Rabin and the leader of the opposition, Menachem Begin, each sent messages of congratulations and gratitude to the team. The next day, the last minutes of the game were repeatedly broadcast in schools around the country, and the country's newspapers fixated their coverage on the incredible accomplishment, with headlines that included "Maccabi Tel Aviv did it!" (*Haaretz*), "It is really a dream" (*Maariv*), and "the night when all of Israel danced in front of the unbelievable vision" (*Yedioth Ahronoth*).

On the Map

Maccabi Tel Aviv's 1977 victory over CSKA Moscow, made even sweeter when Maccabi Tel Aviv defeated Italy's Mobilgirgi Varese in the next round to win the tournament championship and hoist the European Cup, is arguably among Israel's greatest moments, sports-related or otherwise. At the time, the State of Israel was a youth in its twenties and was just four years removed from a war in which it tee-tered on the brink of its very existence. In addition, the USSR, home of CSKA Moscow, did not recognize Israel's right to exist, so Maccabi's victory was much more than just one professional sports team defeating another. It was a country's bold and public pronouncement of its arrival on the international stage. It represented the hard-earned right to exist not only formally, but meaningfully. It represented the fact that life, in this instance represented by international-level sporting accomplishment, was happening in Israel. And when Brody, one of the stars on the team, was interviewed during the postgame celebrations, the significance of the moment was not lost on him.

"We are on the map, and we are staying on the map," he said in Hebrew in a memorable television interview. "Not just in sports, but in everything!"

For a country like Israel, a tiny sliver of land which was at the time arid, undeveloped, and lacking in cosmopolitan appeal, Maccabi Tel Aviv's victory, and Brody's quote, was a unifying and galvanizing moment. It was a singular example that all Israelis, and all Jews, could point to as evidence that Israel could not only compete but thrive on a world stage against the very best. It was also an internationally visible victory that took place outside the battlefield, an area of previous victories by which Israelis hoped never to be defined again in the future.

In proclaiming that Israel was "on the map, not just in sports, but in everything" Brody leapt high above the generic bravado of a typical victorious star athlete. Still, the work of some academics suggests Brody's words could be considered objectively accurate. Sociologist Grant Jarvie, author of *Sports, Culture and Society*, noted that international sport and the success of international athletes have often been among the most important symbols of integration for many emerging nations. Victorious athletes not only tended to legitimize their nation within the international arena, they further embody a positive image of that nation. Essentially, Maccabi's victories in 1977 engendered a positive image of Israel, but even more importantly it contributed to the legitimacy Israel badly needed in the international arena at that time.

And none of this would have been possible without Aulcie Perry.

"Those were the best nine months of my life," Perry said. "After we beat Russia and came back to Tel Aviv, I felt a lot of Israeli nationalism. I think that was the most memorable experience I've ever had."

Peace in a New Home

By that point, Perry's plan to return to America and take another shot at the NBA was in the distant past, and his personal transition from "foreigner" to "Israeli" was in full force. After his success in Israel, Perry was invited to the New York Knicks' training camp and the Detroit Pistons showed interest, as did the New Orleans Jazz and various top European teams. Perry wasn't interested—he knew what he had found in Tel Aviv was more than a new team. He had found an adopted home in which he felt more at peace than he ever had in New Jersey, where he was no stranger to the racism that pervaded parts of the United States in the 1950s. "Maybe it's because I play ball, maybe it's because my friends on the team are cool, but I've never experienced it [racial discrimination in Israel]," Perry said in a 1978 interview in *Ebony* magazine. "For the first time in my life, I felt free! The fact that I am Black [and the only Black player on the team] made no difference to my teammates or to the people of Tel Aviv."

Israeli fans chanted his name and carried signs saying "Aulcie Perry for Prime Minister." The actual Prime Minister received him and his teammates and thanked them for "bringing honor to the people of Israel." Perry could be seen on television pitching local products in commercials, and his name became an endearing term for stature, with parents of growing youngsters being told they've "got a real Aulcie Perry there." By his second year in Israel, Perry knew he was there to stay.

Perry was one of the first pure "import" players in Israel—a gentile with no discernible connection to the country other than Maccabi's desperate need for a big man. Brought in on a two-month contract to help break the squad's mounting streak of first-round losses in European competition, Perry surpassed all expectations. He not only became an integral force on a championship team, but also a beloved figure in Israel and, eventually, a Jewish convert, permanent resident, and citizen, staying in the country long after his playing days ended. Aulcie Perry, an African American from Newark, New Jersey, helped put Israel on the map and in turn forged a storied path for the hundreds of African American basketball players that followed, all with stories of their own.

2

THE PATH TO ISRAEL

Upon touching down in Israel, visitors are known to feel excited, happy, spiritually uplifted, and occasionally frankly manic. Vidal Massiah, an African Canadian professional basketball player from Toronto, felt only nervous. Very, *very* nervous, in fact.

When Massiah agreed to play for a first-division team in the small Israeli city of Ramat Hasharon, Mickey Berkowitz, the team's owner and a legendary former Israeli player in his own right, had told him that to ensure smooth entry into the country Massiah should mention Berkowitz's name at the customs desk on arrival. But that offered little comfort to a player who was already wary of security issues in the region and who was taken aback by the intensity and rigor of Israeli airport security in Canada. Prior to his boarding the flight in Toronto, Israeli airline personnel went through his luggage piece by piece and asked for the phone numbers of his contacts in Israel along with "a million" other questions. Airline security apparently even followed him into the bathroom!

This level of cautious vigilance matched nothing he had seen before. Even with the widespread intensification of airport security following the terrorist attacks in the United States on September 11, 2001, travelers to Israel undergo security that surprises them with its rigor and intimidation. Massiah began to seriously wonder if he would even be allowed into the country, let alone whether or not he would enjoy it there. His first minutes in the airport once he arrived did little to reassure him.

"So I get there, and there's an American guy ahead of me in customs, and I watch and I see that they sent him back," Massiah said. "They turned this guy back! So now I'm like really, *really* nervous. They just sent this guy back, and I'm like 'Damn, what am I going to do?' So I get up to the counter, and the officer asked 'Why are you here?' and I said 'I'm here to see Mickey Berkowitz.' He's like, 'OK, go right ahead.' That's when I realized basketball had to be pretty big in Israel!"

Looking for Winners

"Big" may be an understatement. Massiah was granted entry into Israel in 2003 with a simple name-drop. In earlier years, though, teams' eagerness to get top-notch basketball talent into the country involved machinations that reflected just how fanatic Israelis were about the game.

In the 1950s, basketball teams in Israel were, not surprisingly, made up primarily of Israelis, but that was to change in the next few decades. Teams felt increasing pressure to achieve domestic and international sporting success, prompting them to look elsewhere for stronger players. One of Maccabi Tel Aviv's first efforts was the recruitment of American Tal Brody, who was Jewish by birth. Although Brody had been a first-round pick in the NBA draft, he opted to join the Israeli team after his graduation from the University of Illinois. He brought exceptional skills as well as an entertaining, up-tempo style that helped to reinvent his team. Witnessing how much Brody could do to elevate his squad drove Maccabi and the rest of the teams to broaden their talent search even further. Now they wanted players who could line up against Europe's best whether they were Jewish or not.

Maccabi Tel Aviv was especially aggressive about recruiting new players, including the prime example of Aulcie Perry. This led it to further domination of the local league and to successes that sparked what became an arms (and legs) race of sorts. "Every other team in the

Israeli league had to find foreign players to break Maccabi or risk going out of business. It was survival of the fittest," said former Israeli league coach, and current broadcaster, Simmy Reguer. Soon there was hardly a team in Israel without a tall American player, most of whom were African American.

But adding foreign players was tricky business and put teams in more than a bit of a quandary. The issue was clear: league rules allowed only a restricted number of foreign players per team and so, in order to fill the roster with more elite players, teams had to be sure many of those elite new players *became* Israelis. Although challenging, the task of finding ways for players to quickly attain Israeli citizenship did not turn out to be impossible. How? It was thanks to an historic policy Israel's founders developed to ensure persecuted Jews the unencumbered right to emigrate to their homeland, a policy hardly intended to further the ambitious goals of enterprising basketball teams who would later capitalize on it.

The Holocaust of World War II resulted in the systematic murder of almost two-thirds of Europe's Jewish population. This terrible tragedy raised great anxiety and concerns about just how close the Nazis and their collaborators had come to exterminating an entire people. The modern State of Israel was founded in the dark shadow of this horrendous event and its founders were determined to have a new country that would "open wide the gates of the homeland to every Jew." Shortly after the State of Israel declared its independence, the leaders formalized that proclamation. The Law of Return legislation was enacted in 1950, granting Jews (including converts), those of Jewish ancestry, and their spouses, the right to migrate and to settle in Israel and, importantly, to gain citizenship.

Chutzpah is a Yiddish word defined as the quality of audacity, for good or bad. That word comes fittingly into play to describe how someone, or a group of people, could leverage a law so revered and well-intentioned to benefit—of all things—competitive basketball in Israel. Fortunately (or unfortunately, depending on your point of view) there were plenty of folks in Israel with ample chutzpah who were willing to do precisely that. Enterprising minds soon found the Law of Return, meant to provide safe haven for any Jew wishing to migrate to Israel from the Diaspora, to provide an invaluable loophole they could exploit to improve their basketball teams.

The Law of Return in Basketball

In the earliest days of teams importing players, the Israeli basketball league only allowed foreign players (including Perry) to participate in games against European teams. In the late 1970s, the Israeli league modified the rule to allow one foreign player per team for domestic games as well. This opened the door for teams to ponder how they might be able to squeeze additional talented Americans onto their rosters while staying in compliance with league rules. While most professional basketball leagues around the world had similar limitations on the number of foreigners per team, only Israel had the Law of Return. It didn't take long for teams to capitalize on the fact that if a player converted to Judaism or married a Jewish woman, he could earn citizenship without delay. After becoming a citizen, a foreign player could stay on his team's roster as an Israeli, which, of course, meant the team could now bring over another talented American to fill the sole foreigner slot.

As if on cue, in the late 1970s and the 1980s American players were, en masse, suddenly converting to Judaism or marrying Israeli women and obtaining citizenship. According to broadcaster Reguer, it was hardly a coincidence. "Being the son of a rabbi, it was quite insulting," Reguer said. "[I felt] like these people were making a joke of religion and of citizenship. People just started doing it, fictitious marriages and things like that. It was stupid, it was ridiculous. It was insulting to the religion and insulting to the country. It was just crazy. They were making fun of being Jewish," he said, obviously irritated.

The circumstances were intensified by the passionate religious, social, and political debate in Israel that surrounds the question of "Who is a Jew?" Orthodox Judaism discourages proselytizing. In fact, a rabbi's first step in the process of an Orthodox conversion is actually to attempt to dissuade the prospective convert in an effort to test his or her commitment to the transformation. Those who persist must complete a year or more of rigorous studies and pass tests about what they have learned before they can finally be accepted as "Jews by choice," as converts are sometimes known. Conservative or Reform streams of Judaism offer less intensive conversion processes, but within Israel the validity of even those conversions is a source of contentious debate among the country's rabbinical and political leaders.

Because converting to Judaism is meant to be a lengthy and thorough undertaking that requires spiritual commitment, exhaustive study, and careful adherence to customs and traditions, the numerous examples of African American players undergoing quick conversions eventually raised eyebrows. Some Israelis were upset not only by the quantity of conversions, but especially by their "quality." According to an article in *Sports Illustrated*, an example of how extreme the situation had become concerned a former college star that was playing pick-up games in a Brooklyn gym. A representative of an Israeli pro team approached him saying, "Do you want to play basketball in Israel?" He then added, "And would you like to be a Jew?" After the player agreed to both, the rep introduced him to a rabbi in Manhattan who handed him a book entitled *What is a Jew?* The rabbi then asked the player some perfunctory questions and told him to come back in a few days. On the player's next visit, the rabbi talked to him for ten minutes, shook his hand, and said, "Welcome to Judaism."

As disturbing as this example is, it was not an uncommon occurrence. Prospective converts interested more in rebounds than religion were known to start and finish the process in mere days with the help of one of a number of "basketball rabbis," no doubt an unfamiliar theological sub-specialty to many. These rabbis were alleged to have been paid or otherwise compensated by teams who arranged for their players' conversions to take place in the United States in an effort to avoid the stringent requirements of the Israeli rabbinate. Motti Rosenblum, then a writer for *Maariv*, a Tel Aviv newspaper, recalled that there was one rabbi in New York who advertised that he could give conversions and easily make anyone a Jew for a few dollars. "[Players] were looking for many ways to get Israeli citizenship. It was a big lie in basketball," Rosenblum said.

The increasingly common practice did not go unnoticed by the Israeli media. The *Jerusalem Post* once dubbed the questionable conversions as "circumstantial circumcisions" and an editorial cartoon depicted a trio of rabbis working together, one standing on the shoulders of the next, to give an African American player a Hebrew name and place a kippah on his lofty head. Eventually, enough was enough. The National Religious Party, a political wing of Orthodox Jews, began raising serious objections. However, a certain hypocrisy was in play and not lost on secular fans. The National Religious Party was affiliated with the Elizur Netanya club, a team that essentially carried the flag for religious Israelis in the field of basketball (most sports organizations in Israel are tied to a political party). While the team did not play or practice on the Sabbath, nor were its members permitted to eat in non-kosher restaurants, it had six African American players on the team at one time. Furthermore, it was reported that none of the Americans were genuinely observant Jews, leading the team to become known in more critical circles as the "Orthodox Globetrotters."

Nevertheless, in spite of the irony the objections were real and they eventually led to an overhaul of the eligibility requirements in Israeli basketball. The National Religious Party alone might not have brought about change, but the cases of two American players in particular, Philip Dailey and Chris Rankin, apparently pushed the situation over the line. Dailey and Rankin arrived in Israel in 1982 with conversion certificates signed by three Milwaukee rabbis. Coincidentally or not, their team, Maccabi Petah Tikvah, donated $6,000 to the rabbis' synagogue. In 1983, the Interior Ministry invalidated the conversion certificates when it was noticed that they were dated four years *before* the alleged conversions took place. However, the team was not to be deterred. In its next attempt to facilitate Dailey's and Rankin's immigration, it claimed citizenship for them through arranged marriages to Jewish women thirty years their senior—*uber-chutzpah*!

The daily newspaper *Yedioth Ahronoth* published a front-page picture of the twenty-something Dailey and Rankin and their fifty-something wives, leading the team's coach to admit that the organization had found the wives for the players. Reaching further back, one of the Milwaukee rabbis who had signed conversion papers for these and other players denied ever having met them in the first place. While the Dailey and Rankin "conversions" were especially galling, they were far from being aberrations. "I knew a girl who got married three different times, with three basketball players," basketball writer Rosenblum said. "One of the girls got $5,000 and a ticket for a nice weekend in Cyprus." In all, about forty players converted to Judaism from the mid-1970s to the mid-1980s. The negative publicity and media backlash led to the petitioning of the Israeli Supreme Court, at which time the Israeli Basketball Federation finally decided to close the much-abused loophole. Eventually, the rules changed to permit each team to have a maximum of two foreign players and to require any new immigrant to Israel, including those born Jewish, to live in the country for at least three years before becoming eligible to play as an Israeli. However, the rules have changed repeatedly over the years. The Federation continuously tries to maintain a balance among needs: the desire to bring in as much high-level foreign talent as possible, to maintain the integrity of religion and citizenship, and to ensure that the Israeli league will continue to feature local Israeli players.

An Honest Conversion

Almost lost in the controversy were those African American players who insisted that their conversions were legitimate. Carlton Neverson converted in 1984 in his hometown of New York City before he came to Israel, where he would go on to play for 16 seasons and settle after his retirement. Neverson was born a Catholic and says he did go to church as a child, but in time he lost interest. The decision he made to become a Jew was based on considerable soul-searching. "In the beginning, I wasn't 100 percent sure," Neverson told a newspaper reporter

in 1992, "but I saw a rabbi three times a week and became more interested. Sometimes now I really do feel like a Jew. Especially when things
get tough."

African American player and former Baptist LaVon Mercer played
for Hapoel Tel Aviv from 1981 to 1988 and for Maccabi Tel Aviv from
1989 to 1995. He told the same reporter that he and his American wife,
Sharon, both converts, practiced Reform Judaism and were fluent in
Hebrew, as were their two children. After more than a decade living in
Israel, though, he admitted that his wife was the one in the family who
was more active in Jewish practices.

And, of course, there was Aulcie Perry. In spite of his icon status,
for having led Maccabi Tel Aviv to a European Cup in his first season,
resentment flared when he returned to Israel for his third season as a
converted Jew and citizen (allowing Maccabi to sign Earl Williams, a
rugged African American big man who would become one of the best
and most beloved players in Israeli history). Many made the assumption
that Perry, like so many other foreign players, was simply converting to
the "religion" that was Israeli basketball. At the time, Perry said, "I want
to join the fold," but Maccabi's archrival, Hapoel Tel Aviv, charged that
Perry was converting to allow his team to hire an additional foreigner.
One of the political parties in then–Prime Minister Menachem Begin's
coalition even threatened to leave the government if the Interior Min-
istry approved Perry's conversion.

The conversion, which Perry clearly stated was authentic and
Orthodox, was ultimately accepted, although there are those who continue to question its legitimacy to this day. "[Perry's] full of shit," Reguer said. "It was ridiculous, it was stupid, it was insulting. It wasn't
an Orthodox conversion, it was a joke. It was rabbis getting paid off."
However, Perry stands by the legitimacy of his conversion. I spoke to
him in the bowels of Tel Aviv's Nokia Arena (now known as Menora
Mivtachim Arena) following a 2010 Maccabi victory while he took me
through the mind-set that led him to convert.

"I started to fall in love with the country and the people, and I
was up in the air as far as religion," Perry said, speaking thoughtfully

and quietly amidst the hoots and hollers of the celebrating present-day players. "I started to study with the rabbi, and I started to fall in love with the religion. So I said, 'OK, Aulcie, convert. If during the process [you realize] it's not for you, you'll stop.' But I went on and went through the whole process of Orthodox conversion. It was fantastic, because I didn't know the scriptures that well. My family is Southern Baptist, and the difference between Judaism and Southern Baptism is that in Judaism, if you ask the rabbi a question, there's an answer. In Christianity they say, 'Oh, you just have to have faith.' That's what grabbed me most. If my rabbi didn't have an answer, he'd say, 'Come back next week, let me go ask *my* rabbi—but I'm going to get you an answer.' That impressed me."

Perry said he observes kosher dietary laws and the Jewish High Holidays, and he continues to practice Judaism to this day. Eventually the legitimacy of his conversion and his adoption of the religion won over many cynics. His choice to lead a Jewish lifestyle led even more Israelis to embrace him. Not surprisingly, though, his decision was not popular back home. "I come from a devout Baptist family, and my parents could not accept my conversion," Perry said. "My mother still hasn't accepted the fact that I'm Jewish, but she's happy if I'm happy."

* * *

The Hebrew name Perry chose to take with his conversion, Elisha ben-Avraham (translated as Elisha, son of Abraham), is replete with historic and religious significance. The biblical Abraham was the first Jew, and thus he was by definition, a convert. Although there is no mandate that a male converting to Judaism need to adopt the Hebrew name of Abraham, as Perry did, it is a longstanding tradition for several reasons. First, the Bible (Genesis 17:5) speaks of Abraham as being "the father of a multitude of nations." Because converts come from diverse peoples and backgrounds—a "multitude of nations"—it is appropriate for them to be called the sons and daughters of Abraham. Second, in Jewish tradition, Abraham becomes known as "the father of proselytes," *proselytes* being a term which applies to non-Jews who have converted to Judaism. Their conversion for the most part severs their legal connection with their former non-Jewish families, thus the family of Abraham becomes their family. Offering the convert the name of Abraham is explained by the *midrash* (the ancient rabbinic commentary interpreting Jewish texts) as an expression of deep love. The midrash says, "God loves proselytes dearly. And we, too, should show our love for them because they left their father's house, and their people, and the Gentile community, and have joined us."

Perry did indeed "join" the Israelis, and he would be far from the last African American player to do so. Although Israeli officials closed the loophole that encouraged basketball-based marriages and convenient conversions to bolster rosters, Israel retained its popularity as a destination for African American players. In subsequent decades, more and more arrived to play in the Israeli leagues and, importantly, more and more chose to stay. Creative use (or misuse, depending on who you ask) of the Law of Return may have catalyzed the "African-Americanization" of Israeli basketball, but the story of how the phenomenon has been sustained for more than forty years is far more complex.

3

WHY ISRAEL?

TIME AFTER TIME, MACCABI TEL Aviv approached former University of Michigan standout and NBA player Maceo Baston about joining their squad, and time after time the club was rebuffed. Baston would eventually go on to become a beloved star for Maccabi, helping carry the team to two European championships, but he ducked the team's initial recruiting efforts for more than three years. It wasn't the money being offered that was the problem, nor was it an issue with the club itself. It was the country—Israel. Baston's father hated the thought of his son's being in harm's way, and his father was certain that would be the case in a nation known for its ongoing conflicts. In fact it wasn't until his father's untimely death that Baston began to seriously entertain the thought of giving Maccabi, and Israel, a try. Baston had thrived playing for teams in Italy and Spain, but it was taking the plunge and heading for Israel in 2003 that was, as he later said, "one of the best decisions" of his career. Sitting in the locker room of the Toronto Raptors, whom he joined in 2007, Baston talked about his path to Israel.

"My father was very influential in my decision-making, and he was always like 'Nah, just stay in Spain, don't go over [to Israel], there's a lot going on.' When my dad passed and I finally chose to go there, it was like destiny. I was hesitant from what I had heard, but [when I got there] I was like, 'Wow, Israel!—Beautiful country, beautiful city [Tel Aviv].' It was summer and really hot, and it was kind of like being on vacation."

Baston's late father's attitude was nearly identical to that of the friends and family members of many other African American players, who routinely ask the same question when those players announce an intention to go to Israel: "Why?!" Why would they choose to play in a Jewish state, which has been in virtually perpetual conflict since its very founding?

Indeed, why Israel?

* * *

I spoke to more than thirty African American players in researching this book, and there is one word that best summarizes their collective initial reaction to Israel: *surprise.* Player after player told me about being braced for the omnipresent sense of danger he expected to feel, and the sights, sounds, and smells of war he anticipated experiencing, only to have his eyes widen and a smile spread across his face as he described just how much the reality of the country pleasantly differed from his perception. More than anything, the players were astonished to find they actually felt safe. Indeed, one of the advantages the players frequently mentioned about living in Israel turned out to be a feeling of security. Cory Carr, an African American from tiny Fordyce, Arkansas, spoke of the unexpected discrepancy between what players anticipated and what they found.

"Any time you're watching something about Israel, it's usually on CNN or Fox News and it's usually some terrorist attack, or something going on in the country between the Palestinians and Israelis. It is always conflict," said Carr, who first came to Israel in 2001, became a citizen in 2009, and continues to live there today. "The picture the media presents of the country is very intimidating. You're a little bit afraid to come because of that. But once you get inside the country, and you see what goes on, and how the Israelis live, it's an immediate connection for a lot of the foreigners. The transition here is very easy. My first impression of the Israeli people is that they were kind people, they were warm, and they really tried to extend their arms to make sure I was comfortable."

However secure Carr began to feel about life in Israel, his family continued to worry. "They were terrified for me," Carr said. "They didn't know; they weren't prejudiced, just blind. They had no idea [of the reality], and they didn't want me to go. When I got here and they realized how comfortable I was, they felt a little bit better, but they were still hesitant about coming themselves." His mother told him she could never visit and that she would have no idea what to expect. But eventually, "My mom came, and she loved it! I had to knock her over the head to get her on the plane and send her back!" he said, laughing.

Nonetheless, violence is an unfortunate fact of life in a country surrounded by hostile nations, and I discuss the impact and specter of violence on the experience of African American basketball players in Israel in Chapter 5. Briefly, though, the common message of so many of the players was that the frequency and scale of the *coverage* of violence dwarfed the real *impact* it had on their lives in Israel. On a day-to-day basis, it just wasn't something they had to deal with, which isn't the case everywhere. Rodney Buford, for example, played in Israel for a few months and recalls it as a time he enjoyed immensely. Years later he played in Lebanon but left after just a week, overcome by the fear so many anticipate but never actually experience in Israel.

"It was night and day," said Buford about being in the two countries. "In Lebanon, walking through the streets of Beirut, man, I was so scared. I'm walking down the street and there are guys walking with guns, looking at me, staring at me. I'm like, 'Yo, I'm not doing anything. I don't want any problems; I'm just trying to go get something to eat.' There are tanks driving down the street, the soldier on the top manning the gun is circling at me, pointing the gun at me, I was like, *Oh crap, this is not for me.* The hotel I was staying in, I looked out the window right across the street and half of buildings are blown off, there are bullet holes. Everywhere you walk, you just see rubble. It was crazy, man. I had to get away from there."

A Second Safety Surprise

In addition to the surprising discovery that Israel was not the war-torn country they feared, many players shared their surprise at feeling safer going about routine activities in Israel than they had in America.

"I do things here I would never do [in the United States]," said Fred Campbell, who first played in Israel in 1992 and lives there as a citizen today. He recalls a conversation with another long-time African American Israeli-league player, Kenny Williams. "We walked through an alley on a Sunday night after a game. And I said, 'Now Kenny, you know, if we were in America, we would never have made the left turn down this alley.' And he said, 'Damn right.' In the States, I would never chance that."

Deon Thomas, an African American from Chicago, spent five seasons in Israel and married an Israeli woman. Prior to that he starred for the University of Illinois and played for the Dallas Mavericks of the NBA, and today he is the radio voice for his alma mater and a commentator for the Big Ten Network. Even with his successes in various high-profile roles in America, he said when people find out he played in Israel, he gets pummeled with question after question.

"'Oh wow, how is it in Israel? Is it this? Is it that?'" he says. "But the biggest question is, 'Is it safe?' And I tell them all the time, 'I feel safer in Israel than I do here [in the United States]. In Israel, my kids run around and play, and I don't have to worry about them. [My wife] drives at night—I don't care if she stops at the gas station or at the ATM. Here [in the United States], I don't allow any of this because of the fear. There [in Israel], I don't have that."

Although recent statistics indicate a rise in the Israeli crime rate, the stats continue to confirm the players' impression that in some ways the country is indeed safer than the United States. According to the United Nations Office on Drugs and Crime in 2011, Israel had 2.1

intentional homicides per 100,000 inhabitants, compared to 4.8 per 100,000 in the United States. Anecdotally speaking, a striking example of safer living in Israel came to my attention unexpectedly as I was reading through my Twitter timeline in February 2012. I read a tweet from African American player Alex Tyus saying he had lost his wallet in Israel. Later he was shocked to find it with all of its contents intact. He noted that if he had lost it in the United States, its contents would have been "gone forever." Tyus used the last of his 140 characters to simply say, "Love Israel."

Not Far from Home

In a blog post about life as a basketball player overseas, African American point guard Eugene "Pooh" Jeter confirmed the commonly held sentiment that Spain's ACB League is the best outside of the NBA as far as quality of play, but he asserted that Israel might be the best place for Americans as far as their experience off the court. His rationale was concise and enthusiastic:

"Mostly everybody [85 percent] speaks English, the food is GREAT, the party scene is real cool, and the WOMEN are BEAUTIFUL. Women out here are a lot like Kim Kardashian out this way. LOL!!! You should've seen my girlfriend's face as I wrote that statement. She got that look on her face saying 'You better not write that.'"

Although Jeter's post may have landed him in the doghouse at home, it also touched on some frequently noted responses to the commonly asked "Why Israel?" question. One of the primary issues for players transitioning to life overseas is the language barrier, so the prevalence of English-speakers in Israel (Jeter's 85 percent figure is accurate) effectively removes that problem. I touch on Israeli cuisine in Chapter 4, but the country is replete with its own takes on American food as well, not to mention American chains themselves—a potentially homesick player is never too far from a McDonald's, Burger King, Domino's, or KFC. As for nightlife, Tel Aviv has been called the "Miami of the Middle East," and it's a regular on top-10 lists highlighting the world's most vibrant places to party, boasting club after club playing the best of American hip-hop. These and other similarities between life in Israel and in the United States are among the most frequently mentioned draws of playing there. An Israeli sports television show even produced a short feature in the 1990s on a local barber known as "Zalman the Man" frequented by African American players because of his skills at giving them the fades and high-tops they grew used to at home and struggled to find overseas.

Nightclubs, fast food joints, and American-style barbershops provide welcome relief for the many African American players who incorrectly assumed that Israel, land of the Bible, had not advanced very much since those ancient times. Derrick Sharp, an African American from Orlando, Florida, came to Israel in 1993 and stayed for twenty years, eighteen as a player and two as a coach. He recalls just how skewed his sense of the country was before he first arrived and how it was tempered only by the much-needed advance notice he received from a few college teammates who played there before he did. "If I didn't know [my former college teammates], I would have thought people would be walking around with camels, wraps in their hair, and donkeys pulling carts," Sharp said. "I would have been clueless. [Other foreign players] can be ignorant to the fact that Israel is actually very Americanized and a great place to be."

What players find on arrival is that about 90 percent of Israel's inhabitants live in urban centers, which boast all of the amenities of the typical modern-day metropolis. The misperception they report having of the country is not uncommon according to Ze'ev Chafets, author of *Heroes and Hustlers, Hard Hats and Holy Men: Inside the New Israel*. He noted that the enormous disparity between the country's image and reality greatly complicates the task of writing about Israel. "Outsiders customarily perceive Israel in grandiose terms as the Holy Land, or the mysterious reincarnation of an ancient; as an embattled and heroic David, or an overbearing, militaristic Goliath," Chafets wrote. "Admirers and critics alike tend to see and judge Israel in moral, even metaphysical, ways that are not usually applied to normal societies. Yet there is another Israel, a nation of four million people (now more than eight million) engaged in routine daily pursuits. They may inhabit a uniquely evocative geography and live in the shadow of great, even inexplicable, events, but they are not, themselves, larger than life. Israel is their home, a place to live and work, have fun and raise families —in short, a country like any other."

One way in which Israel does differ from many other countries is the absence of the subtle distrust or outright dislike of America that can be unfortunately common elsewhere. Unlike locals in many other countries around the world who view the United States as an enemy or aggressor, Israelis view it as their closest friend as the two countries enjoy an interdependent relationship that is expressed on economic, military, social, and cultural levels. The United States and Israel have long been staunch political allies, and American food, music, and movies carry considerable cachet in Israel. In a 2011 interview, Prime Minister Benjamin Netanyahu said that "Israel is the one country in which everyone is pro-American."

To learn about how playing in Israel compares to experiences elsewhere, I spoke to a number of African American players who spent the bulk of their careers in other countries overseas. Former NBA player Randolph Childress raved about the decade he spent in Italy, but recalled his biggest discomfort there being the anti-American sentiment he sometimes felt. He told me about one memorable instance when a police officer pulled his car over for an unknown reason. The officer spoke only Italian and forced Childress to stand outside his vehicle in the cold for more than an hour. When a representative from his team arrived to deal with the situation, Childress said while he couldn't understand much of the conversation, he could make out that the policeman was making multiple and increasingly angry references to George W. Bush, the internationally unpopular American president at the time.

Joe Dawson, an African American from Tuscaloosa, Alabama, has lived in Israel since 1991. He said that unlike in some other places he had played, being an American in Israel is reason to be loved, not loathed. He pointed out the frequency with which Israelis travel to the United States and the number of Israelis who have family in America. According to Dawson, the result is that the transition to life in Israel for African Americans is bound to be easier compared to transitions to life almost anywhere else. Dawson had played in Greece and France as well, two countries that are also popular with African American players. However, he pointed out that the lifestyle in Israel, unlike that of Greece or France, is particularly suitable to the players. In those countries, he said locals are "so caught up in their culture that they're less [appealing] to Americans." Israel, on the other hand, was a whole different story. "Israeli and American are like one culture together," Dawson said. "The people want to speak English, they wanted to bring in American foods, American television. It made it an easier fit ... Israel isn't another state," he said, laughing, "but it's close."

Jeffrey Rosen, a Jewish American businessman from Aventura, Florida, is the owner of the Maccabi Haifa club in the Israeli league, and he holds open tryouts in the United States for players looking to go to Israel. Rosen echoes Dawson's sentiment that notwithstanding all of the differences players prepare themselves for before they arrive in Israel, most experience an almost immediate and comforting feeling of familiarity.

"We have images of Israel being a war zone with missiles landing, Palestinians and Israelis fighting every day, and rocks being thrown," Rosen said. "You nuke this vision, this idea, the minute you drop in an athlete, particularly a non-Jewish athlete. They have what they perceive is going on from the news, and then they get there and see this beautiful, modern, working country, with roads and highways and phones and stores, and suddenly it's remarkably similar to home. Not the same, but hardly foreign. And unlike the experiences of athletes that have played in Europe or elsewhere, not only are the Israelis friendly to our athletes, they also speak English! Suddenly you're in a warm country, you feel safe, you can speak English walking into a store, you can buy a hamburger or get a hot dog or slice of pizza. I think Israel's an ideal place for the North American athlete to play."

To Rosen, Israel's welcoming reality is also part of why so many players choose to return year after year. "Why does an African American player choose to come to the Jewish country?" Rosen asks. "Because he loves basketball. He wants to pursue his art. And why does he come back? Because he finds himself with an audience that's warm, in an atmosphere and a country that's friendly. Then he says, 'I'm living here, and I *like* it here! It's like home. It might be better than home. It might be equal to home. Maybe it's not as good as home, but it's not *cold*.' I know some guys playing in Russia or in Eastern Europe, and I'm not trying to disparage it, but [they find that] winter in Eastern Europe and Russia is culturally cold and physically cold. Israel is a modern country with the attributes of a modern society—open and liberal—that make it a really encouraging and inviting society. And the misconception that this is a country at siege ... is washed away when you're sitting there hanging out at the Mediterranean or going up to have falafel on Mount Carmel or visiting the sites in Jerusalem. Suddenly, it's 'Wow! What Israel are they talking about?'"

That Loving Feeling

The warmth and hospitality of the Israeli people is consistently mentioned by African American basketball players as one of the most significant benefits of playing there. Andrew Kennedy, a Jamaican American, did not know any Jewish people before he played in Israel. He has lived in the United States for more than fifteen years since retiring from playing, yet he points out that most of his close friends today are Israeli and/or Jewish. He tried playing in other countries over the course of his career but never found anything like he had in Israel, where he ended up spending 12 seasons, at that time the most ever by an import player.

"Israel really gave me that feeling of home," he explained. "[The players and citizens] have an interesting, interesting dynamic and relationship. I don't know necessarily why that is, but I did feel and sense a closeness to a lot of the people who lived in the towns that I played for all over Israel. You're recognized wherever you go, and there is an

unusually strong bond between basketball fans and a lot of players ....
I was greeted with nothing but love, to be honest with you. I was
inducted into a family. It was great. I had nothing but positive vibes
from the very beginning."

Dean Thomas had been a beloved college player at the University of Illinois and played in prime international destinations including
Turkey and Spain. But he was floored by the reaction of the Israelis
who followed him when he played for Maccabi Tel Aviv.

"The fans honestly love you, and they treat you as if you're one
of their own," Thomas said. "I'll tell you a little story—when I broke
my leg, before the 2005 Euroleague Final Four, I had [Israeli American] fans fly to Tel Aviv from New York to visit me in the hospital.
They brought their whole family! It was a grandfather and his two kids.
That's not going to happen in the US. If Kobe Bryant hurts himself,
nobody from New York is going to fly, with his family, all the way to
LA to bring him flowers. [In Israel] we were considered part of the
family."

Israel, of course, does not have a monopoly on warmth. Mediterranean countries in general are considered warm, welcoming, and hospitable.
Yet there are factors that make the Israeli fan-player relationship unique.
Amir Gissin was the Israeli Consul General to Toronto and Western
Canada from 2008 to 2012, and also the driving force behind Brand
Israel, an initiative to make Israel relevant worldwide in a non-political
way. He once explained that the distinctly warm relationship between
African American players and Israeli fans in part has to do with similar
experiences in terms of longstanding exclusion by the religious/racial
majority, whether nationally or regionally.

"The Israeli society, because of geopolitical reasons, wants to be
loved," said Gissin. "Israelis want to be loved. This is one of our nationwide, psychological characteristics. Those who come to play with us,
and like us, get the same treatment [as native Israelis]. Compared to
other cultures, Israeli culture is very open and passionate. The value
and the essence of friendship, comradeship, is very developed. If somebody has a problem on the street in Israel, ten people would run to

give a hand .... The ultimate test is to be with your friends, out of all times when they need help, when they have problems. This is certainly a characteristic of Israelis and Israeli society."

Exceptions to the Rule

Despite its advantages for players, Israel doesn't work out for everyone. Like all international basketball destinations, Israel has had African American players who came, failed to make a satisfactory transition, and left. But because so many players spoke so highly of the country and so few had anything negative to say, I began to wonder, why *wouldn't* a player enjoy his time in Israel? I posed the question to some of those with the most experience in the country.

"I don't see how someone could come and be like, 'Oh, I didn't like it,'" said Jeron Roberts, an African American who played more than a decade in Israel, earned his citizenship, and even played on the Israeli national team. He pointed out that some players have on-court experiences that are not to their liking, for example too little playing time or clashes with coaches. "That can take away from the actual experience of being in Israel," he said. "But Israel as a whole? I've been a lot of places, and just the getting around, the people, the life ... it's not like this in other countries."

Then again, while the country itself is a consistent variable, there can be significant differences in players' attitudes. "Some guys come over here and do crazy things and act wild," said Chris Watson, an African American who, like Roberts, played more than ten years in Israel, earned his citizenship, and played for the national team. "If you're cool, and a good person, you'll get treated that way. But if you're an asshole, you're going to get treated a different way. I've seen guys come over here with a bit of a chip on their shoulder, and they think that America's the best, and 'I'm American, and you need to respect me,' and those guys get treated with no respect. I think it's all about the way you carry yourself and the way you behave—you'll get that in return. And that's the way it should be," he summed up.

Thomas, the player who was so touched by Israelis' response to his injury, said some of the same factors that make the Israeli experience so positive for most African American players can lead to a failed experience for others. He pointed to a vibrant nightlife and said that if a young player doesn't have the discipline to maintain proper priorities, he could more easily make bad decisions in Israel than just about anywhere else. The fact that most Israelis speak English can actually *add* to the trouble.

"For guys that come over and are not focused on what they need to do, [the social life] can be a problem, and again, that goes back to being able to communicate with people," Thomas said. "Because you can communicate, you can get into different things that you probably couldn't [otherwise]. I knew some people who liked to smoke marijuana. Well, it's easy to find if you know how to talk to people. Whereas if you were in Spain or in other countries where you can't really relate or [speak the language], you might not be able to find it. I think that's probably the biggest pitfall that could confront somebody who comes to Israel."

Canadian basketball agent Bernie Lee has placed a litany of players in Israel over the years and visited the country multiple times. Asked for any downside of playing in the popular basketball destination, Lee noted the country's size, saying that "the only issue with it is that it's really, really small. It's kind of like living in a fishbowl, especially when you're a 7-foot African American basketball player." Although Lee wasn't referencing him explicitly, he could easily have been talking about his former client Jeremy Tyler, one of the most scrutinized and criticized foreign players in the country in recent years.

A 6-foot-10 basketball prodigy from San Diego, Tyler became the first player to forgo his senior year of high school to turn professional overseas, signing with Jeffrey Rosen's Maccabi Haifa squad. The news drew considerable media attention both in Israel and the United States, but the experiment failed to work out from the start. A critical *New York Times* feature just three games into Tyler's professional career featured teammates questioning his work ethic, coaches bemoaning his immaturity, and even supporters from America critiquing his overall attitude. Tyler, who moved to Israel alone without any friends or family members, reportedly cried when leaving the United States and missed his first flight because the need for a passport took him by surprise. He left the locker room in tears after playing just 10 minutes in his first game, and he was kicked out of his third regular-season game for head-butting an opposing player.

Although things settled down for a stretch, Tyler eventually protested being benched for the first half of a game by changing out of his uniform and watching the second half from the stands. He parted ways with the team prior to the end of that first season, having appeared in 10 games and averaged an underwhelming two points and two rebounds in about eight minutes per contest. The story ultimately ended well for the youngster, with Tyler eventually developing into the NBA player he always seemed destined to become. And although many pointed the finger at Tyler for his struggles in Israel, Lee said it was simply a matter of a young man caught in a power struggle between a team owner who wanted to make a splash in the media and a coach who had little interest in developing a seventeen-year-old project.

"I just think it was an ill-conceived idea, from the standpoint that it was something that the owner wanted more than the coach wanted," said Lee, who negotiated Tyler's deal with Haifa. "And that put Jeremy in a situation where it was going to be pretty hard for him to be successful. I was trying to get him what I thought was a strong deal in a stable place, where he would be able to grow, but he just became the coach's whipping boy for the disagreements he was having with the owner at the time. Jeremy's situation, being that he should have only been a senior in high school, was a really tough spot for him ... But he was awesome. He tried really, really hard to embrace Israel."

When asked to reflect on reasons a foreigner may not enjoy his time in Israel, some of the most experienced and knowledgeable African American players in the country pointed to two primary factors: the player's attitude/maturity and his basketball circumstances. Both appear to have been relevant to the unsuccessful stint of the teenaged Tyler, who lived alone in a foreign country while planted to the bench—a perfect storm of risk factors for a subpar Israeli basketball experience. So what can be learned about Israel from Tyler's particularly turbulent time there? Perhaps only that the roughest experiences for African American players in the country have little or nothing to do with Israel at all.

A Brighter Spotlight and a Longer Career

As noted, Israelis *love* their basketball, as well as the hoopsters that play it. Sometimes that love can result in African American players getting the rock star treatment—one African American player after another told me about discounts received at local stores, free meals provided at trendy restaurants, and the relaxation of even the strictest of dress codes at the country's top nightclubs. Other times, though, that love can be expressed in a slightly more overbearing way. It's hardly unusual for Israeli fans to corner their favorite players and provide an earful of hoops wisdom and suggestions on how to improve their game. Although at first glance that may seem like an unwelcome reality of playing in Israel, many viewed it as a benefit.

"It's more than just coming to a game, the difference between winning and losing can be like living or dying for [Israeli fans], and I can relate to that because that's how I approach the game too," said Will Bynum, a college star and former NBA player who spent two years with Maccabi Tel Aviv. And what of the unsolicited advice he received so frequently those seasons? "I mean, it's different at first," Bynum said. "But once I started to get used to it, I started to appreciate it a whole lot more. Because I understood they had to be putting hours in and watching the game, and not just to see if a guy scored or if a guy made a highlight—they were really watching the game. That was big for me."

Chris Watson grew up in New York, unquestionably one of the world's greatest basketball locales. On the other side of the spectrum, his career has taken him to some countries, such as Belgium and Sweden, which are hardly considered hoops hotbeds. To him, the fun of playing in a basketball-crazy nation is well worth the scrutiny it comes with.

"Everything is watched," Watson told me of his experience playing in Israel. "It reminds me a little bit of New York. You can be a star one minute and the goat the next. It's pretty much day by day, and that's the way I like it. [In other countries] you can have two or three bad games in a row and there's not really much media coverage or pressure on you. In Israel, if you have one bad game, you're going to hear about it the whole week. When I was playing in those countries, I missed that pressure."

Of course, Israel is far from the only country where players grapple with the pluses and minuses of fanatic followings. Spain, Greece, Italy, and many other nations boast their own zealous fan bases and intense media throngs, each with their own distinct elements. There is, however, another important factor unique to Israel that has a direct and significant impact on African American players and their careers in the country. It may be a surprise, but the actual job requirements for basketball players are less demanding in Israel than elsewhere. There are several reasons for this, not all of them immediately apparent. First, Dawson pointed out that there are fewer big men in the Israeli league, making it easier to play well and put up good numbers. Furthermore, the basketball season in Israel spans from early October to mid-April, much shorter than in other countries where it can stretch to ten months long. Dawson said his time playing in Greece, long considered one of the best places to play basketball overseas, was a rude awakening.

"When I went to Greece, we [had to arrive] like three months before training camp even started [to begin conditioning with the coaches], and went to the mountains for almost a month of three-a-day practices," Dawson said. "And then to come to Israel—if you came halfway in shape, it was OK. If you came out of shape, they just worked you into shape. That part was easy."

Dawson was an active player into his late forties, and Campbell played into his fifties. Stanley Brundy, another African American who also played into his forties in Israel, attributes his extended career directly to the less rigid approach to practice and conditioning. Brundy said he is convinced this is an important reason why a lot of Americans who play in Israel return year after year. "The practices aren't so hard, and the level of play is not that tough compared to some of the other leagues in Europe and the States," Brundy said. "That's probably why my career has lasted so long. The basketball is great here, *and* you can keep your body—you don't have to do all the hard practices they do in Europe, the two-a-days every day. Maybe you might go twice a day at the beginning of training camp or preseason, but once you get the season started, it's not that hard. I think guys know they can prolong their careers."

Those are just some of the unique reasons given by African American players for enjoying their time in Israel and so frequently returning year after year, but it's hardly an exhaustive list. Many also spoke of (and posted on social media about) Israel's warm weather and its physical beauty, boasting mountains, deserts, valleys, coastlines, and other stunning sights. In fact, when one player who had previously played in Israel found out that a friend had just signed in Tel Aviv, he simply told him, "You're going to heaven." Comments such as those are a long way from the concerns expressed by many worried family members. Why Israel then? To Campbell, the answer is as simple as giving it a chance.

"I see a lot of guys [who are nervous] when they come here, and then I see them a few months later and they're all settled," said Campbell. "They're already thinking about coming back for another season. It's a great place to play, but when you talk to people in America, it's always, 'Israel? Why Israel?' And I always tell them, 'If you go there for a visit, you won't want to leave.'"

4

THEY'RE NOT IN KANSAS ANYMORE

AFRICAN AMERICAN BASKETBALL PLAYERS IN Israel clearly enjoy how Americanized the country is. They can converse with its many English-speakers, dance to American hip-hop music at night clubs, watch popular television channels such as MTV and Comedy Central, and eat at familiar fast-food chains such as McDonald's and KFC. Still, there are reminders each and every day that life in Israel is definitely not life in the United States. There are differences, some obvious, some subtle, that for better or worse make living in Israel a unique experience.

Speaking the Language

The most obvious and immediate difference is, of course, the language. Even though many Israelis speak excellent English, the language that surrounds players in newspapers, on billboards, in shop windows, and in chatter overheard on the street is Hebrew. Curiously, despite the number of players who return to Israel for multiple seasons, the majority of them do not progress beyond rudimentary Hebrew proficiency. When it comes to having some fluency in the language, veteran player Cory Carr estimated that only half of one percent of African American players get there. He later reconsidered even that number. "Half a percent might be pushing it," he said. "It's a really, really tough language, with its symbols and its history. I've been here a long time, and I still have a hard time speaking Hebrew. I can understand it better than I speak, but if you throw me into a room of Israelis, I can manage a conversation and wiggle my way out of the situation," he said with a smile.

I asked him, in Hebrew, whether he could speak to me in his second language. *"Ktzat, ktzat. Tedaber le-at, le-at, ani meveen,"* Carr answered. (Hebrew for, "A little bit, a little bit. Speak slowly, I'll understand.")

Chris Watson admitted that his Hebrew was not particularly good, despite more than a decade in Israel. Still he said he was satisfied that he had learned what he needed. Or, as he said, "If I was lost somewhere, and I needed to get out of that place, and nobody spoke English, I think I'd be able to speak well enough to get out."

Generally, the African American players I spoke to invoked two main explanations for the reason so few pick up Hebrew. First, players point out that not only do many Israelis know how to speak English, they *want* to speak English; local citizens generally are more focused on improving their English than the basketball players are on improving their Hebrew. Second, they point to significant and complex differences between the Hebrew and English languages.

"Hebrew is one of the hardest languages to learn," Marcus Fizer, then of Maccabi Tel Aviv, told me. "I picked up Spanish in two or three weeks. In Spain, it's easy. Even if I don't know the correct pronunciation of the word, I can read it. And if I'm reading it, people can understand what you're trying to say and they can teach you the proper way to pronounce it. But it's totally different here. The alphabet is different—you can't correlate what's 'A' from our alphabet to what's 'A' in Hebrew because it's not recognizable. I'm thankful that pretty much everyone [in Israel] speaks English … In Spain, [almost] nobody did."

Mixed Messages in the Media

Generally speaking, limited knowledge of Hebrew does not seem to create any barriers or challenges. But that is not the case in one area in particular. Players cited a lack of familiarity with Hebrew as a main source of problems dealing with the Israeli media.

"That's the biggest thing," former NBA player Fizer said. "You can talk to [the media] in the tone and intonation that I am speaking to you now, and they will take something out of the middle of a sentence and put it into a headline. You don't know what it says! And instead of [the organization] telling you what's being said, they're not, and now it causes a rift within the team. You just have to know who to talk to and who not to talk to."

Media conflict reached the point that longtime player Joe Dawson no longer conducted interviews with Israeli reporters unless he could independently tape record the conversation. Having been a victim of too many out-of-context or inaccurate quotes, Dawson keeps his own record in case he needs to dispute any misleading articles. As the father of two talented basketball players who have begun to garner attention in their own right, Dawson insists on having them follow suit.

Although issues about accuracy of quotes in the media are not uncommon in North America, the fervor of the Israeli media makes such issues especially sensitive. Members of the media there aren't hesitant about displaying themselves openly as passionate supporters of the teams they cover. For example, when Maccabi Tel Aviv defeated the Toronto Raptors in an exhibition game in Toronto in 2005, the Canadian press members were astonished to see Israeli media cheering on "their" team, yelling at the referees, and generally blurring what is usually a well-established line between reporter and fan. According to Andrew Kennedy, who spent twelve seasons in Israel before retiring in 2002, some Israeli media members were better to deal with than others, but passion was a trait they all shared, for better and worse. "There's normal media, there's paparazzi—they run the gamut, but all of them are pretty fanatical. The [language barrier] was definitely an added element.

Some things got lost in translation, and the media sometimes wasn't as professional as I thought they could have been."

Getting by in Hebrew

None of this is to say that African American players in Israel don't pick up *any* Hebrew. Indeed, a few players even go to *ulpan*, Israeli language schools set up to teach immigrants the language and assist in their integration into society. Jitim Young, a Chicago native and Northwestern grad who spent three seasons in Israel, didn't attend ulpan, but he made an almost immediate commitment to learn Hebrew. For him, embracing the language was a way to express his love for the country and its people.

"I have friends that teach me Hebrew, and I'm definitely making a conscious effort to learn as much as I can," Young told me. "Every day I try to learn new words and to put them in a sentence. And so I'm just getting better at it. It's funny, because I was in Greece, and I was picking up Greek, but with Hebrew, it just seems like it's been so much easier for me. It just seems like it flows, like I really, really understand it. I don't know if it's because I'm so open to being in Israel and so open to Hebrew culture, but I really enjoy learning the language and it feels like it's been easy to pick up."

Young acknowledges that he doesn't fully understand why so many players make little effort with the language. However, he notes that for him it is a big deal to be in Israel and says, "Other players may just come here and go through it like a job. But it's a huge opportunity to be in this country with the weather, the culture, the history of this place. The Israeli people are such a strong people … you [have to] commend them as a people. And to be in this land with everything you've read about in the Bible since you were a kid? I'm just captivated and captured by this culture and this country. I love it, I really do."

Gene Banks, an African American from Philadelphia, played six years in the NBA in the 1980s and was an assistant coach with the Washington Wizards when he and I spoke. Although he spent three seasons playing in Israel in the 1990s, he actually began learning Hebrew decades earlier. "My mother had us learning Hebrew when I was ten or eleven years old," Banks said. "The connection is really quite strange. My mother was a member of the Pentecostal Church, and she wanted us to know more about certain scriptures in the Bible that have Hebrew in them. I had no idea that's what she really wanted to do!"

The more usual patterns are for players to pick up some Hebrew informally from Israeli girlfriends, wives, and children as well as just being around the language every day. There are plenty of opportunities to learn the less refined side of Hebrew, as Ramon Clemente, a native New Yorker, said he initially did. "When I first got there, they taught me all the bad words," Clemente said. "Once I learned how to curse everybody out, I started to put little things together [such as] pick-up lines for chicks. And from that I started getting the words they teach you in practice, like *left* and *right*, those little phrases. And then I went from there—how to order my food and stuff. I did pretty good," he said with clear satisfaction.

In Clemente's case, language-acquisition priority followed the order of trash talk, then flirtation, followed by basketball, and finally sustenance. Others, however, gave basketball terminology greater attention. In his one season in Jerusalem, former NBA player Brandon Hunter learned to say *shalom*, meaning hello, goodbye, or peace; *yalla*, which means "let's go"; and *arba*, the Hebrew word for *four*. Why, of all words or even numbers, did Hunter pick up arba?

"We have a couple of plays, four side, four down—and four down is my play," said Hunter. "I'm definitely not going to forget that!"

The most famous example of an African American player displaying proficiency in Hebrew is Derrick Sharp, who, perhaps not coincidentally, is also one of the most beloved players in Israeli basketball history. Sharp began his career playing in the second and third divisions before playing for 15 years with Maccabi Tel Aviv, in the most Americanized and English-speaking city in Israel. Even so, Sharp developed a rare comfort level with Hebrew.

"I'm pretty good, I can hold a conversation," Sharp said, humbly. "I understand a lot, but I've never been to any formal lessons or anything like that. Just from my teammates and asking questions, I've picked it up a lot. I speak mostly Hebrew [day to day]. Everybody knows I speak Hebrew so they'll talk to me in Hebrew, unless I meet someone who wants to impress me with their English. Either way, it's fine with me."

After 18 total seasons on Israeli courts, Sharp retired in 2011, taking a position as an assistant coach with Maccabi Tel Aviv. His grasp of Hebrew no doubt came in handy in the role, assisting with his interactions with both Israeli players and media. For other players, the transition from a playing to a post-playing career is a major impetus to focus more on learning Hebrew. "My wife is always telling me," Carr said, "if I ever want to have a business or create some basketball school, I'm going to have to learn how to speak the language a little bit more fluently."

Dawson, the player who became so vigilant about his interaction with Israeli reporters, recalled how he didn't pick up much Hebrew in the first part of his career in Israel, notwithstanding that the star married an Israeli woman. He attended *Ulpan Aleph* (the beginner course), but he admitted he wasn't really interested in putting forth much effort. After a divorce, a humbling drop to playing in the second division, and one too many business negotiations in which he felt taken advantage of, Dawson committed himself to learning the language. His decision led to more than just a better understanding of Hebrew words; it also gave him a greater overall comfort about living in Israel.

"I decided that I had to really get into the Hebrew, because I had all the lessons I'd learned from *not* understanding it. I knew it was hard, and [only made progress] when I met my second wife. She started to help me and insisting on me speaking it, and helping me speak and speaking to me. Then I started to understand [Hebrew], and then once I started to understand then I could understand all the people around me—what they were saying in the elevator, what they were saying in meetings, what they're saying to their kids. It's not like you're just walking around and hearing voices. Now you're understanding!"

Cuisine: Charm and Challenges

Although Israel is home to a multitude of American food brands, it also has its own distinct style of cuisine incorporating traditionally Middle Eastern and Mediterranean fare along with dishes brought by Jewish immigrants from Eastern Europe, North Africa, Ethiopia, and elsewhere. Players can easily avoid Israeli food altogether, but, unlike learning Hebrew, most are eager to embrace it.

"I loved Israeli food!" said Kennedy, who spent 12 seasons in Israel before retiring in 2002. "I eat hummus to this day, and falafel. I loved, *loved* the food." Hummus is one of the most well-known Middle Eastern delicacies, a dip made with chickpeas, tahini, olive oil, lemon juice, salt, and garlic. Note that hummus is described as Middle Eastern—this dish, like a number of other beloved regional dishes, has complicated origins and claims by many nations. In 2008, Lebanon was reported to be mulling a potential lawsuit against Israel for allegedly marketing hummus as its own. Iteratively raising the bar in recent years, Israeli and Lebanese chefs have been one-upping one another to enter the *Guinness Book of World Records* with the largest plate of hummus. The current winning plate weighed in at more than 23,000 pounds!

Of course, though, there isn't anything that can be *everyone's* favorite. "I've tried just about everything, but I hate hummus," said Clemente, who spent four years in Israel. "That's like an insult if you say that to an Israeli, but I just didn't like it. It's too dry for me." Others vehemently disagreed with Clemente, many claiming hummus as one of their favorites. Other dishes players mentioned as winners at the table included *falafel* (a deep fried ball or patty made from ground chickpeas) and *shawarma* (shaved lamb, goat, chicken, turkey, beef, or a mixture thereof, with a variety of sauces and other toppings, served in a pita bread). There are a host of additional delicacies to choose from in Israel, and those players who spent the most time in the country had the deepest rosters of favorites. Stanley Brundy, for one, has lived in Israel since 1999, long enough for him to change his once-skeptical tune about Israeli food.

"I'm going to be honest with you, I didn't like it too much at first, because it's always the same," said Brundy. "In the States we always have a different variety of food you can try. Here everyone's got the kababs, the shawarma, hummus—everything is almost the same! But I'm adapting to it. I'm not too much of a meat man—I like all the salads, like the cabbage salad. I had never tasted that until I got here, and I can't stop eating it! I'm telling you, I love it, I really do! I don't see people in the States eating cabbage salad, but now I've got to have it."

Fred Campbell has spent 25 seasons in Israel and remained an active player at age fifty-four. Clearly, eating well and keeping his body in top condition is of utmost importance to him. In 2011, I had coffee with Campbell and his then–twelve-year-old son, Toi, in Tel Aviv, and Campbell admitted to taking some liberties with his diet when his favorite Israeli dishes are available.

"Man, my favorite food is *dag chareef* [Hebrew for spicy fish]. What else do I like, Toi, *shakshuka*?" Campbell asked his son, referencing a dish of eggs poached in a sauce of tomatoes, chili peppers, and onions, often made spicy. "I had shakshuka just last night."

"He was sweating from it!" Toi interjected.

"Yesterday, when I was eating shakshuka, my whole face was [covered] with sweat, and I'm like this [mopping his brow], but I'm still eating it!" Campbell said. "I've just got to have it. Got to have it! Even last night, I woke up out of the middle of a sleep, went to the refrigerator, grabbed the shakshuka and some crackers. I was standing at the sink with my eyes closed, eating shakshuka and crackers. And then I put it back, rinsed my teeth, and went right back to sleep. My wife, it drives her crazy. She'll say, 'How can you just get up and walk in the kitchen and just stand there and eat, and then go back to sleep?!' But it's just me," he said with a grin.

To former NBA player Hunter, sampling the local cuisine is part of the fun of playing international basketball. "I like Israeli food, the shish kebabs, the hummus," Hunter said. "To me, [not trying local cuisine] is narrow-minded. I'm here, I might as well try it out, accept the culture. I think you should [do that] anywhere. When I was in Italy, it was pastas and lasagnas, when I was in Greece, it was Greek salads and other Greek food. It's stuff we have in America, but it's not the same as when you're in the country itself. I think you should try everything, but I really do like the Israeli food."

Too Close for Comfort?

Whereas Israeli food is something African American players can choose to partake of or avoid, all of them must interact with Israelis themselves and those interactions involve their own unique nuances. Israelis are said to be aggressive in their day-to-day interactions, both in terms of what they say and how they act. The African American players I interviewed spoke glowingly about the warmth and helpfulness of the Israelis they encountered, but didn't mince words about the pushiness either.

"People here are right down your neck," said Chris Watson, who as a New York City native knows a bit about urban aggressiveness. "You go to the bank or the supermarket and they're all … on your back. They don't give you space! When I'm at the supermarket, they're killing me at the supermarket! They rush, they cut me off in line, they don't care! They go right in front of me in line. It's crazy. It took a little time to get used to, I'll tell you that."

Others had similar impressions and examples, and, as if those stories weren't enough evidence, I witnessed some classic Israeli pushiness myself in 2009 when I went for lunch in Ra'anana with Carr, then a veteran of almost a decade in the Holy Land. Toward the end of our meal and in the midst of our interview, Carr received a phone call on his cell phone. It was a friend, another African American playing in Israel, calling to discuss a visit from that player's mother—describing what they had done so far and asking Carr what else they should do while she was in town. After Carr and his friend exchanged a few comments and ideas, an Israeli woman seated at a nearby table—with a group that had actually moved from a distant table to a table closer to ours over the course of our meal—began to interrupt, telling Carr, "Excuse me sir, you are not alone here."

"Why are you being so rude?" Carr answered.

"You are not alone here," she said back. "You are shouting in my ear."

"You're standing right beside me!" Carr exclaimed. "It's a free country, no?"

Back and forth they went for a short while longer, before Carr ended the phone call with his friend and the conversation with his new acquaintance.

"All right business-lady, have a good one," he told her, before turning back to me, head shaking. "Just another antic in Israeli society right there."

Beneath the Abrasive Surface

Joe Dawson is an Alabama native who, after 14 seasons playing Israeli basketball, has remained in the country since his retirement in 2005. But his laid back, polite, Southern personality made his transition to Israeli life extremely difficult at first. In fact, although Dawson (like Campbell, Watson, and Carr) eventually became a naturalized Israeli citizen, he almost left for good after his first season because he had such a struggle getting along with people on a day-to-day basis. Dawson said, however, that over the years he came to understand that the aggression of Israelis wasn't about any actual anger they felt, but rather pressure they were under.

Living in Israel means living with constant international scrutiny, constant political pressure, and the constant threat of attack from neighboring armies or terrorist suicide bombers. Then there is the history of the Jewish people even before the advent of the modern State of Israel, with one exodus or tale of persecution after another, culminating in the Holocaust. Maceo Baston, a veteran of four seasons in Israel, describes Israelis as having a "matter-of-fact personality," one he found

understandable since "maybe that's how they got through all the trage-
dies and turmoil they went through."

Furthermore, the history of tragedy and turmoil is one shared by
Jews and African Americans, an important connection I explore in
greater detail in Chapter 12. For Dawson, time and a better understanding of the Israelis' circumstances helped put him at peace with the
"Israeli Way," even if he still can't help but notice it.

"When we're coming back to Israel [from the United States], and
I'm sure you felt it when you came, in the terminal at the airport every
gate has a line, except the one going to Israel," Dawson told me. "There's
no such thing as a line in Israel. There's an opening and everybody tries
to get there first. That's how it goes. Instead of feeling pressured by it,
I understand that's just the way they are, from birth."

Many players agree that the pushiness Israelis exhibit is the flipside
of the warmth they are also capable of. Like Dawson, Deon Thomas
needed time to realize that and to understand the seeming contradic-
tion that an Israeli who is yelling is not necessarily an Israeli who is
angry.

"That's how they are in Israel. You say 'personal space,' but to them
there is no personal space," said Thomas, who spent five seasons in
Israel. "It's, 'We're here together, sharing together.' They're a lot closer
[than Americans]. The things they do are different than the way we do
things here. I don't necessarily see that as a bad thing, it's just different.
I'll give you a quick story. My wife used to speak on the phone to her
best friend, who is also Israeli. When we first got married, I used to
always ask her, 'What were you guys fighting about?' She's like, 'What
are you talking about? We're not fighting, we're just talking.' I was like,
'Oh my God! That's talking?! You guys were screaming and yelling at
each other!' She's like, 'No, we were just talking.' It took me a couple
of years to be able to relate to the tone of the voices and the way they
speak to each other."

Campbell said he has been in Israel for so long that he not only
better understands the Israeli mentality, he has begun to embrace it.

"Even my Israeli friends always say, 'No, he's not American. He's Israeli,'" Campbell told me. "Some of them will tell me I'm too Israeli! But, you know, certain people you have to deal with them in the Israeli mentality, and I know how. And that's when it becomes funny, when [locals are] like, 'Ohhhh, this guy's Israeli.' Sometimes it's just being in your face. I'm from the South, so I'm not naturally in your face. Sometimes [Israelis] tell you exactly how it is right then and there, no cutting corners, and sometimes I have to push a button to go over to my Israeli mentality in order to understand. Because if you can't, then you will never understand what's going on."

His adjustment notwithstanding, Campbell still expresses some disbelief when describing how that Israeli mentality manifests itself.

"The thing about me is, I can never lose my Southern hospitality," Campbell said. "But at the same time, I have to switch over to the Israeli mentality, just to cope, especially when driving, or standing in the bank line. I'm a token in the bank line! Everyone comes in and gets in front of me, and then goes like this [peers up at him from a spot in front]. I'm like, 'I know you saw me. I'm the biggest man in here!' And they're like, 'Oh, I didn't know you were in line!' Well, how could I not be in line? It happens to me every time I go to the bank!"

Reckless Driving

The aggression of Israelis is probably most apparent in how they drive, reflected by the fact that since the state's establishment more Israeli lives have been lost on the road than on the battlefield. Players called driving in Israel "horrible," "crazy," and one actually compared it to a "video game." Marcus Fizer diplomatically described driving in Israel as "an experience" and added some examples to make his point.

"I've been in situations where I'm four cars away from a red light, and the fifth car behind me could be a bus, and the light just turned green like half a second ago and they're blowing their horn!" Fizer said. "Honestly, where can you go? One time we were stopped behind an eighteen-wheeler, and so we couldn't go, and there are cars behind me blowing their horns. Like, where am I going to go? It's just really frustrating. The horn is supposed to be used as an emergency thing, and it startles people! You hear a horn blowing and you're looking around trying to figure out what's going on. But that's how they are. I guess they're used to it," he added with a sigh.

Coming Around

In spite of the years Campbell has been driving in Israel, he *still* has not been able to get fully accustomed to the rudeness he sees from drivers around him. "You don't see common courtesy," he said. "You see someone pull up in the car, and they slow down to parallel park. This whole line right here will go around that car, and that car has to sit and wait. As opposed to, 'Let the man park and then everyone can go!' No patience, no patience. Everyone's in a rush to nowhere. Talking on the phone, driving, texting, driving. It's amazing." And it is no wonder, as Campbell points out, that "Israel is number one in car accidents."

Israel's traffic lights offer drivers a chance to display their impatience on a regular basis, said Jeron Roberts, another naturalized citizen. In preparation for a switch, the light changes from red only to red plus a yellow light below it and after that to the green light alone. Obviously this is meant to give notice to cars and pedestrians that the switch is coming, but Roberts explained that it effectively provides Israelis with a countdown to start honking their horns.

"One thing I learned," said Roberts, "is you know here how the light goes from red/yellow to green ... how it gives you a little time? As soon as that light turns green, if you're not gone, you're going to get honked at from everywhere! I'm like, 'Man, I didn't even get to process that the light went green before everybody starts honking at me to go!' That's one of my favorites. Yeah, I got used to it," he added. "After a while, getting honked at enough times, you get used to it. You just have to understand that they seem to be in a rush, but they have nowhere to go—that's what I always say."

Although some players tolerate the Israeli way of driving and others remain frustrated with it, a third approach is the way of "if you can't beat 'em, join 'em." As Brundy explained about his transition to driving in Israel, "I'm driving just like them now! I don't like when they flash you, you know, like get out of the way? If you're in the fast lane, and they want to pass you, they flash you and they keep the high beams on you until you move. I didn't like that at first—I was like, 'Why are they flashing?' I didn't know! I guess I was driving too slow for them. But now," he said with a chuckle, "I'm driving just like them!"

5

VIOLENCE

VIOLENCE, AND THE THREAT OF violence, have always been unwelcome realities for Israeli society. In its long history, Israel's capital city of Jerusalem has been destroyed at least twice, besieged twenty-three times, attacked an additional fifty-two times, and captured and recaptured forty-four times. The modern State of Israel was born in war in 1948 as the fledgling state triumphed over the armies of Lebanon, Syria, Iraq, Jordan, and Egypt, which had coordinated a simultaneous invasion on the day the British Mandate terminated, just one day after Israel's independence was officially declared. Israel has been involved in at least one war during each decade of its existence, and it has been the focus of two Intifadahs, violent and non-violent Palestinian uprisings that lasted a combined total of eleven years. And the violence in Israel isn't limited to war between nations—Israel is also constantly in the crosshairs of terrorist organizations for attacks both within its borders and on its representatives abroad. Car bombs, bus bombs, bombs in packages, shootings, and stabbings by terrorists are an unfortunate commonplace occurrence in day-to-day life in Israel.

Nonetheless, as discussed in Chapter 3, most African Americans who come to Israel to play professional basketball are actually surprised by the *absence* of signs of war there. Some, however, have been introduced far too quickly to the threat—and overt displays—of violence in the country. Shortly after he arrived in Israel in 1990, Donald Royal, a 6-foot-8 forward from New Orleans who would later become a starter with the NBA's Orlando Magic, went shopping with an Israeli friend at a Tel Aviv mall. He gave no pause when an elderly Arab woman walked by them and stopped in the middle of the food court to place her shopping bag on the floor. But when she then declared what he later found out was Arabic for "God is great," Royal's friend grabbed his arm and shouted frantic instructions for him to run. The two of them raced across the mall's concourse. "We were running, everyone was running, and I was saying, 'What's going on?'" Royal recalled. "The next thing I know, behind me, *boom*, the bomb she left in her shopping bag went off," he said.

"To hear about these things happening is one thing," Royal said, "but to be involved in one … it was the worst experience I've ever had. I didn't feel anything hit me, but it was way too close. I learned right there that if you ever hear that phrase, 'God is great,' start running. That's something the people who become martyrs over there typically say just before they kill someone or sacrifice their own lives for whatever their cause."

Although Royal narrowly averted disaster that day, his experience in Israel would again be marred by violence a few months later when Iraq began launching Scud missiles at Israel during the Gulf War. Fearing for his safety, the Maccabi Tel Aviv swingman asked team chairman Shimon Mizrahi if he could leave Israel and meet the team on the road for its games, a request Mizrahi understandably granted. Royal spent two weeks in a hotel in Switzerland, where he stayed close to his room, riveted by the sights he was seeing on the television. Although he was safe, Royal recalled feeling more lonely than lucky during those weeks. "I'm from New Orleans, and I never had my hometown bombed before," he explained. "I had been in Israel since the summer, and I'd gotten to know so many people there and I was scared, wondering if anyone I knew was hurt. I wandered around in a daze. I couldn't sleep."

So despite his mother's pleas for him to return to the United States, Royal chose to go back to Israel, where he was warmly embraced. The security guard in his apartment building shook Royal's hand when he saw him. "He said, 'I'm proud of you for coming back,'" Royal told *Sports Illustrated* at the time. "I know some people would not have made the decision I did, to come back to Israel, but I'm proud that I did. Once I got here, I realized I had made the right decision. I learned I had a lot of character. To know what the Israelis were going through and to decide to go through it with them made me feel good. I'm glad I came back."

Andrew Kennedy, a 6-foot-7 forward from Kingston, Jamaica, arrived in Israel in 1988, and he, too, lived there during the Gulf War. Later in the 1990s a border conflict forced him to stay inside his northern Israel apartment at times, because Katyusha rockets were being fired into the country from southern Lebanon. Though more than twenty years have since passed, he vividly remembers them whistling overhead, and the booms he would hear as they landed after passing over his home. Still, he chose to stay in Israel throughout.

"I just felt so much respect for Israelis," Kennedy said. "They showed so much courage, the way they conducted their lives, and their belief that this is their country and where they were meant to be. I know it might sound weird, but I never felt my life was in immediate danger," he said. "Having me stay was a source of inspiration for the Israelis, and they drew comfort knowing I could have left."

During times of conflict, Kennedy would visit injured children in area hospitals and kids in bomb shelters. "In Israel, every house has a 'safe room' where they go for protection in case of rocket attacks," he explained. "People sometimes lived in there for days on end, so we would visit occasionally." I asked Kennedy if, when he visited children in shelters or hospitals, he felt like a foreigner or a visitor to their nation. He responded immediately and unequivocally. "I was in it with them, an Israeli who came to visit. There was a definite sense that we were all in it together. I don't want to say as basketball players we were looked at as heroes, but we were admired, and our presence brought smiles to a lot of kids' faces and people in need. That was a really nice feeling."

Joe Dawson, an African American native of Tuscaloosa, Alabama, first moved to Israel in 1991. Although he spent the following few years bouncing back and forth between playing in Israel and in other leagues in Europe and the United States, he would eventually settle in the country permanently upon his retirement in 2005. Asked about coping with violence in Israel, Dawson recounted a years-old story as if it had taken place only days before. March 4, 1996, was the eve of the festive Jewish holiday of Purim, one of the most joyous days in the Jewish calendar, partaken in by religious and non-religious alike with costume parties and lavish meals. It is a holiday celebrating the redemption of the Jewish people from a planned genocide, but the celebrations were scuttled that night when a Hamas suicide bomber detonated a forty-four-pound nail bomb outside the Dizengoff Center, the biggest shopping mall in Tel Aviv. It was the country's fourth attack in nine days—one had taken place in Ashkelon and two others in Jerusalem. A total of sixty-one people were killed.

In 2011 I met with Dawson, then fifty-one years old, a citizen of Israel, and the father of two Israeli sons. He explained that he hadn't gone to the bombing site right away. "A few days later I walked through the mall and, amazingly, everything was back to normal," he said, clearly in awe that regular life could replace violence so quickly. As we sipped our iced coffees in the *kenyon* (shopping mall) in his adopted hometown of Rehovot, Dawson continued that he found the resilience of the Israeli people extraordinary and that it held true throughout the country. "The message the people gave after those attacks was that whatever their enemies did to them, they would not allow it to disturb their daily lives. Israelis live their whole lives like this, and it has become my commitment to Israel now as well," Dawson said. "It makes it acceptable to send your kid off to the army, which I'm about to face. You just have to believe in it," he added firmly.

The Israeli Army—Everybody In

In most countries today, soldiers comprise a self-selected subgroup of the larger population, people who have volunteered to serve their country. Compare that to the conscription in the Israeli army, a fact of life for everyone eighteen and over with the exception of ultra-Orthodox Jews, non-Druze Arab-Israelis, and a few others. Israeli women are required to don the uniform for two years of service and Israeli men for three, plus one month a year in the army reserves until their mid-forties. It is a true "citizens' army."

To understand the Israeli people's support of their army and their acceptance of the necessity of mandatory service, it is important to recognize the precarious nature of this young nation. Israel is only the 152nd largest country in the world, just slightly bigger than the state of New Jersey. Israel is not only small, it is surrounded by enemies or former enemies—twenty-two Islamic nations which are 640 times bigger in size and sixty times bigger in population. There is no buffer zone standing between Israel's citizens and its conflicts. Accordingly, a strong military, and the existence of conscription, is a national necessity.

Walk around any town in Israel for even a few minutes and you will notice the ubiquity of the country's young soldiers. They are the same bespectacled engineering students or lithe athletes you could see walking around elsewhere, except in Israel they are wearing the green uniforms of the Israel Defense Forces (IDF), and have guns slung over their shoulders. For Israelis, the IDF is a great unifier and equalizer; rich or poor, famous or anonymous, an Israeli is expected to serve, because the nation's very existence is always at risk, and it must employ its tiny population fully. There are approximately eight million people living in Israel, compared to, for example, 23 million in Syria, 36 million in Iraq, and almost 79 million in Iran—all sworn adversaries of the Jewish state.

At first many of the American players in Israel find the commitment to army service strange and somewhat perplexing. For example, Jeremy Pargo, an African American player from Chicago, recalled asking an

Israeli teammate shortly after he arrived in the country what would happen if a citizen left Israel to avoid army service. Pargo said the player didn't mince words in responding: "If you do that you should never come back!" So serious is the obligation that in 2013, following a successful freshman season playing and studying at Seton Hall University in New Jersey, Israeli point guard Tommy Maayan reportedly spent forty-eight hours in prison for failing to return to Israel in time for an army-imposed enlistment date.

Another African American player, Cory Carr, from tiny Fordyce, Arkansas, moved to Israel more than fifteen years ago, ultimately becoming a citizen in 2009. Carr has no issues with mandatory army service in Israel, a perspective informed by the years he has spent immersed in that society. He explained to me that he saw first-hand the value of that service and in turn, the value Israelis put on those in the army.

"This is a way of life," Carr told me, during a wide-ranging conversation we shared in his apartment in the cosmopolitan city of Ra'anana. "You live in Israel, you've got to protect the country and so you go into the army. Obviously, most of the people here are Jewish and have to serve. Everybody's together, and the Jewish mentality is togetherness, that's what I like," he added. After pausing to take a sip of his drink, Carr leaned forward and continued, his voice growing increasingly serious. "When there's a holiday in the country, everybody celebrates it. When there's triumph, it belongs to everybody. And when there's tragedy in the country, everybody feels it. The Jewish people, when a soldier's killed or people are hurt, the whole country gives all of its attention to that. You feel that! You feel the pain of the country, feel the mourning of the Jewish people," Carr reflected. "To get one soldier back who's been taken or held hostage, or even, unfortunately, sometimes to get back a body bag, the country will release 500 or 1,000 terrorists. That says something about the mentality of the Jewish people," he asserted.

It surprises many African American basketball players to discover that military requirements and conditions apply as much to their young

Israeli teammates as they do to any other citizens. During the years when American players would be on a college team, developing their game and partying after hours with their new friends, Israeli players would be serving in the IDF. In the United States, college players in elite basketball programs train and play at state-of-the-art athletic facilities, receive private academic tutoring and advising, and often live in exclusive team housing, separate from the regular student body. By contrast, only a very few exceptional Israeli athletes are granted minimal concessions to allow them to continue playing during their army service. For American players who are often used to receiving special treatment as athletes, the mandatory military service of their Israeli teammates offers an early and important lesson about the State of Israel.

"Sometimes it was weird," said Kennedy. "I mean, seeing one of your teammates leave early or miss practice altogether because he had to go serve in the army that day or knowing a player would be spending the night on guard duty in a particularly dangerous area," he said, pausing briefly. "You couldn't help but admire them and think, 'Wow, these people are really putting their lives on the line for their country, for the right to live.'"

Over time, African American players in Israel begin to adapt to the constant threat of violence and the need for a conscription army. In fact, their concerns about war and terrorism in Israel actually tend to strengthen the connection they feel to the country and its native citizens. Players described a process they go through that could aptly be characterized as "Israeli-fication," that is, changing from nervous visitors to confident Israelis, who cope resolutely with the threat of war or terrorism. "After a while you develop a thick skin about the potential for violence," noted Anthony Parker, who jump-started a sputtering NBA career with five great seasons in Israel. "I went from my early years wondering how the Israeli guys did it to my last years here telling the new guys, 'Don't worry, it's nothing, we'll be OK.'"

Players also start to recognize the impact of the intimate relationship that exists between soldiers and civilians. "You know, in the States we might have somebody we know who served in the military and maybe was on the battlefront," Parker continued. "But I think in Israel it's more immediate. You have brothers that are actively in Gaza or in the West Bank. You have uncles, you have fathers, you have so many people that have been touched—and I say touched because I don't know how else to say it—by the conflicts, so it's really, *really* personal."

Parker ultimately adapted thoroughly to the Israeli way of life, which he clearly demonstrated shortly after he left. Parker's success in Israel led the Toronto Raptors to sign him to a three-year, $12-million contract. He departed Israel for Florida to prepare for the NBA season, but he had scheduled a return trip to conduct a basketball camp for Israeli youth. As he was about to leave the States for Tel Aviv, Hezbollah kidnapped two Israeli soldiers and a battle between Israel and Hezbollah began. That fighting eventually escalated into a full-scale war, during which hundreds of thousands of Israelis were displaced from their homes, and 165 Israelis were killed.

So, with all of this happening, what did Parker do? Exactly what he had originally planned—he returned to Tel Aviv as scheduled. No longer a member of Maccabi Tel Aviv and already safely back in the United States, he nevertheless flew back to Israel, kept his promise, and held his camp. Interviewed by *SLAM* magazine for a feature about basketball in Israel, Parker reminisced about the strength and resilience of the Israeli people in the face of conflict, a resilience he himself had exhibited. "In the midst of war, you don't feel it. You go to the mall, you go to school, to the grocery store, you keep everything as normal as possible."

The specter of terrorism, like the compulsory military service, unites Israelis regardless of race or class. LaVon Mercer, an African American from Atlanta who played more than ten years in the country, often explains this element of Israeli life using a simple, but compelling, metaphor—the "brown paper bag test." In Israel, Mercer explains, it is literally a matter of life and death that all Israelis remain aware of their surroundings and be vigilant for anything that is out of the ordinary, no matter how innocuous it may seem.

"You learn to watch out for things that don't look right," Mercer told an American crowd during one of his many speaking engagements on behalf of Israel. "Like a bag lying somewhere by itself. Or strangers hanging around. Anything out of place. You [have to] become aware of everything. When I lived on Rehov Pinkas, a street in Tel Aviv, a bomb went off on the corner. There was a bag sitting there that we had walked by numerous times, as had other people. I was on my way to practice when it went off. Some people got injured and were maimed from that attack."

Mercer uses the metaphor to teach his audience that in Israel, something as simple as an out-of-place brown paper bag can actually be a threat that should be noticed, avoided, and reported. And although Israelis are born into that reality, they reserve a special admiration and appreciation for those, like African American basketball players, who *choose* to live in Israel and allow themselves to be a part of it.

Players as Soldiers

All African American players in Israel, no matter how short their stay in the country, experience the omnipresence of the nation's military, known as *Tzahal* (an acronym for Hebrew words that literally translate to Army of Defense of Israel, though the army is known in English as Israel Defense Forces, or IDF). Whether it's having teammates in the army, being checked by soldiers before entering a grocery store, or simply passing a group of young soldiers on a popular waterfront boardwalk, crossing paths with the IDF is part and parcel of living in the country. But for those players who decide to obtain Israeli citizenship, their relationship with the Israeli army can change from brushing shoulders with those who wear the olive-green uniform, to donning it themselves.

Perhaps befitting an army known for its flexibility and non-hierarchical nature (*Start-up Nation*, among other works, describes the phenomenon in great detail), whether or not an African American-turned-Israeli actually enlists and the duration for which he would serve, can vary based on a variety of fluid factors. For some who wish to become citizens but not join the army, their teams are successful in having the requirement waived. Some receive the same mandatory enlistment notices as any other Israeli citizen and are threatened with the same legal consequences if they fail to show up. Others voluntarily enlist but are allowed to leave after completing *tironut* (Hebrew for basic training). For those African American players that have served, their responses to being in the IDF were as varied as the men themselves.

Derrick Sharp, the Florida native who climbed all the way from the lower leagues of Israel to multiple Euroleague championships with Maccabi Tel Aviv, said he chose to sign up for army service to show his commitment to his adopted home. The powerful Maccabi organization may have been able to pull some strings to free him of his military obligation, but his commitment to even a limited stint with the IDF contributed to his status as one of the most beloved players in Israeli basketball history. He spent 18 years playing in Israel, but when I spoke with Sharp in the bowels of Nokia Arena (now known as Menora Mivtachim Arena) following a Maccabi Tel Aviv victory, he could not overstate the significance of his army days in particular.

"I did nineteen days in tironut, and it was great," he said, his tone turning resolute in the midst of the postgame frivolity taking place around us. "I really wanted to be looked upon as someone who takes being Israeli seriously. I'm sure the people respect me more for doing that, being a part of the Israeli culture by serving, just as they do. I'm glad I did—it was a good thing for me."

James Terry, an African American from Cleveland who ended up playing more than a decade in Israel, also served in the army as a nationalized citizen. His memories of IDF training were decidedly less romantic than those of Sharp. "The army was definitely an experience, although I wouldn't want to repeat it," he said. "I don't even remember exactly how much time I spent on the base, but I do remember that every day was too long ... the desert, the cold showers, and the food—it was awful! We learned how to shoot an M16 and how to dismantle it, but I just wanted the whole thing to be over. I did meet a lot of friends there, though."

On the debut episode of *Israeli Yellow Nation*, a television show about the Maccabi Tel Aviv organization, Sylven Landesberg and David Blu exchanged stories about their respective times in the IDF. The two African Americans share other similarities in terms of their backgrounds—each is Jewish by birth, each starred at major college basketball programs before taking his career overseas, and now, each is a veteran of Tzahal. The two shared laughs about gun maintenance, avoiding army jail, taking pictures with their fellow soldiers, and the rules surrounding their "five-star meals."

"You can only start eating when your commander, your *mefakedet*, comes over," Landesberg said. "You've got to sit with your hands behind your back before you can even touch your food. You're sitting with the food in front of you, and it can take five or ten minutes until she comes to you. Then she tells you how much time you have to eat—you usually get ten minutes to eat, fifteen minutes if you're lucky. Then you eat, and when I say 'eat' I mean you scarf it down, because when she comes back ten or fifteen minutes later, you've got to be sitting with your hands behind your back again. If you get caught taking an extra bite when she comes to your table … trouble."

Fred Campbell started playing in Israel a few years out of college in 1992 and remains an active player in Israel's lower-level leagues twenty-five years later. In between, he became a citizen and received a conscription notice and follow-ups like any other Israeli citizen would. Only, Campbell didn't realize this was serious business. "You know, they sent me this letter, and I threw it away. I got another letter, and my wife was like, 'Fred, you got another letter from the army. They want you to go to Be'er Sheva, to some army base there.' I never called, and I never went. Then I got a *third* letter," he said emphatically, "and it said someone was going to come to my house to arrest me if I didn't show up on Sunday. I showed up, but I only went because I was threatened with jail," Campbell said, laughing.

While Campbell was conscripted just like a typical Israeli, the 6-foot-7 basketball player, then thirty-four, was well-known and stood out immediately upon arrival. Even on the first day, waiting for his paperwork, Campbell drew a crowd of curious enlistees and active soldiers. "I did everything that was expected of me," Campbell said, "but it was funny trying to get clothes I could wear. Pants that fit in the waist were too short, so I ended up tucking my pants into my boots. And the other soldiers laughed at me because I would iron my uniform. You know, Israelis don't do that, but I come there like an American, with creases down the middle of the pants, creases down the sleeves of the shirt, and my boots shined. When it came to the running and all the physical training, I helped the other soldiers, but they helped me a lot too with taking the gun apart, putting it back together."

Campbell was in the army for only a month because his commanding officer, a basketball fanatic, offered to get him a release. He had expected to serve for two years, and said that, frankly, getting out so early was a welcome reprieve. But Campbell quickly added that he greatly enjoyed the time he did serve. "I'm still in contact with a lot of the guys even now, all these years later. I always joke with them, and they're like, 'Where are you Fred?' I tell them I got *Miluim* (reserve duty), and they're like, 'Where?' And I say 'Lebanon!' They're like, 'Really?' And I'm like, 'Nah!'"

Shortly after receiving his Israeli citizenship, Dawson *wanted* to serve in the IDF, as a statement of fulfilling his civic duty. At age thirty-two he married an Israeli woman he had met during his first year in Israel and shortly after that he drove—unsolicited—to sign up for duty. When he arrived at the military base, he was asked why he was there. "I said I got married recently, and I know that every Israeli has to serve in the army, and I just came to let you know. The guy looked at me funny, and just then someone came out of a nearby office who recognized me. He asked me to come into his office, and he said, 'We really respect that you're doing this, but service is not mandatory after age thirty. There's no shortage of soldiers right now, so you don't need to be here.'"

Dawson acknowledged that one reason he attempted to enlist was that he didn't want the IDF to come after him, but he also had a principled motive. "I think they were shocked that I would volunteer, and everybody was looking at me like I was crazy," he said. "But that's just how I am. I tried to join the army because I'm here, and I'm supposed to help protect the place where I'm living."

Heroes in Their Own Way

For the most part, the African American players I spoke with reported remarkably similar perspectives on the issue of violence in the country: they typically felt surprisingly safe. In fact, their families back in the United States were usually more worried about violence in Israel than they were. Viewed from the perspective of those American relatives, war is something that takes place somewhere else, somewhere distant. For them, the prospect of living a normal life, working and socializing in the midst of war, is tough to imagine. But as player after player told me, those are often the circumstances under which day-to-day life in Israel carries on, even flourishes. What those players fail to mention, however, is the vital role they play in enabling the country to maintain that normalcy.

The heavy reality of violence in Israel underscores the importance of distraction for its citizens, and for that, basketball is high on the list. Yaron Talpaz, then the head of sports news at *Arutz Ha'Sport* (The Sports Channel), Israel's equivalent of ESPN, explained why in times of conflict or threat of conflict, television ratings for basketball games tend to soar.

"In troubled times, you realize two things about sports," he said. "One, it's not that important, and [two], somehow it's very important. What do people in the shelters or those staying in their homes, hoping a missile won't land on their heads, have to do? They watch sports."

In one notable circumstance, watching basketball in a bomb shelter would have been a welcome alternative to an even harsher reality. Gilad Shalit was a nineteen-year-old corporal serving in the IDF on June

6, 2006, when Hamas and other militant groups crossed the border and attacked Shalit's tank unit, killing two Israeli soldiers. Shalit was dragged from the tank with multiple injuries and held captive for 1,941 days before Israeli Prime Minister Benjamin Netanyahu eventually agreed to swap Shalit for hundreds of Palestinian prisoners being held in Israeli jails, many of them convicted for deadly terrorist attacks. The years-long ordeal was an international incident, and Shalit later wrote that during his captivity he drew strength from listening to sports (including Israeli basketball) on the radio, finding it a rare break from the reality in which he found himself. He even watched games together with his captors, with sports providing a unique common denominator he could share with them.

Basketball continued to be a source of comfort and normalcy for Shalit after his release. One of his first public appearances was attending a Maccabi Tel Aviv game, and not long after that, he had a chance encounter with Mark Brisker, a retired African American player best known for his time with Maccabi. It was an interaction that made a lasting impact on the former hoopster.

"I had just finished ulpan, and I invited everybody from my class to my house for a barbecue," Brisker said. "Afterward we decided to go to the pool, and Gilad Shalit was there! He knew me from Maccabi, and *he* wanted to take a picture with *me!* Just as [I was thinking about asking for] a picture with him, one of his friends came and said, 'Hey, Gilad wants to take a picture with you!' Then we started talking, and I played two-on-two with him and some of his friends. I told him he was a true hero. To me it was a blessing—I was really proud to meet him."

As much as *watching* basketball helps the Israeli people during troubled times, the game's biggest impact may be in what it *demonstrates* about the Israeli people—their amazing resilience. Consider the prime example of Maccabi Tel Aviv during the Gulf War, when Iraq lobbed Scud missile after Scud missile into Israel, a demonstration of Saddam Hussein's anger about America's opposition to his Kuwaiti invasion. Israel was under attack for six long weeks, but throughout, Maccabi Tel Aviv remained a visible, international symbol of national defiance.

Israelis, including the most prominent basketball players among them, refused to let the war bring the country to a halt.

It was not easy. After the Scuds began to fall, the local Israel Basketball Association suspended its games, leaving Maccabi Tel Aviv (through its participation in the Euroleague) as the only team the nation had to support. But the International Basketball Federation, basketball's international governing body known as FIBA, decided to prohibit any games from being played in Israel. As a result, Maccabi Tel Aviv would have to play all of its scheduled home games on the road. Not only would the players now have to deal with the obvious difficulties those circumstances presented—such as twice the travel and competing exclusively in front of their opposition's antagonistic hometown crowds—they also faced the threat of terrorist attacks against the team itself. All Israeli sports teams were considered prime targets, but Maccabi was the country's most prominent one. Still, the team persisted, flying out of Ben Gurion Airport on Tuesdays, playing their games in Europe on Thursday nights, and then flying back to Tel Aviv every Friday. This allowed the Jewish players to celebrate the Sabbath at home, from sundown Friday to sundown Saturday, and for them to spend at least part of the week with their families. Circumstances were difficult, but continuing to play was viewed as the only option.

Israeli player Nadav Henefeld, twenty-two at the time, explained the drive behind the country's focus on sports during such distressing events and the motivation it provided him and his teammates. "We *want* to keep playing," he said emphatically. "Sport is something everyone can feel close to. It can unify. When we are on the road, we show people outside Israel that we are still living, still working as a society, as a people, and that is important. Israel has not shut down. Israel still works. The situation for my country has never been easy, but we still have our lives and we want to make a statement to the world," he concluded.

But it was one thing for the Israeli players such as Henefeld to shoulder the excess burden and risk. It was, after all, their country, and the citizens whose existence they were showing off to the world were their brothers, sisters, cousins, and friends. But what of their African American peers? This wasn't their fight. These weren't their people. They would have been well within their rights to pack their bags and go. You could argue that anyone in his right mind would do so. And yet they didn't.

Mercer, Maccabi's power forward, recalls how his parents begged him to return to the United States. "What are you trying to prove?" his mother asked. "What are you doing over there? Explain it to me." And so he did.

"Of all the bad things that have happened here, Maccabi Tel Aviv has been one of the few good things," Mercer told her. "Team players can't go anywhere and not be noticed. We're not just Maccabi of Tel Aviv. Or Maccabi of Israel. We are, really, Maccabi of the Jewish nation. It's an important thing we're doing. We're helping each other. We're giving something back. There is nothing like this team in the United States. No analogy. It goes a lot deeper than sports. We are like ambassadors for Israel." (Mercer actually *became* an ambassador for Israel in 2002, being officially designated as the ambassador to the Southeastern United States by the Israeli consulate general to the Southeast.)

The significance of Maccabi's continuing to perform as normal was not lost on team chairman Mizrahi. Although he referred to the Israeli players in particular, his comments are arguably just as applicable to the African American members of the team. "Some Israelis serve in the military, and others, like the Israeli members of this team, serve by playing basketball," he said at the time. "They are serving the people, too. All our games have been televised. This has been important during the war, when most people go home at night. Millions watch us on Thursday night, according to the polls. In one very close game there was an air-raid alarm, and many people wouldn't go to the shelter."

Of course, some American players did choose to return home rather than stay in Israel with their respective teams. Interestingly, one of strongest statements on the issue of players staying or leaving came from Earl Williams, an African American player from Levittown, Pennsylvania, who ended up playing more than a decade in Israel. An

Israeli writer once said that Williams's "Zionist spirit would do credit to any blue-and-white blooded Israeli," and his comments on the matter back up that assertion. "They knew where Israel was before they agreed to play here," Williams said at the time. "Israel and Tel Aviv is my home, and I won't move from here." Years later, he reflected again on the decision to stay: "I thought, I'm not going to leave my people when I was needed," he said. "Israel is my country just as much as America."

To get a better sense of the Israeli perspective on various issues, I went to the Israeli Consulate in Toronto to speak with Amir Gissin, the consul general of Israel to Toronto and Western Canada. As an added reminder of the constant threat of violence, not just in Israel but to Israel's representatives abroad, I was subjected to a series of questions before I could even get onto the elevator that led to the consulate's floor, then to a longer, more drawn-out series of questions to get into the office itself. My belongings were put through a metal detector, and my digital audio recorder was tested to prove that it actually did what I purported it would and nothing else. These safeguards, used in all official Israeli government institutions, demonstrate all too clearly the reality that the nation is perpetually under the threat of violence. When I finally met the consul general, and asked him about the significance of African American players staying in Israel during times of conflict, I was particularly curious to hear his response.

"That is the *ultimate* test of joining in," said Gissin, pausing for emphasis before continuing. "If somebody stays, he's certainly one of us. I think that those who choose to stay continue to feel the love and appreciation from everybody, always. They are among the heroes of the nation."

Violence and the threat of violence shaped the Israeli society these African American players lived in, and the personalities of the Israeli people they interacted with. From those, like Dawson, who would become Israeli citizens and send their children into the army, to those whose stints in Israel included narrowly avoided terrorist attacks, to the many who never felt so much as a nervous moment, the experience of every African American basketball player in Israel was affected by the nation's history of conflict. These players, however, are more than just bystanders observing the impact of violence on Israeli society—in many ways they act as ameliorative agents. A primary goal of terrorism, for example, is to generate fear and panic, to cause a change in behavior. By playing in Israel, African American basketball players provide not only an invaluable distraction during difficult times, but a public symbol of the lack of that fear and the resistance of that change. While they may be American by birth and African in ancestry, their performances and success on the court are sources of tremendous pride to Israelis and to Israel. But most important is the character, poise, and solidarity that these players demonstrate by choosing to stay in the country when they have the option to leave, by standing side by side with Israelis and looking out for the same brown paper bags, visiting the same local hospitals, and watching and listening to the same missiles fly overhead.

6

RELIGION

BRANDON HUNTER, WHO ONCE PLAYED for the Boston Celtics, is a fighter on the court—a true portrayal of the term "power forward." Listed at 6-foot-7 (and likely standing an inch or two shorter), he's more diminutive than most players he matches up against, but his 260 chiseled pounds worth of brute strength compensate for anything he lacks in stature. I saw Hunter play for Boston in 2003 and again in 2010 when I joined the frenzied fans in Jerusalem's Malha Arena to watch him and his Hapoel Jerusalem teammates battle the opposition. In both cases I was struck by Hunter's intimidating presence, with his shaved head, intense glare, and generally menacing on-court demeanor.

A few days later I met with Hunter and his girlfriend at Kenyon Malha (a Jerusalem shopping mall) and his expression was far more perplexed than fierce. The couple had been invited to Friday night dinner to celebrate *Shabbat* (the Jewish Sabbath) at the home of one of his team managers. Our plan was to meet at the mall after practice so that Hunter could buy a small gift for his hosts, after which we would head to a nearby coffee shop for our interview. It was still mid-afternoon, but when we got to the mall we saw that the chain-link gates were already being lowered and the stores were closing. Unable to shop, we headed to the nearby café. The server told us they too were about to close in anticipation of Shabbat. Only some good-natured cajoling from Hunter (surprisingly charming and funny off the court, when not tossing opponents around on it) convinced the proprietors to allow us to stay, at least for a little bit. We sat down, but having the staff sweeping the floor under our feet and placing chairs on the tables around us made it obvious that preparation for Shabbat would not wait for the café's celebrity guest.

Americans play basketball in dozens of countries around the world. In each of those nations, players have many stories about adapting to life in a strange land. But part of what makes the experience of African American players in Israel so unique is that it is a religious state, a Jewish one at that. Although the nature and extent of its influence varies somewhat depending on specific situations and individuals, it is readily apparent that religion is a constant presence in Israel, with Israeli basketball being no exception. The doorways to team locker rooms, for example, are adorned with *mezuzahs* (parchment scrolls contained in a decorative case which are inscribed with specified Hebrew verses from the Torah and affixed to the door frame in Jewish homes) and teams announce not only those fans in attendance at their games who are celebrating a birthday (as they do in North America), but those who are celebrating a Bar Mitzvah or Bat Mitzvah as well (those being the Jewish coming of age rituals marking thirteen-year-old boys' and twelve-year-old girls' transitions to adulthood). Indeed, the unique religious aspect of players' Israeli experience sometimes becomes apparent even before their flights touch down in the country.

"It was a bit strange on the airplane," Vidal Massiah, an African Canadian who spent time with two Israeli teams, recalled. "People were praying, walking down the aisle [to pray together at the back of the plane]. It seemed like everyone on the plane was Jewish except me. I'm sure that wasn't the case, but it seemed like it, so that was kind of strange." However, Massiah said that having arrived in Israel, he didn't feel overwhelmed by religion and was in some ways quite grateful for its traditions. "When I got there we had almost back-to-back-to-back holidays," he noted. "At that point it turned out to be a good thing because we got more days off. There were more holidays, more food. Every time there was a holiday they brought in more food!"

Holidays and Shabbat

Massiah, like most players, arrived in Israel shortly after Labor Day, which roughly coincides annually with the most widely observed holidays on the Jewish calendar: *Rosh Hashana* (Jewish New Year) and *Yom Kippur* (the Day of Atonement)—known collectively as the High Holidays—and *Sukkot* (the holiday of gathering). These take place over a period of just three weeks. Given the significance of the High Holidays many Israeli Jews, even secular ones, follow the traditions closely, including not using electricity or driving any kind of motor vehicles on the holidays. As you can imagine, witnessing this makes quite a memorable first impression, including on Marcus Fizer, then newly signed with Maccabi Tel Aviv and previously an NBA lottery pick with the Chicago Bulls.

"When we got here in September, it seemed like there were more holidays than I'd ever seen in my life," Fizer said a few months later. "Every other day we couldn't do something, or something was closed, or something was going on because it was the holiday season. The most memorable was two and half days of not driving cars. That was really weird. Seeing four or five hundred people in the middle of the street, just walking in the middle of the street! It was peaceful, though," he said.

Players quickly discover that the countrywide peaceful feeling Fizer described is not just connected to the High Holidays. In Israel this happens weekly, in celebration of Shabbat, which starts at sunset Friday and lasts until nightfall on Saturday (officially, after three stars have become visible in the sky). One of the biggest adjustments African American players in Israel have to make, as my Friday afternoon with Hunter reflects, is getting accustomed to just how much of the country grinds to a halt for those twenty-four hours. Businesses close and a day of tranquility and rest replaces the hustle and bustle of daily life.

Additionally, for the religious and secular alike, Shabbat in Israel brings together all the family.

Andrew Kennedy, who played 12 seasons in Israel, shared Friday dinners with many families he befriended in his time there. And when he did, he noticed that even family members who lived in different cities around the country returned home for the weekly meal, something that made a lasting impression on him.

"I loved the fact that on Shabbat, even if someone is away from home, they would still come back, get together, and break bread," Kennedy said. "I loved that, I thought it was great. The fact that people could sit down and talk about their day and their week and what's going on in their lives and stay in touch. [Israelis] protect the family structure and preserve it, and I think that's very important and something that's missing in [American] society today. I have a lot of respect for [Jewish] culture."

Kennedy was also pleased to discover that Israelis welcome others into their family gatherings. He recalled how he spent his years in Israel getting to know his teammates, their friends and families, and many other native Israelis. Often friends and new acquaintances as well would invite him to Shabbat dinners and celebrations of the various Jewish holidays. Eventually, Kennedy said, he began to consider these people to be his extended Israeli family, and he still keeps in touch with many of them, having spoken to some earlier on the very day I interviewed him. The warmth of his Israeli hosts ensured invitations were always extended to Kennedy, and his warmth and inquisitive nature made him happy to accept them and make the most of his Israeli experience.

"I ate countless dinners and shared many, many holidays—you name it, I spent it with [my Israeli friends]," Kennedy said. "I was inducted [into their families]. Not only was my team my family, but I had an extended family as well. It was great. I learned a lot about the culture and the way Jews interacted, Israelis interacted. There is so much celebration. Obviously, Yom Kippur is one of the darkest holidays, I don't even know if I should say it's a holiday really, but the

Jewish New Year, it's a celebration … Purim, [people wear costumes] like Halloween. I've always been the type of person that even if I don't agree, I can appreciate and understand why, appreciate the differences, and can celebrate along with people and respect it."

Like Kennedy, fellow-American Stanley Brundy has also spent the majority of his decades-long basketball career playing in Israel. Unlike Kennedy, who returned to the United States after retiring, Brundy married an Israeli woman and remains in the country today. Holidays, of course, fill his calendar as well, but he said he is somewhat less enthusiastic than others seem to be. "Wow, man, do we have to get into those holidays?" Brundy asked me, laughing. He quickly assured me that he has adapted well to most, but, in truth, not all of the holidays. "I really do not like Passover," he said, touching on the biblical holiday commemorating the Jewish people's liberation from slavery in Egypt, which involves an annual retelling of the story of that liberation. "All the reading and all that stuff you have to do *before* you eat? You've got to count the hours. I'm so hungry, I'm ready to eat right away, but you have to go through all the reading and stuff like that … [Every year I] go to someone's house because they invited me over, and I would sit with the family, listen to what they had to do, and then eat!" I asked him if he ever took part in the readings that are integral to the Passover celebration. "No, man—I can't read Hebrew! I was observing. I was very observant," he replied with a chuckle.

Bigotry of a Different Kind

To gain a better understanding of how religion impacts African American players' experiences in Israel, I called on Rabbi Yaakov Gloiberman, who is uniquely qualified to comment. Gloiberman is the spiritual adviser to former Maccabi Tel Aviv coach Pini Gershon as well as to other prominent members of the Israeli basketball community. He observed that the passion Israelis have for basketball was actually in keeping with the Jewish religion—the ancient scholar Maimonides (also known as *Rambam*) wrote that being active in sports is in fact a requirement. Gloiberman then explored the religious context for some of the other unique advantages African Americans report experiencing while playing in Israel, including the relative lack of perceived racist experiences.

"It is written about the priest Aaron [brother of Moses] loves peace, searches for peace, loves mankind," Gloiberman told me, in Hebrew. "It doesn't say he loves these ones or those ones, it says he loves mankind. Everyone is a human being in front of God. Racism? Sir, there is no room for racism. He who is racist, hates God. Who created us?" Gloiberman asked me. "God," I offered. "Very good," he said. "If I hate you, I hate God."

However, the fact that many African American basketball players in Israel report a lack of discrimination does not mean that the country is the race-blind utopia Martin Luther King Jr. dreamed of, a topic I deal with in Chapter 12. Setting aside the issue of anti-Black discrimination for now, players found they were sometimes confronted with a wholly different type of bigotry—anti-Semitism. Cory Carr, an African American player who has been in Israel for 15 years and a citizen since 2009, said that he hadn't known many Jewish people before coming to Israel, other than his agent, Mark Bartelstein. But he discovered that playing for Israeli teams and representing Israel abroad during games in Europe gave him a taste of *being* Jewish.

"We experienced anti-Semitism in a couple of places—in Turkey, in Croatia," Carr said. "Name-calling ... in Croatia, over the bench we have a protective plastic covering. The whole game people were throwing batteries, coins, gum, rocks, whatever they could throw—the whole game, *bang, bang, bang.* We definitely got it worse because we were an Israeli team. This is the one country that's a little bit different from the rest ... I can feel [Jews'] pain. Any of the people that struggle—I'm African American so I can understand that struggle."

That sense of identification with Jews was not limited to Carr. Many African American players talked about the strange emotions evoked by hearing anti-Semitic chants or seeing swastikas exhibited in protest of Israeli teams in foreign gyms. In a 2007 game against CSKA Moscow in Russia, a pregame laser show depicted Maccabi Tel Aviv as a long-bearded Orthodox Jew wearing a traditional fur hat, while CSKA was depicted as a steam train running over the Jewish caricature.

Basketball provided some African American players with the opportunity to gain a better understanding of the Jewish people's tragic history. The Israeli Super League recently organized visits for its players to Yad Vashem, Israel's acclaimed Holocaust museum. Years earlier, James Terry, a veteran of more than ten seasons of Israeli basketball, made time in Europe to visit the Auschwitz concentration camp. "It was a very important and emotional event for me, and it made me understand how it feels like being Israeli and Jewish. I know how much evil came out of that place, and it was very sad for me, but I am happy I visited there. You can read about it in books, but it can't really demonstrate what really happened in that damned place," he said.

A Place for Christians

For many African American players, the opportunity to live and play ball in Israel provides not only a way to learn about the history of the Jewish people, but a thrilling and up-close look at their own Christian roots. Israel, of course, was the cradle of Christianity, and, as such, can be a strong draw for players. Indeed, Fizer, then a highly touted acquisition of Maccabi Tel Aviv, reported that his faith was a main reason he came to Israel in spite of his concern about possible violence in the region.

"My biggest thing was that this is the Holy Land, this is where everything I've been taught in the Bible took place," Fizer said. "Of course there is concern of sorts [about violence]. But my father is a minister and a preacher and my mother is a missionary. I've been raised in the Church, and we have a strong belief and faith in God. Bad things can happen anywhere. But I have faith that whatever happens is His will. I have faith that I'm covered. If I'm at the place where that takes place, then I'm there for a reason. I pray that it doesn't happen, but I'm not going to allow it to disrupt my thoughts and my ability to live life and live abroad."

Living in Israel means that African American Christians can visit a host of holy sites that they have heard about since childhood—places like the Church of Nativity in Bethlehem (the birthplace of Jesus and what some feel is the world's most important Christian site), the town of Nazareth (Jesus' childhood home), the Jordan River (the site where Jesus was baptized by John the Baptist), and the Church of the Holy Sepulcher (believed to be where Jesus spent his last hours and was crucified). Other countries can offer players passionate fans, friendly locals, good competition, and generous salaries, but only Israel can also provide them with this connection to their religious backgrounds.

Carr said that he had visited just about all of these sites. "Sea of Galilee [where it is believed that Jesus walked on water], Jerusalem, Bethlehem—it's an experience, man, a really good experience. I did a lot of those things when I first came to Israel … when my parents first came they did all those tours. Just to learn, just to see for themselves, get that experience. It's a very big advantage to playing in Israel … Everything we read about, it's right here! History is right here!"

Roger Mason Jr., who played in Jerusalem between stints in the NBA, talked about poignant moments that he experienced driving to and from Tel Aviv, where he visited friends. While Mason enjoyed the slower pace of life in Jerusalem, he liked to combine it with the more active Tel Aviv lifestyle, but it was on his trips between the two cities that he would realize the uniqueness of his circumstances at the time. "To live there and be driving home and see signs for Bethlehem, sometimes I would do a double take," he said. "It's pretty neat to call that place home."

Carr and Mason are both mature players with years of life experience under their belts, but younger players have also shown interest in Israel's religious and historical significance. Jitim Young, who signed with a second-division team in Ramla in just his second pro season out of college, said he established his plans for religious sightseeing before he even got on the flight to Israel. In our phone conversation shortly after he arrived he told me he had grown up in the Church and had been reading the Bible since he was a child. He excitedly explained that he was thrilled "to walk the same roads I've read about my whole life!" Given his attitude about living in Israel, I wasn't surprised to hear that he signed to play another season there. When we spoke during that second stint, Young told me he had been to even more sites and gained an ever deeper appreciation of being in the country.

"I've gotten to see Harris Gate, the Mount of Olives, a lot of the traditional places that people grow up in Church reading about," Young said. "All these places … I've gotten to walk the land and see it with my own eyes. It's just an amazing experience. Words can't really express how honored I feel being here, just to get the opportunity to experience all this—it's so great."

In the fall of 2011, for the third straight year, Young packed his bags and left his Chicago home for another season of Israeli life. Unlike the previous two years, he did not come with a signed Israeli team contract in hand. What Young did have was an Israeli girlfriend, a desire to explore more of the country's biblical sites, and faith that despite the professional uncertainty, he was better off in Israel than anywhere else. In December of that year (during a conversation we joked had become an annual tradition), Young told me he wasn't finished seeing everything Israel had to offer, but he was enjoying ticking one destination after another off his list. He most recently had been to Eilat, Israel's southernmost city at the tip of the Red Sea.

"That was the first time I've been," Young said. "You're driving toward Eilat, you see Jordan, and then you get to Eilat, and you see the Red Sea, and they show you that right across, there is Egypt. I'm looking at the Red Sea and thinking, 'This sea right here is the sea that parted. This big old thing right here.' It just made you feel like, faith-wise, there's nothing that's impossible if you pray. [The religious aspect] is important. It's a big deal to me."

One of Israel's most famous religious sites is the Western Wall, the closest remaining connection of the Jewish people to the Second Temple (which was destroyed by Rome in 70 BCE) and a popular destination for visitors of all faiths. After the destruction, only one outer wall remained standing, which was not even a part of the temple itself but rather an outer wall surrounding the Temple Mount. For Jews, however, the remnant of what was once the most sacred building in the Jewish world has become the religion's holiest site. Also known as the *Kotel* (from *Kotel ha-Ma'aravi* being Hebrew for Western Wall), it eventually began being referred to as the "Wailing Wall" for the heartfelt nature of the prayer there. That name rung true with Alysha Clark, a WNBA star who spent five seasons in Israel and became a citizen (by virtue of having Jewish ancestry, though she was raised Christian).

"One [experience] that jumps out immediately is [visiting] the Western Wall," Clark said of her time in the Holy Land. "I didn't really know what to expect when I went there. You kind of hear that it's the holiest place and the closest to heaven and God that you get to go to. But when I actually went, I can't even explain how I felt. My heart was just so happy. I was in tears when I just walked in through the gates there. It just immediately took me over."

There are, of course, players, particularly younger ones, who are more interested in nightclubs and video games than historical touring. Most, though, according to Carr, eventually come around to investigating the rich history around them, especially when encouraged by new friends.

"A lot of players are so caught up in being in Israel, the overall perspective and what they see on television, they're a bit afraid to move around," Carr told me. "For the most part though, when they get here and talk to the right people about how things really go over here, they want to go see some things, see some of these sites, experience some of this history. They usually have an opportunity, especially when they meet those pretty little Jewish girls! [The girls] always want to take them somewhere! Guys are like, 'Yeah, I went here, she took me here, we went there.' [I'm like], 'It's a good experience man, go! See, see these things. [The girls] enjoy it. They enjoy you coming here, wanting to learn about the country. So go do that!'"

It would appear that for an African American basketball player in Israel, even dating has an historic and religious element to it.

Separation of Church and Hoop

Perhaps not surprisingly, a topic as sensitive as religion did give rise to the occasional challenge for African American players in Israel. Billy Thompson is one of only a handful of basketball players to ever win a high school state championship, an NCAA championship, and an NBA championship. Even more uniquely, to my knowledge he is the only basketball player to be taken to task in Israeli newspapers for proselytizing to his Jewish teammates and attempting to convert them to Christianity.

Thompson was a high school star in Camden, New Jersey, claimed an NCAA championship under legendary coach Denny Crum at Louisville, and earned two NBA rings with the Showtime-era Los Angeles Lakers in 1987 and 1988. A man of intense faith, Thompson felt a calling to preach the gospel so he retired from playing a few years later and took a job as an assistant pastor with the Jesus People International Church in Miami. Shortly thereafter, a churchgoer told him the Lord was going to bring him back to the court. Intrigued, Thompson began fasting and praying, and he decided to contact his agent to see what teams might be interested in his services. He was completely unprepared, however, for the return call he received asking how he felt about moving to Israel to play for a team in the Galilee. "All I could do was laugh," Thompson said. "They play basketball in Israel?"

Multiple rounds of negotiations started and stopped, each with a different Israeli team and each without success. "I had never even considered visiting the Holy Land, but I couldn't keep ignoring the messages for me to play in Israel," Thompson said. "It wasn't about basketball anymore—I started dreaming about going to Israel and tracing my Christian roots." Finally, a one-year contract was finalized with Hapoel Jerusalem in 1990, and Thompson rewarded the team by leading them to a magical season and a stunning State Cup victory over Maccabi Tel Aviv.

Thompson subsequently signed a multiyear deal with the club, which was widely celebrated by fans who've since called him the greatest foreigner ever to play for the team. Yet, some outside the basketball community were less pleased with the continued presence in Israel of a basketball star nicknamed "the Priest," who signed autographs with "Jesus Loves You." The morning after signing his deal, Thompson awoke to the front pages of the country's Hebrew newspapers scrutinizing his faith, with some viewing him as a threat to the Jewish people and calling for his removal from the team and the country. Thompson balked at his classification as a missionary, saying instead that he was simply expressing his faith, not proselytizing. The threats and concerns eventually subsided, and Thompson, now a full-time pastor in Florida, maintains a positive connection to the country to this day. The likable Thompson even ended up bonding with his fiercest opponents.

"Billy certainly was not shy about his faith, nor embarrassed to pray," said Dr. Jonty Maresky, Hapoel Jerusalem's longtime team doctor. "There was a rabbi on the Jerusalem city council that objected to the way Billy said 'Hallelujah' all the time, and wanted him out. But in the end, the two of them became best friends."

Reminders of Judaism

In an interesting twist, not only does religion impact the experience of African American basketball players in Israel, the players affect the religious identity of their Jewish fans as well. This can be seen in ways both symbolic and practical. Rabbi Gloiberman explained to me that one way for people to identify more closely with their Judaism is by having passion for Israeli sports. In order to strengthen people's Judaism, he continued, the first thing is "to remind them that they are Jewish." And this is where basketball comes in.

A terrific example of how sports can enhance a sense of Judaism occurred with a solitary jump shot, one that became famously known as the "Zalgiris Miracle." It was the spring of 2004, during the Jewish holiday of *Pesach* (Passover), when Maccabi Tel Aviv was hosting Lithuanian team Zalgiris Kaunas in the fifth and deciding game of their best-of-five Euroleague quarterfinal series. With a berth in the Final Four on the line, it would have been a critical game in any season, but circumstances that year made it particularly significant. Maccabi chairman Shimon Mizrahi had lobbied for years to have Tel Aviv host the Euroleague's Final Four, but in 2000, after Israeli-Palestinian fighting broke out yet again, Israel had been banned from playing host to most international events. Mizrahi finally convinced the Euroleague to let Tel Aviv host the 2004 Final Four, but in the months leading up to the event increased hostilities brought the safety issue once again very much to the forefront.

Fearful of the conflict, Euroleague teams had refused to travel to Israel, and several Spanish and Italian clubs were clamoring for a last-minute change of venue. Once again Mizrahi made an impassioned plea at a Euroleague meeting for confirmation that the Final Four would indeed take place in Tel Aviv, just weeks before it was to occur. His plea was successful, but for Mizrahi's hard-fought plan to truly succeed a question remained: would Maccabi qualify to play? In addition to the pride that would come with the home team's participation, there was considerable anxiety that many international fans, fearful about their safety, would stay away. If the home team didn't qualify, local fans would also be likely to stay home, the media would put a negative spin on the sure-to-be sparsely attended event, and in short, Mizrahi's dream would turn into an unmitigated disaster. All of this work, worry, and the need to "stay on the map" set the stage for the "Miracle."

With only two seconds left in the game, Maccabi found itself trailing by three points and without possession of the ball. Forced to foul to stop the clock and allow the team more time to make up its deficit, Maccabi ended up sending Zalgiris player Giedrius Gustas to the line. In his previous 18 Euroleague games, Gustas hadn't missed a single shot from the charity stripe. Making just one of his two allotted shots from the line would seal the win. A Zalgiris victory appeared so certain that players and fans responded in kind. One of Maccabi's star players was already walking over to the opposing bench to congratulate the Zalgiris coach, and a multitude of fans were heading for the exits. Remarkably, Gustas missed the first shot. And the second one. This was obviously good fortune, but Maccabi fans were still facing the unwelcome reality that their team had only two seconds to cover the entire length of the court and make a three-pointer. That's when, coming out of a timeout, Israeli player Gur Shelef threw a three-quarter-court Jewish-equivalent of a "Hail Mary" pass to African American teammate Derrick Sharp, who caught it, took a dribble, lofted a leaning three-pointer as the buzzer sounded, and nailed it.

The crowd erupted instantaneously in a Hebrew chant, "There is a God! There is a God!" The miracle continued when Maccabi went on to win the game in overtime, and Maccabi coach Gershon made clear his belief that the shot was a result of divine intervention. "You have witnessed a miracle," he said excitedly in his postgame media comments. "I am a believer. And if this is not a miracle, I don't know what a miracle is." Sharp, who could hardly speak after the game, sat on the bench crying tears of disbelief. When he was able to collect himself, he too ascribed the shot as "a gift from God." Adding to the miracle of it all, the next morning's headline in the Israeli daily newspaper *Maariv* read, "The Finger of God," and inside the paper a full-page spread featured the word "Hallelujah" across it in large, bold type. The paper went on to declare, "Can you believe what one ball can do to an entire country, can you believe that one basket can change the national mood? Two seconds from the end, everything was lost and depressing. Suddenly God wore yellow [Maccabi's team color]. God is yellow."

The immediate reaction of the crowd that watched the game, the headlines chosen by the journalists who covered it, the bombastic words of the coach who drew up the final play, and the hushed whispers of the player who executed it each exhibited the symbolic connection between Israeli basketball teams and religion. If indeed to strengthen someone's Judaism the need is "to remind people that they are Jewish," as Rabbi

Gloiberman had told me, after that game there couldn't have been a Jewish Israeli who didn't have his or her faith reinforced.

But Rabbi Gloiberman insists that basketball can do more than provide a symbolic reminder of people's Judaism. It can also, he said, spur practical change.

"I'll tell you a story, an example of how people become connected," Gloiberman said to me. "I was at the grave of the *Baal Shem Tov* (a rabbi considered the founder of Hasidic Judaism) two years ago. When I exited, I was approached by a woman who told me, 'Rabbi Gloiberman, my father is eighty years old. He just began putting on *tefillin*' [two small black boxes Jewish men wear during weekday morning prayers— one on the forehead, the other on the arm—that contain verses from the Torah]. I said, 'What happened? Why the change?' She said, 'He saw Pini Gershon putting on tefillin on TV, and he too wanted to put on tefillin, even at eighty!' Here is a man who had never put on tefillin, and all of a sudden, his soul had a desire for Torah."

Gershon was, of course, a basketball coach, not a religious figure, but his participation in a religious custom was a television-worthy event because he had so much success leading Maccabi Tel Aviv. This success was made possible by the African Americans who played for him including Sharp, Maceo Baston, Anthony Parker, and Deon Thomas. All of them and others contributed to Maccabi's excellence, leading fans to take pride in the Israeli team, which, in turn, led to greater identification with the team's religiosity, and finally, as we saw, at times even prompted participation in religious customs. The influence of African American players is a distal contribution in the chain, but one with important significance.

Basketball's contribution to a stronger sense of Judaism is especially noteworthy when Israeli teams battle on foreign soil. "In every Euroleague game outside of Israel, I organize a meal for thousands of people for Friday night," said Gloiberman, acknowledging Maccabi's notoriously mobile fan base. "And at that Friday night dinner thousands of people come, and this one wears a kippah, and that one lights the Shabbat candles, this one suddenly remembers that he's Jewish. I don't tell them to pray! But suddenly you see the Jewish heart in each. It is written, in every Jew beats a Jewish heart. Suddenly, you see that they are all connected to their Jewishness. Where? At a basketball game in Spain, at a basketball game in Prague, at a basketball game in Moscow. It suddenly connects people! Even more so in a foreign land, it connects many people with their Jewishness. Suddenly you hear someone say, 'This is the first time I've prayed.' We organized a dinner in Prague for a few thousand people at the Hilton Hotel, a man came to me and said, 'For twenty years I haven't been to synagogue, but as I hear the singing of the songs welcoming the Shabbat, it inspires me to pray.'"

Journalists often describe basketball at a given school or city as a religion, perhaps the best word to capture just how feverishly certain communities follow the game—how the fans' commitment to basketball rivals even their commitment to their chosen faiths. But in Israel, basketball and religion are intertwined. The game actually *impacts* that faith, both of the players and their fans. Only in Israel can African American players learn about and experience the customs and rituals of Judaism, as well as walk the paths and visit the sites most fundamental to Christianity. In the same week, they can celebrate Christmas at the birthplace of Jesus and light the Hanukkah candles at the home of one of their Israeli friends. And sometimes, their successes on the court can even inspire Israeli fans to light those candles in the first place.

7

ON-COURT IMPACT

When Omri Casspi tore off his warmups and checked into the Sacramento Kings' season opener on October 28, 2009, he became the first Israeli to play in the NBA. It was a huge accomplishment and milestone for Casspi and for Israeli basketball as a whole. But it also led to a natural question: what exactly took so long? It's not surprising that players from basketball powerhouses such as Russia, Australia, and Spain had become part of the NBA before Israelis, but why did players from such non-basketball hotbeds as Estonia, Iceland, Uruguay, and even Iran also make NBA rosters before Casspi? Israel's late arrival to the NBA begs a key question that is central to basketball followers in Israel. Do African American players in Israel help, or hinder, the development of local Israeli players?

Too Much Foreign Content?

With the explosion of basketball's popularity internationally, high-level professional leagues now exist in countries around the world. And with the United States still considered the preeminent source of basketball talent, producing both the best individual players and the greatest number of high-level players, Americans are sought after all over the globe, including, of course, Israel.

Observers on one side of the often heated discussion point out that African American players fill roster spots that would otherwise be given to Israelis, earn minutes that would otherwise be played by Israelis, and get a multitude of shot attempts that deprive Israelis of their share. Viewed from that perspective, it could be argued that the influx of African American players in Israel over the last decades cannot help but stunt the development of local Israelis, giving fewer of them a chance to play, and relegating those that do play to smaller roles.

"It's much cheaper to buy a ready-made player," an Israeli coach explained. "I personally object to having so many foreigners with us. It blocks the way of our own young generation. We are cutting the branch on which we are sitting," he added grimly.

Critics on this side of the discussion also say that in addition to stunting the growth of young Israeli team members, the presence of African American players takes away from the accomplishments of Israeli teams. One writer boldly stated that there was precious little connecting the European victories of Hapoel Jerusalem and Maccabi Tel Aviv to Israeli basketball. "To call a team that is 80 percent foreign 'Israeli' is absurd," he wrote, "especially when the lie is so obvious." The same writer stretched his point further by comparing basketball to internationally traded goods marked with their country of origin. Israeli goods can be sold without duty in the European Union by virtue of being "Israeli," but only if they include at least 35 percent Israeli workmanship. Along this same line, the writer asserted that Israeli basketball teams playing in Europe do not qualify as Israeli because they often play four Americans and only one Israeli at a time. He closed his argument by noting that in basketball, as with any industry, "we retard the local market by preferring imported goods to local ones."

Modeling Experience

Others, however, support the presence of African American players, pointing out that they actually facilitate the development of homegrown Israeli talent. African American players are recruited to Israel precisely because of their superiority to Israeli players on the court. Proponents argue that their presence raises the level of play in Israel, allowing Israeli players to benefit from better competition and giving them higher goals to work toward. The rationale is that by practicing and playing against elite foreign, particularly African American, players, Israelis improve their games more than they ever could playing only against each other.

The late Kevin Magee (who was killed in a car accident in Louisiana in 2003), an African American who played for Maccabi Tel Aviv in the 1990s, is considered one of the team's greatest players ever. Magee also had a reputation for being blunt, once admitting that he had no particular affiliation with Israel beyond the fact that it was a convenient place to play basketball. He openly dismissed the abilities of some Israeli players, including saying that the idea of Israeli Nadav Henefeld, then a player at the University of Connecticut, being on an NBA team was "a joke." For all his bluntness, however, Magee had a strong practical perspective on the issue.

"Hell, if I was in America and thought a foreigner was taking away my chance of playing in the NBA, I wouldn't like the idea either," Magee once told an Israeli reporter. "But having American players here raises the level of the whole game, which really helps the local players. Anyway, look, I'm just here trying to make an honest living," he added.

Magee's quote reflects a very American view of basketball: a sport that can be a means to an end and a chance to turn a game into a career. In Israel, players tend to view basketball more as recreation and to treat it as such. According to longtime Israeli coach Pini Gershon, signing American players is a crucial way to help Israeli players change that mind-set.

"The Americans take it more seriously," Gershon said in a straightforward evaluation of the situation. "If I bring a good, professional American player to Israel, he starts to run the tempo. The Israelis start to play to his level. The Americans here have better fundamentals. They are more athletic. The Israelis don't take it too seriously. They want to be good players without really working."

Cory Carr, an African American player from Fordyce, Arkansas, who has played more than 15 years in Israel, echoes that sentiment. For Carr, basketball was the means for him to get from a sleepy town of fewer than 5,000 people, to a scholarship to study and play at Texas Tech, to a roster spot with the Chicago Bulls. He then went on to spend time playing in France, Italy, and Israel, where he eventually got married, became a citizen, and settled. As we sat down to lunch at a local café in his adopted hometown of Ra'anana, Carr told me how basketball had taken him to places he never could have imagined but, he explained, he could not have made the journey without hard work, focus, and a thick skin, just some of the attributes he hopes to pass on to young Israeli players.

When I asked Carr what young Israeli players needed to do in order to improve, he responded, "Go get that Bobby Knight on you," referring to the legendary American coach widely known for his tough and demanding, no-nonsense style. "Get that mental toughness," Carr continued. "Be able to take some criticism—learn that a coach can jump down your throat and still want the best for you. A lot of time with Israelis, I hear, 'You can't talk to him like that, can't say this to him.' In basketball, as a coach you've got to be able to jump down your players' throat sometimes. Israeli [players] don't like to work; they can be lazy. For a lot of players in the States, basketball is a way out, especially in my culture. It's a way to get you out, to see the world. For [Israelis], it's more of a hobby. It's not the forefront of what they want to do, so they don't take it on that way—they take it on as something to do. If you want to be good, you've got to work at it. I've played for some of the best coaches in the States at [different points] in my career. That experience can be carried over here and it can help [these Israeli players]—I just want to be able to share it."

Fred Campbell, an African American from Macon, Georgia, is a veteran of more than 25 seasons of Israeli basketball, and at fifty-four, he is among the oldest professional basketball players in the world. He has played with countless Israelis in the first, second, and third divisions, and he knows Israeli basketball as well as anyone, whether native to Israel or otherwise. So it was with great anticipation that I sought out his insight on the topic, scheduling a phone interview one spring afternoon after Campbell had picked up his son, himself an aspiring Israeli basketball player. Campbell, like many others, echoes Carr's and Gershon's sentiments about the work ethic of Israeli players and the effect African American players can have on that work ethic.

"The thing about Israeli players is that they don't like to work during their offseason. They like to go to Thailand," Campbell told me, laughing, about that popular vacation destination for young Israelis. "That's why I always say, 'No Thailand this summer. Work out with me!' I work out hard. I work out like a teenager over the summer. Guys are like, 'Whoa, man, what did you do to your body?! You became buffed!' I say, 'You know me. I work out all summer.' Israelis do as they're told—we [Americans] do things to get better. An American player might get up in the morning and be in the gym two hours before practice, because he's trying to get better. Israeli players will only get in the weight room when you tell them too," Campbell continued. "They think it's all about basketball. I tell a lot of these young guys, 'When I was fifteen and sixteen years old, my coach was more focused on developing my body so that I will be able to do those things, spin around when I'm jumping and all that type of stuff. You guys try to do it backward. You try to get all the basketball [benefit] without working on the body, and it doesn't work like that. You'll find that if you work on the body and keep those muscles elastic, you'll be able to do more things. You'll be able to spin and move.' But they want it now. They don't want to put the work in. But I tell them, 'You don't get better during the season. You get better in the summer—you just sharpen your skills during the season.'"

Having spent decades training year-round, treating the game as a serious vocation, and playing it at the highest levels, African American players can be a true resource for their young, Israeli teammates. Legendary UCLA coach John Wooden once said, "Never try to be better than someone else. Learn from others, and try to be the best you can be. Success is the by-product of that preparation." Without foreign players in the country, the amount young Israelis could learn would be capped at the knowledge of other Israeli players. However, by bringing in Americans, usually African Americans, Israeli youngsters can benefit from knowledge and experience beyond that attained by anyone locally.

"As the foreigner, your basketball IQ and basketball skill set is higher than most of the Israelis," observed Jitim Young, a fellow Northwestern graduate and veteran of three seasons of Israeli basketball. "Israel should look to Europe for an example. American basketball players have been going overseas and playing in Europe for a long, long time, and now, European basketball has caught up. They've beat [America] in the Olympics, and you've got a lot of European players now in the NBA. Obviously, American basketball has impacted the European game, and I think in Israel it can do the same thing. You [should] only play at levels that are at a higher level than you can perform at. If you have good people around you, your game will be better. If you just play against average people, you're going to be average," Young pointed out. "If you continue year after year to bring in more and more really good players to Israel to play, you'll see more players like Omri Casspi in the NBA. You're going to see two, three, four, five, or more Israeli people in the NBA, just like there's a caseload of European players on every NBA team."

A Casspi Study

Another Israeli, Gal Mekel, subsequently appeared in a total of 35 games over two NBA seasons, yet Casspi remains the only Israeli to stick in the league, where he is now an eight-year veteran. Accordingly, he remains the best player to study as a model for ways to help develop young Israeli players. Casspi displayed his desire to play in the NBA from childhood, evidenced by, among other things, an amazing Nike commercial showing a home video of him as a youngster, standing in front of the NBA Store in New York City, saying in Hebrew that he would one day play in the league. But Casspi went far beyond hopes and dreams alone. He bolstered that desire with the work ethic to make it happen and the resources, including foreign teammates, to help him along the way. I spoke to Casspi after he finished his pregame preparations for a match-up against the Toronto Raptors. Dripping in sweat in the NBA warmup gear he had worked so hard to earn the right to wear, Casspi acknowledged the influence and impact of those African Americans who played alongside him at Maccabi Tel Aviv.

"Those guys were not only great basketball players, they were great leaders and role models," Casspi told me. "To learn from a guy like Anthony Parker, Marcus Fizer, Will Bynum—there were so many of them. I remember myself as a seventeen-year-old kid, asking them 'How is the NBA? What's it like? How many pairs of sneakers does each player have? How are practices? What are the coaches like?' They really took me under their wings and showed me how to work, what to do, and how to get better individually. They helped me tremendously... Those players come in with a different mentality as far as hard work and dedication. Their love for the game is something different. Most of my inspiration was from those guys—watching how much they love the game and how much they were willing to work for the game."

One of the players Casspi noted working with—and learning from—was Will Bynum, an African American who forged his basketball skills at rough-and-tumble Crane High School in Chicago. Before signing with Maccabi, Bynum had played in an NCAA Final Four, participated in an NBA Summer League, and played for the Golden State Warriors. He then spent two seasons playing in Israel alongside Casspi before returning to the NBA with the Detroit Pistons. Speaking with him in the same visitor's locker room in Toronto in which I had interviewed the young Israeli, Bynum recounted the Casspi of those years as a focused, determined player and a true student of the game and the Casspi of today as a great source of personal pride.

"I spent hours with Casspi in the gym, and he was always asking me tons and tons of questions," Bynum told me. "How to do this, or what guys are like in the NBA, or what do I do in this type of situation, how do I approach the game? There are so many questions he could ask me that I don't know if anyone else could have answered," Bynum said thoughtfully. "When you have a guy like Casspi, especially someone who works as hard as he does—he's so passionate about the game and loves the game—to see him doing well, it's just a different kind of feeling. It's like a younger brother making it big, when you know you gave them advice. You can't really find words to describe that feeling."

Not Too Many, Not Too Few

Casspi's learning from Bynum and ascending to the best basketball league in the world is an ideal example of an African American player positively influencing a young Israeli player's career. But there continues to be the problem of determining the right balance of American players to Israelis, since the benefits of Americans' influence can be outweighed by their overwhelming presence. The Israeli Basketball Association has altered its rules numerous times in an attempt to find the best mix for all concerned. Once upon a time, the IBA prohibited Israeli teams from having any foreign players; then the IBA limited foreign players to one per team and subsequently two. At one point in the history of shifting rules, teams were allowed as many as *eight* foreign players on a roster, bolstering the argument that foreigners were taking away more from Israeli players than they were providing. The benefits gained by having American players on teams can be watered down, if not drowned out, by allowing such a large proportion of them in the Israeli league. At that point Israeli players would no longer have sufficient playing time or on-court responsibilities to properly develop better skills for the game.

In 2013, the issue became so significant that most of the Israeli league's local players actually went on strike for a portion of the season, with multiple games having to be postponed. The ultimate resolution allowed for teams to sign five foreign players, but with the league offering financial incentives for teams that sign fewer. Teams were also required to sign at least two Israelis under the age of twenty-two and another under the age of twenty-five. Finally, the league also agreed to implement what's known as the "Russian Rule." Named for its country of origin, it requires two Israeli players to be on the court at all times.

The idea behind the rule is to incentivize teams to sign up and develop good Israeli players, since they will always make up 40 percent of a team's lineup, no matter how talented its foreigners.

Even the Russian Rule, however, hasn't really changed the influx of foreign players and some, including African American players, are uncomfortable about that. Campbell has seen the Israeli league through its various rule changes and commented on how the shifts have impacted Israeli players. He pointed out that the limit on foreign players under previous systems encouraged teams to spend big money on the best Americans they could find. At that time, teams brought in top-notch players who were talented, experienced, and mature enough to provide tangible benefits to their Israeli teammates. In his view, once teams started bringing in six or seven Americans, the caliber and professionalism of those players was lower and this negated some of the benefit of bringing in foreigners in the first place.

"I think that [the increase in American players] stunts the growth of the Israeli players, the young ones," Campbell said. "It's not so much an Israeli league now, because each team has [so many] Americans on it. Even though they can only have three on the court, it's impacting the [Israeli] players because they're sitting too long. You've got players that can play the three [small forward position], but almost every team has got a foreigner at the three spot. It's pushing players back, and then you've got players leaving teams for that reason, only to find when they get with another team they're going through the same problems. Now you see some players that I thought were going to be good, and now they're done. At twenty-four, they're done. They just got tired of trying to find a job, switching from team to team, and every time they get to a team, the team brings in a foreigner at that position. And because they're paying [the foreigner] more money, they've got to keep him on the court. And these foreigners that they're bringing in now, a lot of them don't have a lot of experience, so they really can't give our young guys the experience that they need, not just on the court, but to sit and talk to them."

Note Campbell's use of the word "our" with the young guys he referred to being the young Israeli players, not the African American players who make up as many as 90 percent of the foreign players in Israel at a given time. Even though he is an African American who initially came to the country to play basketball, Campbell identifies himself as an Israeli, and he takes the development of young Israeli players personally. His commitment to their improvement is a prime example of the positive impact an African American player can have on young Israelis when the veteran foreigner is committed to mentoring and the young Israeli is committed to learning.

"I [teach my teammates] all the time, I take it very seriously," Campbell said. "Even some of my teammates, the big guys, they find it amazing. They'll be like, 'Fred, I finish the army at 12:30,' and I'll say, 'OK, so let's go over to the gym at one o'clock. I want to work with you on some one-on-one stuff.' I come all the way from Netanya to Shfar'am [more than an hour's drive] to be at the gym to work with them, and they don't understand it, because I'm not getting paid for that. But if they want to learn a game that I love so much, hey, that's what I'm here for. Our manager, he told the guys on my team, 'Fred is a walking *beit sefer*, a walking school. You guys should take advantage of that!'"

The impact of African American players on Israeli players is not limited to their professional teammates. Rather, that impact can be felt all the way down to the youngest of aspiring Israeli hoopsters, with many veteran African American players in Israel becoming youth coaches or running basketball camps for children. Aulcie Perry's Sal Stars (*sal* being Hebrew for hoop) and Willie Sims's Play Time are increasingly popular instructional camps run in the summer months for Israeli kids, and many veteran African Americans in Israel coach both boys and girls teams while in the final years of their playing careers or their first years after retiring. The passion of those players for the advancement of the sport in Israel is evident in the seriousness with which they take those roles and the pride they exhibit in the exploits of their pupils. Carr's Facebook page, for example, is packed with pictures of his various protégés, or, as he refers to them in one post, the "future rabbis, politicians, professors, and computer engineers of Israel in action!!" Whether any of his or his peers' young apprentices will also end up future NBA players or Israeli national team members, only time will tell.

Not an Either/Or Scenario

Interestingly, with the passage of time the impact of African American players on Israeli basketball shifts from their *interacting* with native-born Israeli players to *raising* them. As noted throughout this book, a number of African Americans who followed their hoop dreams to Israel ended up falling in love with the country and planting roots there. Now, some of their Israeli-born children are among the country's top up-and-coming basketball stars, with that next generation playing professionally in the domestic league and representing Israel on its national team. These are not African Americans playing in Israel, but rather Israelis, fluent in Hebrew and born and raised in the nation's unique customs and circumstances. Unlike most Israelis, however, they've had upbringings which combine those Israeli elements with high-level hoops sensibilities from the United States—and thus far, the on-court results have been impressive.

The leader of this next generation is Shawn Dawson, the eldest son of Alabama native and former Israeli league star Joe Dawson. A somewhat under-appreciated prospect early on, in part because his family lived in Israel's distant southernmost city of Eilat, Shawn made his professional debut as a teenager with the Super League's Maccabi Rishon LeZion in 2012–13. Year after year his numbers leapt forward, from three points per game to 11 and then to 15. In the spring of 2016, he averaged 21 points per game in the playoffs, leading Rishon to a surprising Israeli Super League championship. He subsequently competed in the NBA summer league and played for the New Orleans Pelicans during the 2016–17 NBA preseason, leading many to believe he will ultimately become only the third Israeli-born NBA player ever.

When it comes to the progeny of African American players and Israeli women making an impact on the hardwood, Dawson isn't the only one in his family, let alone in the country. Although slowed by injuries, his younger brother Tyler also signed a playing contract as a teenager, also with Maccabi Rishon. Derrick Sharp's son DJ was raised in Israel, played some high school ball in Florida, then chose to forego a college career in the United States to return to his home nation and play professionally for Bnei Herzliya. One of DJ Sharp's best friends is Michael Brisker (the son of another former Maccabi Tel Aviv player Mark Brisker), who has starred for Israel's under-18 national team and now plays for Maccabi Ra'anana in Israel's second division. Finally, Campbell's son Toi is a 6-foot-8, Mack-truck-strong 12th-grader with an eye on his own professional career down the line.

Each of these up-and-comers has a chance to meet or exceed his father's respective accomplishments, and if only some of them do so, they could comprise a substantial piece of future Israeli national teams. Time will tell just how far this next generation will go, but their accomplishments could add yet another layer to their fathers' impact on the game of basketball in Israel.

The Controversy Continues

The changing of rules concerning foreign players in Israel continues to be ripe for controversy. Indeed there are some who advocate for more American players in Israeli basketball, taking issue even with the Russian Rule. Essentially this argument is for a free market model based on the idea that if the best players play, regardless of nationality, the best locals will be forced to raise their games. Brandon Hunter, an African American from Cincinnati, Ohio, and an NBA veteran, points to the Italian league as one that has never implemented an equivalent of the Russian Rule, but has produced nine NBA players to Israel's two. On the other hand, Jeffrey Rosen, a Jewish businessman from Aventura, Florida, who owns the Maccabi Haifa club, favors the Russian Rule in part because it prevents big-budget teams from creating a "market of mercenaries." Chris Watson is an African American from White Plains, New York, who played more than a decade in Israel, gaining citizenship in 2003. He also supports the Russian Rule, coming to his conclusion by distilling the debate to its most basic elements.

"I see it from both sides, because I am American, but I've been here so long that I've adopted this culture too and I'm pretty much Israeli," Watson said. "It's a tough debate, [but] this is Israel, and this is their league—the development of the Israeli player has got to be their number one priority. The Israelis have got to get minutes, because at the end of the day, the people of the country need somebody on the court they can relate to. The kids and the people need some Israeli player they can identify with. If you open up the league and make it all five Americans or whatever [some teams] are trying to do, it will definitely bring the interest in the league down, and it will stunt the growth of the Israeli player, for sure."

There is an old adage about the passionate and assertive nature of Israelis, a commonly held view that for every one Israeli there are two opinions. I spoke to a multitude of players, coaches, and basketball insiders about the impact of African American players on the development of native Israeli players, and it became obvious that reaching consensus on this issue was not going to happen. To Watson and others, an unchecked free market that could allow teams to replace all of their Israeli players with foreigners defeats the very purpose of having an Israeli basketball league. At the same time, Hunter and like-minded thinkers argue that a league without set quotas would produce higher quality and entertainment value and would advance the development of those Israeli players by increasing their level of competition.

The Israeli Basketball Super League changed its rules repeatedly in the course of this book's writing, a series of modifications seeking to find a happy medium, with more changes likely to come. Obviously a perfect compromise has been elusive, but what is clear is that when an Israeli player with talent and drive is able to connect with African American players committed to mentoring, optimal results are within reach.

8

LOVE AND BASKETBALL

IT WAS THE SPRING OF 1995. Fred Campbell had just wrapped up his third season in Israel, a successful campaign with Maccabi Haifa. Thirty-one years old and a confirmed bachelor, he went to visit his friend Calvin, a fellow American who was playing for the Israeli team in Netanya. The visit was uneventful; Campbell went to his friend's game, ventured out with him for a night on the town, and crashed on his couch. It was the next day that would change his life.

"I was going to look for a place to eat, and I saw her walking down the street," Campbell recalled to me in 2011, just after his 19th season in Israel. "I tried to introduce myself to her, and she was like, 'Hi and bye.' She wanted nothing to do with it! Anyway, I went on to the restaurant, and I was sitting there eating, and I just happened to look up and I saw her and a girl walking by. So I dropped the food and ran out! I invited them in to eat, and they said 'No', they were going to the beach. I gave up."

Fortunately for Campbell, the story doesn't end there.

"That night I was at my friend's house," Campbell said. "The phone rang when my friend was in the shower, so I told the [caller], 'He's in the shower.'" But the caller wanted to know who this stranger was. "I'm like, 'This is Fred, who is this?' He said, 'My name is Avi, Calvin is helping me with my English class.' And then I heard someone in the background, and it just happened to be *her* again, saying that she had met some guy named Fred that day. And that was me! I always told my Mom I was going to get married when I was in my forties, and she would say, 'You selfish bastard!' But two weeks after I met Liat I told my friend Calvin, 'I will marry this girl.' And he was like, 'No, not you!' June will be sixteen [now twenty-two] years we've been married," Campbell added, a wide grin crossing his face.

* * *

Campbell, Deon Thomas, Cory Carr, Chris Watson, and Joe Dawson are very different people. These five African American players were raised in different areas of the United States, came to Israel for different reasons, and experienced the country in different ways. But they do share one thing—they all found love with Israeli women. While researching this book I spoke to many African American players who met, dated, and married Israeli women, but these five players in particular have romantic relationships that offer intriguing insights into the most important off-court domain of all—that of love.

The story of Fred and Liat Campbell sounds like a page out of a movie script—boy meets girl, girl rejects boy, fate brings boy and girl together anyway in the most unlikely of ways. For those who know Yiddish, the preordained feel to the Campbell's story brings to mind the word *bashert*, which means fate or destiny, and it can refer to any kind of fortuitous good match, such as finding the perfect job or the perfect house. But most often Jews use the term to refer to meeting one's soul mate, a partner whose identity (according to the Talmud, a central Jewish rabbinical text) is said to have been determined even before birth. The concept is that Divine Providence eventually leads every person to find his or her bashert, be that person next door or on the other side of the world.

Campbell wasn't actively looking for a wife, but he found her in spite of himself, in northern Israel of all places, more than 6,000 miles from his hometown. Meeting Liat altered the trajectory of his life in ways he could never have imagined. And he wasn't the only one.

Different Paths to Bashert

While it was Campbell's persistence that allowed him to meet his wife-to-be, for Cory Carr it was his ankles. After playing in the NBA and in France, Carr's first stop in Israel was Ra'anana, where he played both the shooting guard and small forward positions. In an effort to keep his precious ankles and legs in top shape for as long as possible, Carr had a regular appointment with his team's physical therapist. One week the usual therapist was on vacation, so the team retained the services of a temporary replacement from the local hospital.

"She was only with the team for [four or five] days, but I met her, we continued to talk, and the rest is history," Carr said, clearly still delighted about the turn of events. "We hit it off, became a couple, got married, had a baby girl, and we have a life here. She's been very, very supportive of me, and she's stuck by my side through a lot of tough times, man. She's a great woman, and I'm very lucky to have met her."

Carr feels strongly that the good fortune he has with having a loving wife relates not only to his off-court happiness, but to his continued on-court productivity as well.

"She's good at her job—that's why I'm still on the court!" he told me with a laugh as we lunched together at Ra'anana's Arcaffe, a popular Israeli chain of coffee shops. "I've had ACL surgery, ankle surgery—her rehab kept me going."

University of Illinois legend Deon Thomas has an airline mix-up and a telephone company's mistake to thank for meeting and, after a long and winding road, marrying his bashert, Dafna. The eventual Mrs. Thomas was vacationing in Spain from her home in Israel and because of a mistake with her ticket, she had to stay an extra week. It was, she would later realize, a lucky mistake. Years later, I joined Thomas and Dafna, their daughters, Gabrielle and Liel, and their nephew, Daniel, for lunch in St. Louis. Deon and Dafna shared their story, one that started while he was playing in Spain, after his NBA career ended and before his Israeli career began.

"I'm in Gijon, Spain, and we played against the team there," Thomas said. "Her and one of her friends are walking down the street that night, and I'm like, '*Hola.*' She said, 'I don't speak Spanish.' I was like, 'Good, because neither do I.' We exchanged phone numbers, she went back to Israel the next day, and we talked on the phone for the next three months. Then she came to visit. Then she went back, and we talked on the phone for another month and a half, two months."

But the long-distance relationship was to become even longer distance. After another visit to see Thomas in Spain, Dafna took advantage of an opportunity to go to school in the United States, moving from Israel to Florida. Thomas wasn't ready to get serious with anyone at that time and didn't protest her move. In fact, although Dafna gave his agent her new American phone number, she did not hear from Thomas for two years. At that point, Thomas said, he had grown up and knew that he wanted to be with her. What he didn't know was that he had almost blown his chance.

Dafna had moved from one Florida apartment to another. "I called the company, BellSouth, to change my number. But what they do is, they [have a recording that] says, 'The new number is...' I told them, 'Don't do that.' I didn't want anybody to have my new number." Dafna continued, now laughing, that the phone company didn't listen and this was the reason Thomas was able to find her. "So one day I was out," she said, "I was in college, and I was working in a gym, and I came home and had one message on the machine. I pushed play thinking, *OK, it's probably my friend looking for me.* And it was him!"

Her first instinct was to ignore his call. Two years had passed since she had left her number with his agent, and she wanted a clean start. Life was good for her in Florida, and life was good for him playing ball in Europe. But there was one thought she could not shake.

"I knew he was going to be my husband," she said. "The first time we met, I told him, 'You're going to be my husband.' And I called home and said, 'I met my husband.'"

Aulcie Perry warming up before a game at Yad Eliyahu Stadium, now known as Menora Mivtachim Arena. Perry signed with Maccabi Tel Aviv in 1976, helped the team win the European Cup in 1977, and converted to Judaism in 1978. He is generally credited with being at the forefront of the sea change in Israeli basketball that led to hundreds of African Americans playing in Israel in the decades since. Perry continues to live in Israel today. *National Photo Collection of Israel, Government Press Office (Sa'ar Ya'acov).*

Legendary Israeli military leader and politician Moshe Dayan greets Maccabi Tel Aviv players, including Aulcie Perry, in advance of a game at Yad Eliyahu Stadium. *National Photo Collection of Israel, Government Press Office (Sa'ar Ya'acov).*

Legendary Maccabi Tel Aviv star Earl Williams hugs Israel's then-Prime Minister Menachem Begin at a celebration of Maccabi's European Cup championship in 1981. Aulcie Perry looks on from his seat. *National Photo Collection of Israel, Government Press Office (Herman Chanania).*

Anthony Parker parlayed five great seasons with Maccabi Tel Aviv into a successful return to the NBA, signing a multi-year deal with the Toronto Raptors in 2006. As a tribute to Israel and his fans there Parker chose to wear the number 18 for the Raptors, a number signifying life and good fortune in Judaism. Here, he poses with his agent, Henry Thomas, and Toronto's then-President and General Manager, Bryan Colangelo, at his introductory press conference. *Photo by Ron Turenne/National Basketball Association/Getty Images.*

When Tyrese Rice signed with Maccabi Tel Aviv for the 2013–14 season, a friend who had previously played in Israel told him, "You're going to heaven." Here, Rice celebrates having led Maccabi to the storied club's most recent Euroleague Championship in 2014, riding on the shoulders of Greek teammate Sofoklis Schortsanitis while Guyanese-American teammate Shawn James raises the Israeli flag in the background. *Aitor Arrizabalaga / Euroleague Basketball / Getty Images.*

Mark Brisker poses in Raanana with his son Michael, for an article in an Israeli newspaper. The Hebrew quote in the upper right corner is from Mark, who said, "I look at him and see Michael Mor Brisker, not a Jew or a Christian." Michael has grown to become a prominent basketball prospect in his own right. *Photo by Adi Avishai.*

Michael Brisker representing Israel at the FIBA under-18 European Championships in 2016. Here, Michael takes a jump shot en route to scoring 12 points in a 103–102 loss to Bosnia and Herzegovina. *Photo courtesy of FIBA.*

(*left*) Stanley Brundy and his wife, Limor, celebrating the Jewish holiday of *Purim*. The holiday commemorates the saving of the Jewish people from near-destruction, and is celebrated by, among other things, wearing masks and costumes. *Brundy family*. (*right*) Brundy celebrating *Yom Ha'atzmaut*, Israel's Day of Independence, with Limor and their sons, Nadav and Dorian. *Brundy family*.

Brundy with his eldest son, Nadav, at the Western Wall in Jerusalem. The *Kotel HaMa'aravi*, as it's known in Hebrew, is considered the holiest site in Judaism. *Brundy family*.

Fred Campbell, who converted to Judaism during his years in Israel, wearing a *tallit*, a traditional Jewish prayer shawl, in a synagogue in Budapest. Campbell and his family spent part of their time in Hungary visiting historic Jewish gravesites and Holocaust memorials. *Campbell family*.

Campbell with his best friend Amit Ben Ezer. After three years working for a company in Israel's thriving high-tech industry, Campbell left to partner with Ben Ezer and run a motorbike company in Netanya, importing bikes and hosting shows and exhibitions. *Campbell family*.

After a difficult five-year process, Cory Carr finally earned his Israeli citizenship in 2009. Here he represents Israel in the FIBA 3-on-3 World Championships in 2012. *Photo courtesy of FIBA.*

Cory Carr posted this picture to his Facebook profile in August 2013 with the following caption: "I figure, since the US and Israel have had such a great International relationship over the years that will never change, and this country has blessed me for sooo many years professionally, it's only right to represent... #honored #connected #protected Live Life Love Life." *Photo courtesy of Cory Carr.*

Sylven Landesberg takes a selfie in front of Haifa's terraced Bahai Gardens at the Bahai World Centre, the holiest place of pilgrimage and the site of the faith's central administrative center. The Gardens are one of the most popular destinations in Israel for tourists of any faith. *Photo courtesy of Sylven Landesberg.*

Camel rides are a popular activity for visitors to Israel, and early in his stint in the country Sylven Landesberg was no exception. He recently completed his seventh season of Israeli basketball. *Photo courtesy of Sylven Landesberg.*

(*left*) Deon Thomas and his wife, Dafna, at the botanical gardens in Ein Gedi. Deon and Dafna have been happily married for almost twenty years. *Thomas family*. (*right*) Then-president of Israel, the late Shimon Peres stands back to back with then-NBA basketball player Amar'e Stoudemire at the presidential residency in Jerusalem on July 18, 2013. Stoudemire, who identifies as a Hebrew Israelite and first visited Israel in 2010, was in the country as an assistant coach of the Canadian basketball team for the 2013 Maccabiah Games. In 2016, Stoudemire signed a two-year contract to play for Hapoel Jerusalem, moving there with his wife, Alexis, and their four children. *Gali Tibbon/AFP/Getty Images*.

Chris Watson celebrating Hapoel Be'er Sheva's 2014–15 championship in Israel's third division, or *Liga Artzit*, at the home of the team owner. Watson also memorably won a first division championship with Hapoel Holon in 2008. *Photo courtesy of Chris Watson*.

"How did you know?" I asked her.

"I just knew," she said.

"*We* just knew!" he added.

She had told her parents as much in a call the first day she met Thomas. Not surprisingly, her parents pretty much dismissed her prediction with a sarcastic, "Yeah, really." Now these years later, she had to decide whether or not to return the call of a man she had once identified as her future husband. "I came back from school, I called him in Seville, and he wasn't at home. I went to my gym, did my training, I came back, and he called. And it was like…"

"Like we had just talked yesterday," Thomas interjected.

"And so I finished the semester and here I am going to Seville to see him," Dafna said. The visit went so well that she returned to the United States only to pack up her life and head right back to Spain and to Thomas. "I had ten days to go to college and clear my semester, clear my apartment, and sell my car. We got married seven months later."

Chris Watson, an African American from the suburbs of New York City, had no trouble connecting immediately with his wife-to-be, whom he met at a party in Tel Aviv. "She saw how handsome a guy I was, and she said, 'Excuse me, Black man, what are you doing in Israel?'" Watson recalled with a smile in 2007. "I said, 'I came out here to work.' She said, 'What job do you do?' I said, 'My job is to put the *cadur* [ball] in the *sal* [basket].' And then she came to a game, and she said I didn't do that very well. Ten years later, here we are."

Watson may have met his wife in a more predictable fashion than did other players, but meeting her mother was an entirely different matter.

"We used to do a lot of sneaking around at the beginning," Watson said. "The first time I met [her] family is when I woke up in her bed one day when I wasn't supposed to be there, and her Mom came in and caught us in the morning. She almost had a heart attack because my big, black toes were hanging out the side of the bed. My wife was trying to hide me underneath [the covers]! That was the first introduction."

Notwithstanding the uncomfortable nature of their first meeting, Watson and his in-laws ended up getting along well, circumstances he does not take for granted.

"That summer, [his now-wife] came to Florida, we went to city hall, and got married—and her family was really cool," Watson said. "Her father was a soccer player, so he was a sports guy. They supported me and took me in pretty good, and my family as well with her. We got lucky, because it's not so often that it happens like that."

Joining the Family

For couples anywhere, "meeting the parents" is often stressful. Differing backgrounds and values, protectiveness about one's child (i.e. "no one is good enough"), and general ambivalence about the transfer of priorities from the family of origin to the spouse—it's no wonder potential conflict hangs in the air. African American basketball players and the families of their Israeli wives-to-be not only have all of that to deal with, they also have to contend with different nationalities, races, and religions. And then, of course, there is also the part about being a basketball player.

"There was a small amount [of resistance at first]," Campbell said of his wife's family's reaction to their dating. "Because there's a reputation of guys that are just here to play ball, stereotypical things [about playboy tendencies and commitment avoidance], but it wasn't that way at all. I guess once everyone saw how serious I was about my wife, all [those concerns] went out the window."

In fact, Campbell ended up being completely embraced by his wife's family.

"You know, I was sitting with my son, and he was talking about my father, who just passed away recently," Campbell said. "He was asking me what it's like to be without a father. And I said, 'You know, my father is always going to live inside of me, and what you remember about him is going to live inside of you. But right now? *Saba* [grandfather] is my father,' my wife's father. My wife's parents, they love me like a son, especially my wife's mom. No matter what I do, she's always on my side. I love my wife's family."

The Thomases expressed a similar feeling of closeness between Deon and Dafna's family. Thomas is currently a basketball broadcaster in Illinois, but Dafna said it is her parents' dream that he take a coaching job in Israel to be closer to them. Amazingly, he did not even meet them until after the couple got married in Las Vegas.

"After the wedding, he got a job in Israel, in Rishon LeZion," Dafna said about Thomas's first stint in Israel. "So I called my family and told them, 'My husband is coming home, go get him.' They were like, 'How are we going to know him?' I said, 'You can't miss him—go get my husband.' And they fell in love with him. They went and got him, and they fell in love with him. He can't do anything wrong."

"I *don't* do anything wrong!" Thomas added, laughing.

Naturally, I wondered if when Dafna called her parents from Spain on the first day the couple crossed paths and told them she had met her husband—and that he was African American, and Christian, and a professional basketball player—were they concerned?

"No," Dafna said, before I could even finish the question. "You know why? Because they know me. They trust me. Our communication has always been open. So for me to make the decision that I made, they knew it was not going to be anything that was just 'OK.'"

"You had to know her family," Thomas said, with a glint in his eye.

Race and Religion

In the United States, despite much progress, mixed-race couples are still not universally embraced. A 2016 University of Washington study suggested that self-reported acceptance of interracial marriage actually masks the deeper feelings of discomfort, even disgust, which some Americans feel about mixed-race couples. Interestingly, however, the players I spoke with told me that their religion was actually a bigger issue to their Israeli spouse's family than their race. Interfaith marriages among Jews and non-Jews are becoming increasingly prevalent, from about 13 percent in 1970 to approximately 50 percent today. That fact causes much consternation to some, who argue that assimilation threatens to do what the Holocaust could not—bring an end to the Jewish people. Those concerns came to the forefront of Israeli public consciousness when, in 2006, Linor Abargil, an Israeli model and former Miss World, became engaged to Šarūnas "Šaras" Jasikevičius, a White, non-Jewish, Lithuanian point guard who played for Maccabi Tel Aviv. Baruch Marzel, chairman of the National Jewish Front party, called on Abargil to turn down the proposal from Jasikevičius. In a highly publicized letter to the model, Marzel wrote, "I have nothing against Šaras, and he may well be a wonderful, charming man, but as long as he has not converted, you must not make such a move."

He went on to write that if she were to wed Jasikevičius, she would be divorcing the people of Israel as well as her family. "The greatest danger to our people is assimilation! I urge you in the last minute not to make this move."

Although none of the players I spoke to experienced anything even approaching Marzel's public criticism, they all acknowledged the importance of open-mindedness in making the relationships with Israeli spouses and their families work. Carr did not convert to Judaism, and he was relieved to find acceptance from his in-laws nonetheless. He said his wife's family kept the Jewish holidays and traditions, but that they were a modernized family who were unconditionally supportive of him. He has been happy to take part in and learn about various customs, and they in turn have never pressured him to convert.

"I've been to synagogue—been there for the prayer, ceremonies, singing," Carr said. "[We don't do] as much in the house, but we light candles, bring in the Shabbat, things like that. When we go to her parents' house it's a bit more formal—reading the passages, blessing the food before eating. I read the English translations—like I said, I've shown interest and I want to learn, [but] her parents never forced me to make some decision based on their daughter."

Thomas, who also did not convert to Judaism, was raised Christian. But he is quick to point out that his upbringing was more spiritual than religious, which made for an easier transition to life in a mixed-faith family.

"[My grandmother] would always say, 'There's one God. I don't care what they name him, what they call him, there's only one,'" Thomas said. "And that's kind of what I bring in [to the relationship]. It's like I said, I'm not religious, so I don't see a difference between [Christianity and Judaism]. My wife and I talk about it all the time, and I'll tell her, 'They're fruit from the same tree. Wherever people took it, that's where they took it, but it's all derived from one place.'"

Although they were married in Las Vegas, the Thomases did end up having a "second wedding" in Israel, in front of family and friends. That wedding incorporated two important and traditional Jewish customs. It was held under a *chuppah*, the canopy under which Jewish marriage ceremonies take place, symbolizing the Jewish home the couple will build together. And Thomas stomped on and broke a glass, which serves as a customary reminder that despite the joy of a wedding, Jews still mourn the destruction of the Holy Temple in Jerusalem, first in 586 BCE, and again in 70 AD.

So did he ever feel pressure from his wife's family to convert to Judaism? I put the question to Thomas during my lunch with him and his family. It was met with immediate chuckles and a smile from wife Dafna.

"Pressure?" Thomas asked. "No, I wouldn't say pressure. Of course, it was *mentioned*. It was *suggested*. But I don't think I have to [convert], because I embrace all of it."

At this point, Dafna interjected, asking her husband to convey the story of Rabbi Pini.

After finishing his playing career in Israel and moving to Florida, Thomas invited a rabbi the couple had met to recite the blessings for their new house and put up the mezuzahs. During their initial and subsequent meetings, Thomas learned that the rabbi was a Maccabi Tel Aviv fan and that they shared friends in common in Israel. Soon, the former player and rabbi bonded and began spending more and more time together.

"Actually, he ended up being a really good friend of mine," Thomas said. "We were talking one time, we were having a discussion and he said, 'You're more Jewish than the Jews that I know,'" Thomas said with a chuckle.

Dafna seconds that observation.

"We have [big] Shabbat dinners—I have twelve people coming this Friday for Shabbat dinner, we open it up like Rosh Hashana (the Jewish New Year)," Dafna said. "And it's funny to see him—he makes sure everybody has a kippah for the blessings. And when we break the bread, if I forget the salt, oh no!" (It is a Jewish custom to salt the bread because the home is likened to a miniature Holy Temple; just as all offerings at the Temple were salted, the bread at home is to be salted, too.)

"If you're going to do it, do it right," Thomas added.

The Decision to Convert

Watson and Campbell, on the other hand, did make the decision to convert to Judaism. And they both made it clear that their conversions were ideologically inspired and not conversions-of-convenience like some that have taken place elsewhere in the Israeli basketball world. Watson told me that the key to his conversion was that he initiated the process directly.

"I think when guys try to [undertake the conversion process] through agents and through basketball, it becomes illegitimate," Watson said. "I took my wife, we went to New York, and I started going to synagogue every Friday. I met with a rabbi, explained my situation, what I do for a living, introduced him to my family, and he kind of adopted me. And once he did that, I started the process of conversion. It took me about a year, I had to read a lot of books, do a lot of studying, do a lot of different things. After he saw that I was serious about it, he gave me the certificate that I was a Jew. Then he gave me the name of a lawyer to contact for getting citizenship, and that's what I did. I came back, contacted the lawyer, and at first, the country tried to fight it. They wanted to make sure it was valid, that kind of thing. But like I said, I went through it on my own. I didn't go through any basketball people. So once they started doing their checks and things, everything came up legit—because I didn't try to sneak my way through it. I actually did the work, and it paid off," he said with deserved pride.

Unlike Watson, Campbell had already married his wife *and* received his Israeli citizenship when he decided to convert to Judaism. The timing shocked friends and outsiders, given that many players convert primarily to make the road to citizenship smoother. But Campbell had his own reasons. He went through an Orthodox conversion (as opposed to the less rigorous and exhaustive conversion processes offered by the Conservative or Reform streams of Judaism), keeping Shabbat, studying, and taking various exams.

"Basically, I went through a [process of] falling in love again with religion," Campbell said. "It touched me deeply, and I knew [Israel] was where I wanted to be. It was an Orthodox conversion. It was tough, it was very tough. And some of my friends were like, 'Why? You've got all your papers and everything.' I said, 'Man, this has never been about the papers. I love my wife. I fell in love with her, and I didn't want to lose her.'"

Today, the Campbell family has a kosher, Jewish home, much to the surprise of those who knew him previously.

"Yeah, a lot of my [American] friends trip out, because they'll be like, 'What are you doing?' and I'm like 'I'm building our *sukkah* [the temporary hut put up during an annual holiday commemorating the way the Jewish people lived during their escape from Egypt],'" Campbell said. "I respect all the holidays—even on Yom Kippur [the Day of Atonement], I'm not eating. Our house is kosher—we don't eat meat with cheese, the whole works. My [American] friends, when they come over, I'll be like, 'Take a fork.' They'll open a drawer and I'm like, 'No! That's [for] cheese, man!' They're like, 'Oh my God, Fred, you've been here too long!'"

Though his friends may be surprised, Campbell's own family was instantly supportive of his decision. Like Thomas, their focus was more on the spirit and morality of the religion and less on its name.

"My family accepted my wife without a doubt, because once she came to the States and met my family, my family immediately fell in love with her," Campbell said. "They knew that she was Jewish, and I told my Mom that I was going to convert. She said, 'Freddy, as long as you've got God in your life, it doesn't matter. You can always fall back on the things we taught you as a child. I trust you to make a good decision when it comes to your religion—that's why I never pushed Christianity onto my children. If you wanted to be a Muslim, Jew, or this or that [it's OK].' That's the way we were raised," Campbell explained.

Parenting Challenges

Raising children in a mixed-race, interfaith environment is yet another challenge facing African American players and their Israeli wives. According to Jewish law, a child's religion is determined by the religion of the child's mother. Therefore, the daughters of Carr and Thomas are considered Jewish, even though their fathers did not convert. But one's identity according to religious law and one's feeling of identity are two different matters. Deciding whether to raise the children as Jewish, Christian, both, or neither; answering complicated questions about identity; navigating the various holiday seasons; explaining the differences between customs observed at the home of one set of grandparents in comparison to the home of the other—all are responsibilities unique to interfaith parents.

"Our daughter is Jewish," Carr said. "She practices all of the Jewish ways and holidays, but my wife does a great job of keeping her mind open to other things and learning about different things. She's a very, very intelligent young lady. She speaks Hebrew and English fluently. She's very educated when it comes to the world. We mix in holidays. If there's an American holiday, we celebrate that and teach her about that, and if there's a Jewish holiday we obviously celebrate that and teach her about that as well."

For Campbell and Watson, their conversions simplified matters, ensuring that their children would grow up with only one religion being practiced in the home. As for the two daughters of Deon and Dafna Thomas, the religion they end up practicing is ultimately in their hands.

"We do both [Judaism and Christianity]," Thomas said. "I respect my wife's religion and I respect my wife. For me, I have no problem participating in any of the prayers or customs because they are all fruit from the same tree—there is very little difference between the two religions. We do both, and, when the girls get old enough, they can decide what they choose to do. I think that's only fair."

During the course of my interviews, I spoke to Fred's son, Toi, and Deon's daughter, Gabrielle, about their upcoming Bar and Bat Mitzvahs. On both occasions I was struck by the negligible impact their mixed-race and interfaith backgrounds had on the content of our conversations. Each of them talked about where the party would be, where the family would travel afterward, and how difficult studying and practicing had been or would be. I could have been talking to any Jewish boy or girl in my hometown of Toronto, or anywhere else for that matter.

However this is not to say that the family environment has no effect on coming-of-age ceremonies for Jewish children, especially when the father does not convert. Dawson has spent almost thirty years in Israel and is raising two sons. Dawson agreed before his kids were born that they would be raised Jewish, but he chose not to convert. Certainly that decision did not affect his children's ability to take part in Jewish ceremonies, but it did have an impact on his role.

"My youngest son just had his Bar Mitzvah," Dawson told me. "The day that he went to the *Beit Knesset* (synagogue), I had to be upstairs, but his grandfather on my ex-wife's side was with him. From everything that has happened [to him], from the *brit* (circumcision) and everything, the grandfather had to do everything. I could watch and be there, but I couldn't participate. For me, it was just an [emotional, not faith-based] experience because it was my son."

Dawson's two sons are from his first marriage to an Israeli woman. He has since divorced and remarried. Although a first marriage is considered bashert, Jewish custom holds that it is still possible to have a good and happy marriage with a second spouse, and the Talmud teaches that God also arranges those second marriages. Although not Jewish, Dawson is convinced that both of his marriages had a predetermined element to them. Arriving in Israel from the Deep South in Alabama, Dawson had a first impression of Israel that was not good. Polite and soft spoken, he had trouble with the intensity of day-to-day Israeli life, telling me that he initially felt the pressure and stress could be cut with a knife. Indeed, after just one year in Israel, he left to play in Greece. But love was in the air in Israel with a woman he met during his first Israeli season. He chose to return to give the country another try. He married his girlfriend, and now, although the marriage didn't work out, he acknowledges the important role she played in his life.

"What I see now is that I was with my ex-wife to have kids and to keep me here long enough to meet my new wife," Dawson said. "And that's how I feel, because I think I've been searching for her [his second wife, Orna] all my life, a woman I can really trust. Because as a basketball player, especially when you're making money … Ever since I was in high school I was told to be careful of women—they want to have babies, they want to get your money, you have to watch them. I never trusted women, even the one I was [first] married to, until I met [Orna]."

Dawson actually met his second wife while trying to salvage his first marriage. Orna was introduced to him and his first wife by mutual friends, and the three of them would spend time together as a group.

"When Orna found out that we were getting a divorce, she tried to keep us together," Dawson said. "She went and talked to my ex-wife, and they went out one time and [Orna] talked to her and talked to her, and the three of us became friends. And once, Orna told me, 'Joe, she [Dawson's first wife] just doesn't get who you are. I don't know how you guys have been together for so long. She doesn't see you at all,'" Dawson said about the eventful period in his life. "I continued my progress with the divorce and we were friends, meeting at the same places. And then finally Orna invited me to her house for dinner—but it was nothing, she never even thought about a relationship. And I ate her food, and she was a great cook. So I started giving her gifts—I would come to her house and she would cook me these great meals and send me home with them," he said. "Then I started to pay attention to her as a woman, and I asked her out one time. She really kept me on hold for about six months. We were friends, only friends, and then after that she said she could relax, that she understood that she wasn't a rebound. And I discovered how good a person she was. But what really helped me was that during those first months, she was like my counselor. She was keeping me balanced and listening to me. And we found out we had so many things in common. And she had a lot of things in common with my ex-wife, except for one thing. My ex-wife, she wanted to be outside—she loved attention. When I would play games, she liked to walk in like a model. My new wife, she was quieter. She wanted to be just with me."

Dawson met his second wife while at a significant crossroads in his life. More than forty years old, in the twilight of his playing career, and dealing with a failing marriage, Dawson was vacillating about whether to move back to the United States or try to build a post-basketball life in Israel. Not wanting to be separated from his two sons, now twenty-three and twenty, Dawson chose to stay, and Orna was instrumental in helping him better integrate into Israeli society. She encouraged Dawson to work harder on his Hebrew and convinced him that despite the apparent mismatch between his somewhat prickly surroundings and his laid-back, southern personality, he could live a happy life in Israel. Orna encouraged him whenever possible to get to know Israelis, beyond their sometimes gruff exterior. Most importantly, Orna's influence led to improved relations between Dawson and his ex-wife, which in turn led to Dawson's ex-wife granting him custody of their two sons, a welcomed change in circumstances Dawson called his "dream."

"After all this, my new wife made the peace between me and my old wife," Dawson said. "Now, with the kids and everything, we go to [his son's] game and [Orna] says, 'We're not going to sit on one side and she's going to sit on the other side. We're going to sit together. He doesn't need to look up and see us separated—he's going to see us together.' This is the kind of person she is. She made the difference!"

The Israeli divorce rate is up to 30 percent, lower than the generally accepted American rate of 50 percent, but substantial nonetheless. For Dawson, his divorce and remarriage ultimately had a substantially positive impact on his life. In the years since we initially spoke, Watson and his wife also divorced, and though he returned to New York after his retirement from playing, he and his ex-wife remain close friends and cooperative co-parents of their daughter. For Campbell, Thomas, Carr, Watson, and Dawson, no matter where their lives will take them in the future, they share the bond of having created a family with an Israeli woman, and as Oliver Wendell Holmes once wrote, "Where we love is home—home that our feet may leave, but not our hearts."

9

THE ISRAELI YANKEES

IN SPORTS, FEW CLICHÉS GET as much mileage as the parable of David and Goliath. When the coach of an underdog needs to make an inspiring pregame speech or a journalist wants an instantly relatable headline, the biblical tale of an undersized child warrior's victory over a seemingly undefeatable behemoth is an obvious choice. Most teams in sports can easily be classified as either David or Goliath. In Israel though, a land of so many contradictions, there is one team that can be classified as both. Even, sometimes, within the same week.

The names of many Israeli basketball teams start with the word Maccabi, followed by the name of the team's city or town (Maccabi Haifa, Maccabi Rishon LeZion, and Maccabi Ashdod are a few that come to mind). Maccabi Tel Aviv, however, is far and away the country's most successful and well-known team, so much so that when "Maccabi" is used as a stand-alone term, it is implicitly understood that the reference is to Maccabi Tel Aviv. On Thursday nights Maccabi plays in the Euroleague, and Israelis eagerly support the plucky Israeli "David" as it battles the "Goliaths" of Europe. It has been this way since the 1970s, when the team, led by Aulcie Perry, Tal Brody, and other formidable players, defeated CSKA Moscow. Fans and pundits lauded it as a shared victory of four million Israelis over 200 million Soviets, a clear David-over-Goliath win. The club is so well supported in its battles with European powers that Israelis were asked to turn off any unnecessary electrical appliances before a big 1989 clash with CSKA because it was feared the whole country would have their televisions on and cause a national power outage!

Come Sunday, though, Maccabi plays its Israeli league games. Now it suddenly becomes the Goliath, dominating the local competition in an unprecedented (and critics would argue, unseemly) manner, in part because of a budget that often surpasses that of the rest of the league's teams combined. In Israel, Maccabi is akin to baseball's New York Yankees, the team that has claimed more than twice as many World Series championships as the next most successful organization, and, not coincidentally, the team with financing that often far outstrips most other teams. As African American Fred Campbell, a veteran of 25 seasons in Israel, put it, "There's the league and then there's Maccabi—everybody else is shooting for second place."

Maccabi's fans are among the most fervent in the world, with thousands of them regularly traveling to watch the team compete abroad, rocking foreign arenas with chants in support of Maccabi's yellow and blue. The team's influence stretches to North America as well, where Israeli expats religiously track the team's exploits and celebrate current and former players alike. Anthony Parker summarized the passion of the Maccabi faithful with an anecdote from his time with the Cleveland Cavaliers, five years after he left the Israeli club to return to the NBA.

"It's 2010, and I'm with Cleveland in Miami [to play the Heat]," Parker said. "[The players are] all at a restaurant eating, having a team dinner, and I happen to be sitting next to LeBron [James]. Some fans come in, and they're like, 'Yo! Oh my God, I can't believe it!' And you know, LeBron is like, 'All right, here we go …' And the fans say, 'Anthony Parker!' [Everyone was] like, 'What in the world?!' … That's Maccabi."

The team's critics, though fewer in number, are equally passionate. They routinely decry the team's monopoly on success in the Israeli league, and pine for the day when Maccabi championships are no longer inevitable. African American players started suiting up for Maccabi in the 1970s and they have been among the most well-known players in Israeli basketball history. They have also faced the most pressure, played in front of the loudest crowds, had the most memorable victories, and suffered the most public failures of all African American players who came to Israel. As Maccabi players, their experience is simply unique.

A History of Victory

An immediate—and particularly telling—symbol of the difference between signing with Maccabi or with another Israeli organization is the facility in which the team plays. While other Israeli squads compete in small multipurpose arenas holding a maximum of 5,000 fans, Maccabi's games take place in Menora Mivtachim Arena (formerly known as Yad Eliyahu Arena and Nokia Arena), a first-class facility with a capacity of almost 12,000. Constructed in 1963 as an open-air court with concrete stands seating a maximum of 5,000, it has since been renovated into the fully modern arena it is today, one that compares favorably to any stadium in Europe.

And as anyone who has attended a Maccabi game there can tell you, the team's home-court advantage is not limited to bricks and mortar. At game time the arena is filled with the team's passionate fans, an experience as intimidating as any in international basketball. ESPN insider Chad Ford wrote about being in the Nokia Arena audience in 2004. "This is my third consecutive Euroleague Final Four. In all three events, the hometown team has played for the championship. Last year, F.C. Barcelona won in Barcelona, Spain, and the city erupted with joy. But nothing I've seen in all my travels in Europe has come close to this. A sea of yellow and blue chants so loudly twenty minutes before the game starts it's literally impossible to conduct a conversation with the person sitting next to you. When Maccabi takes the floor, the decibel level doubles."

Maccabi won the first professional Israeli basketball championship in 1954 and has won fifty more local titles since then, a stunning 82 percent success rate. The team has also excelled abroad, winning six European championships, behind only Real Madrid and CSKA Moscow in the all-time tally. That domination is without question due in part to the presence of some of the best African American basketball players ever to play in Israel, including an unprecedented number of former or future NBA players. For many, Maccabi Tel Aviv was one step removed from the sport's best league, sometimes coming and other times going. For example, Willie Anderson and Terence Morris in the 1990s and Marcus Fizer and Rodney White in the 2000s were former NBA players when they joined the Israeli club, and none would grace an NBA court again. Others, however, used their time at Maccabi to improve their game, increase their exposure, and turn fledgling NBA hopes into long-term NBA success. A third-round draft pick of the Cleveland Cavaliers in 1987 (back when the NBA draft went seven rounds), Donald Royal played two seasons in the Continental Basketball Association (CBA) and one in the Dominican Republic before even making an NBA roster. He then played sparingly and had just one season with the Minnesota Timberwolves. But he subsequently parlayed a successful campaign with Maccabi Tel Aviv into a contract offer from the Orlando Magic, becoming a valuable contributor and sometimes-starter for four seasons.

Ten years later, Parker was a more touted prospect coming out of college than Royal had been. Parker was picked in the first round of the 1997 NBA Draft by the New Jersey Nets (who immediately traded him to the Philadelphia 76ers as part of a multiplayer deal), but he too found immediate NBA success elusive. In his first two seasons, Parker played in only 39 regular season games, averaging just over five minutes per appearance for the Sixers. He was subsequently traded to the Orlando Magic, but his sojourn with his new team was equally flat. Parker put up modest numbers before being released and finishing his season in the CBA. Having failed to break through in the NBA, Parker signed with Maccabi and spent five seasons in Tel Aviv where he at last found professional success. Not only did he become a favorite Israeli adopted son, he also found fame as an internationally renowned basketball talent. With two Euroleague MVP awards under his belt, Parker returned to the NBA, this time with a three-year guaranteed contract valued at four million dollars per season, and he had starting roles with the Toronto Raptors and then the Cleveland Cavaliers before hanging up his sneakers.

Interestingly, Parker sported the number 18 during his time with both the Raptors and the Cavs, instead of the customary number 8 he had worn for most of his career. The number 18 has a special significance in Judaism, representing the numeric equivalent of the Hebrew letters that spell *chai* (life), and Parker chose the number as a tribute to his years in the Holy Land and to his fans there. "I just had such a great time that I wanted to take something from that experience," Parker said. "The number 18, it means 'chai' and it's the symbol for life and good fortune in Judaism. I thought that was something to take away from Israel and let [Israelis] know I'm still representing them."

The Winning Mystique

The satisfaction of playing for a dominant squad and having the chance to display their individual prowess for such a high-profile team, however, doesn't necessarily mean that the Maccabi experience is altogether trouble-free for African American players. Maceo Baston recalled how he and his teammates "got the VIP treatment" and were "like fifteen Michael Jordans" in Israel. But that upscale reception couldn't offset the level of pressure he felt, from the minute his flight landed in Tel Aviv, to take the team to the Euroleague Final Four. As an example of the intensity of media and fan scrutiny of the team, after Maccabi lost the Israeli league title in 1993, having previously won an astounding twenty-three championships in a row, a reporter actually asked team chairman Shimon Mizrahi if, in light of the loss, he intended to resign. Two years—and two Israeli league championships—later, a sports columnist called for Mizrahi's resignation again, saying that "the same

Maccabi is not good enough anymore." He went on to state that Mizrahi had failed to take into account the changes that had occurred in Israeli and European basketball since the late 1970s and early 1980s. Needless to say, Mizrahi kept his post, and in fact put together four more teams that would win the Euroleague championship in the years that followed. But the haste with which Israeli media clamored for a man who had known such success to retire reveals both the fickleness of the media and the pressure Maccabi Tel Aviv endures year in and year out, to win—and to win in style.

Fizer, a former NBA lottery pick who spent two seasons with Maccabi, said the Maccabi fans and media are "adamant about winning, keeping their tradition of what they had in the past years. Being Maccabi Tel Aviv," he continued, "everyone is gunning for you, from guys in the Israeli league to teams in the Euroleague, and it's very tough. People celebrate beating Maccabi like it's a championship. [Opposing teams] can be 1–30, but if the one win is against Maccabi Tel Aviv, they're satisfied."

Fizer's comments may exaggerate the situation, but not by much. Maccabi's dominance affects not only the experiences of African Americans who sign to play with the juggernaut but also those who play on any first-division Israeli team. Players recruited by Israeli teams often arrive knowing little or nothing about the country, but on arrival they are made well aware of their mission: *Beat Maccabi*. However, knowing the goal and reaching it are two very different tasks. Beating Maccabi involves more than conquering the five opposing players on the court— it also means confronting the fifty-plus years of history Maccabi has behind it.

Cory Carr, an African American who has spent more than fifteen seasons in Israel, points out that playing against this dominant team puts the other players at a psychological disadvantage. "It's the whole mystique. [People are] psyched out before you play the game. Nobody expects you to win—even some of the local Israeli players on your team don't think you can win. It's like to beat Maccabi is a miracle!"

Carr has defeated Maccabi multiple times in his career, in fact, but he considers these victories only a relative success. Maccabi, he points out, has won more times than he has beaten them. Carr also raises an interesting point: the power of psychology in sustaining Maccabi's dominance. Young Israelis are born and raised in a local basketball world in which Maccabi is considered unbeatable. They have seen how the many foreigners recruited and teams assembled specifically to beat Maccabi have fallen short. Understandably, this leads many Israelis on other teams to assume that their team *can't* win, even before tip-off. On the other hand, African American players may hardly have heard of Maccabi before coming to Israel, let alone grown up learning to fear the team. They enter Israeli basketball with a completely different mind-set.

"When I played for Eilat, we beat them three times," said Campbell. "The last time we beat them, we had them by 27 at halftime. I had 20 points and 20 rebounds, and they made a big deal about how Victor Alexander [a former NBA player who played for Maccabi in the late 1990s] can be making a million dollars, and I'm making $100,000. I always played well against Maccabi, because I have no fear," Campbell continued. "It's amazing that teams, before the Maccabi game, they'll start saying things like, 'We need to win the game before the Maccabi game,' because they already know they're going to lose the Maccabi game. That just makes me mad."

Campbell was describing a late '90s matchup between his Eilat team and Maccabi, but his reference to the discrepancy that existed in player salaries almost twenty years ago is still true. According to basketball agent Bernie Lee, the median foreign player for a non-Maccabi team in Israel earns about $120,000 per season, with the highest paid non-Maccabi foreigner maxing out at about $280,000. With Maccabi the range is very different—salaries for foreigners on the team can stretch from $750,000 to almost $5 million a season.

It would be easy to assume that salary envy plays a role in the desire to topple Tel Aviv, but according to Carr, this isn't the case; it's sheer competitiveness that drives players. "Every time I come up against Maccabi, I treat them with respect, but I want to kick their ass," Carr said. "I want to come at them and let them know that, even though you're giants, you're about to feel me, you know? That's the kind of attitude you've got to take against those bigger organizations. And they respect it."

Despite the remarkable success of the team and its individual players, Maccabi is not universally respected in Israel, let alone universally supported. As noted previously, Israeli fans tend to cheer for Maccabi when the team is playing powerful European clubs, but when it comes to Maccabi as the overwhelming favorite in Israeli competition, the cheering frequently stops. And there are some fans who would never cheer for the team in any circumstances. Although a minority, this group makes a lot of noise in Israeli basketball circles, arguing that Maccabi's reliance on foreign players has taken the "Israeli" out of Israeli basketball. They point out that, like the Yankees in New York City, the team's massive budget gives it an insurmountable advantage before games even begin, and they allege that Maccabi wields undue influence to ensure its continued dominance. In short, the toughest critics don't see Maccabi as an iconic symbol of the State of Israel; instead they view it as a big, cold-blooded corporation that has always won, and that would do anything to continue winning. As former Israeli league coach and current broadcaster Simmy Reguer said about Maccabi, "If they need you, they use you. You're as good as your last game."

But is this true? The experiences of two African American players in particular suggest that big, bad Maccabi may actually have a rather big heart.

Help Defense

Following a three-year run of two Euroleague titles and a runner-up finish, Maccabi Tel Aviv entered the 2006–07 season in rebuilding mode. Gone were popular coach Pini Gershon and legendary players Parker, Baston, and Šarūnas Jasikevičius, the cornerstones of that dynasty. They were replaced by a relatively unknown coach and a selection of American players pundits considered underwhelming at best.

In addition to Rodney Buford and Noel Felix, veterans of European basketball who were on the downside of their careers, the team signed Will Bynum, a twenty-three-year-old who was just one year out of college and who had no European experience whatsoever.

A playground and high school legend in Chicago, Bynum played college hoops for Arizona and Georgia Tech before spending his one post-college season bouncing between the NBA and its minor league, the NBDL. His Euroleague career started with a bang, as Bynum led Maccabi to victory with 29 points in his debut. But things would not continue that smoothly. Maccabi's 2006–07 season was a disappointment, with the team failing to qualify for the Euroleague Final Four after doing so seven of the eight previous years. Israel's media throngs were quick to establish the theme of the season—Maccabi's apparent demise, its descent from dynasty to disarray. Despite another coaching change, dire prognostications followed for the next season as well. They looked accurate early on. Maccabi, the team that so often went undefeated in the Israeli league, lost three local games before 2007 turned to 2008, some in embarrassing fashion. And Maccabi's troubles were about to extend beyond the court in a rather extraordinary fashion.

On the evening of Friday, January 4, 2008, Bynum went out to celebrate his twenty-fifth birthday with some teammates and his brother, Jerome. The group went to G-Spot, a Tel Aviv nightclub known to be popular with American basketball players. It was to be a lighthearted celebration, a gathering of friends to enjoy the birthday night, but it turned out to be anything but.

"Yesterday night there was a party attended by a number of basketball players in a club in Tel Aviv," police spokesman Micky Rosenfeld told the media the next day. "There was some pushing and shoving outside the club that turned bad, and then Bynum, voluntarily or not, ran over a resident from Dimona, injuring him."

The injured man was taken to a Tel Aviv hospital for hip surgery from which he recovered. Bynum was taken by the police for questioning. The exact sequence of events was never disclosed, but it appears that Bynum and his brother had an altercation inside the club with members of the Black Hebrew Israelite community. This group is made up of descendants of African Americans from Chicago who moved to Israel in the late 1960s (settling largely in the city of Dimona in the Negev desert) and who adhere in varying degrees to the tenets of Judaism. The altercation continued outside, where eventually Bynum's car ran over the twenty-two-year-old man.

As fortune would have it, Maccabi team chairman Mizrahi, in addition to his duties with the club, was also a lawyer who specialized in motor vehicle accidents. He could have distanced himself and his team from the incident and the negative attention it brought, but instead Mizrahi chose to throw himself into advocating for Bynum and pleading with the media and the courts on his player's behalf. Mizrahi said that the player reported he was assaulted with elbows and provoked while inside the club, but he had refused to respond. When Bynum left the club, twenty people were allegedly waiting to attack him, including one wielding a knife. The fact that Bynum's car ran the victim over was never in dispute. His intent, however, needed to be determined in order for authorities to decide whether or not to charge him criminally. According to Bynum and Mizrahi, it was an accident that resulted from Bynum's hurried and chaotic attempt to extricate himself and his brother from a group ambush.

"All that Will was trying to do was to escape the danger," Mizrahi told the media. "There is no doubt that [Bynum] and his brother went out and people waited for them with a knife and pelted them with rocks. All of this was before they even reached the car."

As terrible as the night of the incident was, Bynum's lowest point was to come a few days later. Bynum was kept in police custody immediately following the altercation as the authorities investigated the incident and his role in it. On January 7, Bynum appeared before the court with Mizrahi arguing for an immediate release and the prosecutor arguing for an extension of the player's remand as the investigation continued. According to Campbell, who closely followed television news of the proceedings, it was the way the police transported Bynum to the court that caused him as much distress as anything else.

"When they brought Will to court, I thought they made a big spectacle out of it," Campbell said. "If you're bringing a prisoner to the court, don't you want to drive him in? Why would they want to stop him a block from the courthouse and walk him down the street, shackled and handcuffed?" Campbell asked, still outraged. "He had handcuffs, and shackles on his feet, about fifty meters away from the place where he had to go! They could have driven him all the way there. Just walking in like that, Will said that tore him apart right there, just thinking that his parents were going to see that."

Bynum's case was eventually closed without any charges being filed. The investigation ultimately determined that he had been in tangible danger, that the collision was not intentional, and that his actions were justified. Maccabi Tel Aviv's support of Bynum throughout the ordeal is particularly noteworthy. When one of a team's players is involved in an embarrassing and controversial incident, it's not uncommon for the team to cut ties with the player or at least stay publicly neutral, especially if the team is badly underachieving. International playing contracts aren't necessarily guaranteed, and Maccabi could presumably have tried to terminate Bynum's deal and replace him with a different player (such mid-season replacements are quite common in international basketball). But Maccabi chose not to do so. The team jumped directly into the fray, publicly supporting Bynum, and provided him legal representation on a pro bono basis.

Maccabi's critics wouldn't necessarily view the team's actions as generous. After all, it was to Maccabi's benefit to keep one of its better players on the basketball court, not in the court of law. Critics could say that Mizrahi, in typical "win-at-all-costs" fashion, was not acting sympathetically, but out of self-interest. Joe Dawson, an African American who has been in Israel for almost thirty years (and never played for Maccabi), admitted those thoughts crossed his mind.

"When I first saw it, I thought it was out of necessity, because at that time Maccabi needed Will to keep playing," Dawson said. "Knowing Will, I knew that he didn't do anything malicious that night, and I guess Shimon felt that also, because they got behind him. [Will] was very upset about it—he thought he was going to jail, he didn't know where [he was going to end up], he was ready to go crazy. And Shimon felt it, and I was proud of [Shimon]. That was one of the times that I felt that Shimon was different. He surprised me, on the pleasant side."

In return, Bynum and his teammates would surprise Shimon, and all of European basketball. The struggling club welcomed Bynum back with open arms and immediately embarked on a memorable run, eventually qualifying for the 2008 Euroleague Final Four in an achievement an Israeli journalist once again ascribed to its being "nothing short of a miracle." In the end though, there would be no storybook finish—despite Bynum's team-high 23 points in the finals, Maccabi fell to CSKA Moscow, 91–77. It was of course a disappointing finish, but given the way things started for Maccabi, including Bynum's midseason legal battle and prison stint, most people considered the season remarkably successful.

Bynum eventually leveraged the Euroleague success into an NBA contract with the Detroit Pistons. I spoke with him in the Pistons locker room before a tilt with the Toronto Raptors. Far from sounding like a former hired gun for a heartless Goliath team, he had clearly become a lifelong ally of the Maccabi organization. He said that contrary to what he might have expected, the nightclub incident and its aftermath didn't weaken his bond with the team, its management, and its fans in the slightest.

"No, actually it got stronger," Bynum told me. "It got a whole lot stronger. They really supported me in one of the worst times in my life. For them to do that for me, it speaks volumes. They stuck behind me, Shimon did a great job, and I beat the case. It was really big for me— that's why I'll always feel indebted to Maccabi."

A Long-Distance Call

Decades earlier it was Maccabi who was indebted, to its African American star, Aulcie Perry. After he helped lead the team to the 1977 European Cup in his first season, his unmitigated success continued for several more years. He led Maccabi to a victory over the defending NBA champion Washington Bullets in a 1978 exhibition game, to a European runner-up finish in 1980, and to another European championship in 1981. Off the court, he met and eventually married Israeli model Tami Ben-Ami. An athletic force with an engaging personality, and a converted Jew to boot, Perry couldn't walk down Tel Aviv's café-lined Dizengoff Street without being besieged by autograph seekers. The reason, at least according to his coach at the time, was simple. "He's a sweetheart," said Rudi D'Amico, the coach of Maccabi Tel Aviv in 1980, in explaining Perry's popularity.

Unfortunately, Perry's popularity, career, and life in general was soon to go into a spiral of decline. "Aulcie Perry was a joke," sports broadcaster Reguer said. "[Perry and teammate Earl Williams] were junkies, getting busted all the time." In December 1982, Perry missed a game against Real Madrid. Some attempted to attribute the disappearance to a case of the flu, while others said that the star had become dizzy from a doctor's ear exam, but in actuality it was something much more concerning. It eventually became known that the real reason Perry didn't make it to the game was his worsening drug problem.

In March 1983, Perry was arrested and charged with buying heroin. He pleaded guilty in a Tel Aviv court and was eventually given a fine of $150,000 and a suspended sentence. In 1985, he retired from playing and left Israel to return to the United States, where things only got worse. In 1987 he was convicted on charges of smuggling $1.8 million of heroin into the United States and ended up spending a total of eight years in prison in three different states (one year in Minnesota, two in Pennsylvania, and the last five in North Carolina). During his time in prison, Perry took some solace in attending penitentiary synagogue services and continuing his study of the Old Testament. He also received a deluge of letters of support from his Israeli friends and fans, support he would not soon forget. But perhaps the most significant bit of correspondence from Perry's time in prison was not a letter he received, but rather a phone call he made.

At one point during his incarceration, Perry decided he needed money, so he called Shmulik Zysman, his former teammate with Maccabi Tel Aviv who was also a practicing lawyer. Years earlier, as part of Perry's playing contract, Maccabi had arranged to purchase an apartment for him in the center of Tel Aviv, with the team withholding a percentage of his salary in exchange for the value of the property. Perry's call to Zysman was to ask him to arrange to sell the apartment. However, the legal arrangements made in the original acquisition required Maccabi's written permission for any such sale.

Zysman called Mizrahi to tell him about Perry's desire to sell, and at this juncture the reputation of Maccabi as the heartless Goliath takes another hit. Zysman advised Mizrahi that he was concerned that Perry, with his giving nature, might squander the sale proceeds he would receive. As it turned out, Maccabi had arranged for the purchase of the apartment with much the same thing in mind—knowing Perry well, they felt he would be better served long term by a tangible, appreciating asset than by cash. So Mizrahi was agreeable when Zysman presented his quite uncharacteristic instinct to ignore his client's instructions.

"Knowing Aulcie, that he spends every penny that he has, I decided I wasn't going to [sell the apartment]," Zysman said. "I called [Mizrahi], and I said, 'I got instructions to sell the apartment. What do you think about the idea *not* to sell it?' He said, '100 percent right, we are not going to sell it. I'm not going to give you permission.' And we shook hands that we were not going to do so. For the first time in my life, ever, I didn't do what the client asked me to do, on purpose. The apartment is worth today in Israel millions of dollars, and [Perry's future] is secure. I'm very proud of that, and he is thanking me every day for not doing what he asked me to do while he was in jail. Thank God that Maccabi Tel Aviv agreed with me. They understood also who Aulcie was—a very good person who couldn't say no to anybody."

Perry was also someone who, as the country's then-Prime Minister Menachem Begin had said years previously, "brought honor to the State of Israel." That fact was not lost on a handful of leaders of the Israeli business community who teamed with Zysman after Perry's release from prison to bring him back to Tel Aviv to get his life back together. Zysman handled the legalities of Perry's return to the country, and the group put together $250,000 to purchase a Burger Ranch (part of a large Israeli fast-food chain) location for Perry to manage as he got back on his feet. If there were any doubts about whether Israelis would re-embrace the now long-retired ex-convict, they would be erased immediately.

When Perry returned to Israel in 1995, the Israeli equivalent of the old *This Is Your Life* television show was taping in a town just outside of Jerusalem. The guest of honor was Shmuel Maharovsky, the Maccabi executive who first discovered Perry at New York's Rucker Park all those years before. Maccabi's greatest stars were all on hand for the taping, so when the host introduced a special guest and beamed Perry's face onto a projection screen, everyone assumed that Perry was on the line from his home in the United States. In spite of the thousands of miles he believed to be between them, Maharovsky became overcome with emotion during their brief conversation. That made what happened next right out of a Hollywood drama. As Maharovsky later described the event, "He came out, the son of a bitch! I almost collapsed." Perry strode onto the stage and asked the guest of honor, "You know how many times I've thought of you in the last ten years?"

A ripple went through the crowd as Maccabi legends including Lou Silver, Tal Brody, and Mickey Berkowitz stood and hugged their former teammate. They stayed arm-in-arm and sang, joining the crowd in an impassioned, impromptu rendition of the fittingly chosen "We Are the Champions." "It was a big hall with hundreds of people," Maharovsky recalled. "Everyone was standing and clapping, [chanting] 'Aulcie! Aulcie! Aulcie!'"

Zysman, a former Maccabi hoopster, was instrumental in Perry's return and in purchasing the business Perry was to run in Israel. The player-turned-lawyer praised Maccabi management's long-ago decision to buy Perry the downtown apartment and Mizrahi for agreeing not to sell it during Perry's darkest days. Both were well-intentioned decisions that would prove to secure the former player's future. In addition, the team has set Perry up with youth coaching positions and speaking opportunities, and he remains to this day happily synonymous with the organization and a fixture at its events.

***

Carr, a former foreigner and now citizen with more than a decade of non-Maccabi Israeli basketball under his belt, has the objective credentials to speak knowingly about this polarizing organization. He and I discussed Maccabi at length and about how it should be classified—good or evil? David or Goliath? Not surprisingly, we concluded that it fell somewhere in the middle. Carr feels strongly that there should be a salary cap to level the playing field in Israeli basketball, but he also praised Maccabi's professionalism and hopes other teams would follow suit. He lauded Maccabi for its establishment of a legitimate farm system and its commitment to developing younger players. Perhaps surprisingly, though, his strongest words of praise were for the organization's most important quality, its loyalty to its players. Carr added that all Israeli organizations exhibit such loyalty to a degree, but that Maccabi's level of support meant the team deserved to stand on its own.

Carr observed how in the States, if players get into trouble, "You're kind of on your own." In Israel in general it's different, he said. "Here, when you're a part of an organization it's like being part of a family. That's something that I respect. When you're in that family they support you as much as possible. Obviously if you do well and you do a lot for the organization, it's a connection for life. Not just Maccabi, it's the other teams too." But if you're in the Maccabi family, he said, "They embrace you, put you under that umbrella, so to speak. The thing with Maccabi is that it's a multimillion dollar corporation. It's just on a whole other level when it comes to how they do things."

10

HOW THE OTHER HALF LIVES

THE EXPERIENCE OF PLAYING FOR Maccabi Tel Aviv is the Israeli basketball equivalent of living the good life. Top Maccabi players can live
like rock stars, making millions of dollars per season, competing in a
state-of-the-art arena in front of more than 10,000 fans, and residing
in a shiny, modern, Americanized metropolis. However, the number of
players signed by Maccabi is just a sliver of the total number of African
Americans playing in Israel. For many of the others, life is not quite so
glamorous and the money may not flow as freely—in other words, their
day to day lives more closely resemble those of their Israeli neighbors.
They play in cities as far north as Nahariya on the Lebanon border, in
Eilat on the far southern border with Egypt, and in all manner of cities
and small towns in between.

New York native Ramon Clemente spent three seasons playing
on different teams in Israel's second division (known as the National
League, or Liga Leumit). As such he is well-versed in how the "other
half" lives. One season Clemente played for Yokneam-Meggido, a team
representing a small town in northern Israel along with the surrounding nine *kibbutzim* and four *moshavim* (*kibbutz* and *moshav* are two different types of collective, agriculture-based communities in which residents pool labor and resources and eat and participate in other activities

communally). Clemente lived in one of the moshavim, which made him much more accessible than he might have been as a big star in the big city. He told me about one of his neighborly experiences that started a few hours before a game during the 2010–11 season. Clemente said he was relaxing in his apartment when he heard a buzz at his door. It was a neighborhood kid, about eleven years old, whom Clemente had seen from time to time riding his bike around town. Clemente remembered the kid shouting "Yo, Clemente!" at him once or twice, but that didn't prepare him for the confident request the boy was about to make.

"He was like, 'Yo, can I come to the game with you?'" Clemente told me with a laugh. "I was like, 'All right, make sure it's cool with your parents and stuff and then come on. Just meet me at the exit to my place, and I'll pick you up.' I went to pick him up, and it was him and his whole crew of friends! There were maybe six of them. I just said, 'Jump in!'" Clemente and Nate Miller (an African American teammate) sat in the front seat while the boys piled into the back and off they went to the game. "I got them seats in the front row and everything and we won," Clemente continued. "I had a really good game—it was fun! You've got to embrace stuff like that. Especially when you're not home —your fans are your next family."

Although the request from the diminutive *moshavnik* (as residents of a moshav are known) was certainly unusual, it reflects the closeness players often develop with fans, especially in the northern part of Israel. Andrew Kennedy spent 12 seasons in Israel, nine of them in the north, and he found he enjoyed the slower pace of living that region offers. He explained that fan support for non-Maccabi teams overall was "more local than national," but that didn't reduce their fervor. It was, he said, equally passionate with an "unusually strong bond" between the African American players and the locals. He recalled how he particularly enjoyed the communal activities that were customary in northern cities and the opportunities those gave him to get to know the local residents.

"I went to the moshav a lot," Kennedy said. "I hopped on my bike and went there to eat in the dining hall—that was just part of being in the north. After practice everyone went and ate in the moshav, among the moshavniks. It was nice, man!"

For players used to living in big cities, in the States or in Israel, the abrupt change of pace in a smaller town takes some getting used to. Los Angeles native Jeron Roberts, for one, spent time living in Tel Aviv, its suburb Hod Hasharon, and southern cities such as Ashdod and Ashkelon. In his ninth season of Israeli basketball he played in Nahariya, a northern coastal city with 50,000 residents, giving him a chance to learn even more about his adopted country.

"Nahariya is really quiet," Roberts told me in 2011. "The suburbs around here aren't like the suburbs around Tel Aviv, like Herzliya and Rishon [LeZion], or whatever. Up here everything's a little slower, and a lot quieter. Almost too quiet," he said with a laugh. "Living up here in the north, how can I put it? They make do. In Tel Aviv, you may need a lot of money, you may need this or that. But up north, it seems like people just make do with what they have. People from Tel Aviv, when you tell them you live in Nahariya, they're like 'That's far!' But really, it's only about ninety miles away. Coming from [Los Angeles], you don't think it's that far. But they think that's the end of the world. They're like, 'You live in Nahariya? Wow!'"

City Living

Playing in the northern part of the country doesn't always mean small-town living, though. Haifa, long considered the capital of Israel's north, is the country's third largest city, after Tel Aviv and Jerusalem. Located in a broad, natural bay between the Mediterranean Sea and Mount Carmel, Haifa boasts a population of about 265,000, plus another 300,000 living in neighboring towns.

Haifa is about ninety minutes north of Tel Aviv, considered by Israelis—whose perspective is somewhat skewed by the small size of the entire country—as a bit of a haul. Haifa may not draw tourists to the same extent that Tel Aviv or Jerusalem do, but the city has its own unique sites. For members of the Bahá'í Faith, Haifa is the holiest place of pilgrimage and the site of the faith's central administrative center, the Bahá'í World Centre, whose terraced Bahá'í Gardens are one of the most popular destinations in Israel for tourists of any faith.

"One of the first places they told me about when I got to Haifa, was the Bahá'í Gardens," said Larry O'Bannon, an African American from Louisville, Kentucky, who spent two seasons in Rishon LeZion and one with Maccabi Haifa. "Before I got here, I had never heard of it at all, but I've never seen anything with that precision and of that magnitude. It's really beautiful architecture, very precise, very neat, and very well taken care of. It's just really beautiful to the eye. From the designs you could see that it was a holy place, but I was just really impressed by the precision and the cuts and just wondering how they keep that grass cut like that, at some of those tough angles."

At one time Haifa was a vibrant basketball city, with two representatives in Israel's first division (known as the Super League or Ligat Ha'al)—Hapoel Haifa and Maccabi Haifa. Unfortunately, questionable management doomed both teams, knocking them down to the second division and even as low as the third. Now it appears this situation may well have been turned around. American businessman Jeffrey Rosen purchased Maccabi Haifa in 2007 and set out to help the team reclaim its former glory. He increased its budget to among the largest in Israeli basketball, renovated the team's arena, and produced an English-language television show about the team that is broadcast in Israel and parts of the United States. The players rewarded his investment with a 2013 Israeli Super League championship, upsetting Maccabi Tel Aviv in the final, and the club remains a perennial contender.

Israel's capital city, both politically and religiously, is Jerusalem, which is located in the center of the country. It is represented on the court by Hapoel Jerusalem, the country's second best-known basketball organization and a team some think could eventually knock Maccabi from its perch atop the league standings. Hapoel Jerusalem is the team most comparable to Maccabi in terms of stability, budget, and recruiting power, but the experience of living in these two cities couldn't be more different for the players. Tel Aviv, as the ultra-modern professional/social locus of Israel, is in sharp contrast to Jerusalem, the historic religious/political one. No one summarized the difference between Tel Aviv and Jerusalem as succinctly as Hapoel Jerusalem forward Brandon Hunter, an African American from Cincinnati. Walking to his car in the near-empty parking lot of a Jerusalem shopping mall on a Friday afternoon, his adopted Israeli hometown in the process of shutting down for the upcoming Shabbat, Hunter told me that, "In Jerusalem, the city is so spiritual that you walk around and think that Jesus Christ himself might pop out at any moment. In Tel Aviv, you think a stripper might pop out."

Ramla, also in central Israel, offers yet another dramatically different example of life for players in the country. Unlike the cities discussed thus far, Ramla has been plagued by infrastructural neglect, financial problems, and a negative public image. Its basketball team has bounced between the Super League and lower divisions for decades, and its appeal for players is, not surprisingly, pretty limited. Vidal Massiah came to Israel in 2003 planning to play with Ramat Hasharon, in a suburb of Tel Aviv. In finalizing its roster, however, the organization decided his talents were too similar to those of an American player already on the team and decided to send Massiah, the younger of the two, off to play with Elitzur Ramla, then in the second division. Prior to the transfer from Ramat Hasharon to Ramla, Massiah received the full court press from his new team, being told how much the coaches loved his game and how he could average 30 or 40 points in the second division. Although Massiah was reluctant to accept a position in the lower league, he agreed to at least give it a try, and the team hired a taxi to take him to his proposed new home.

"The cabbie spent the entire ride from Ramat Hasharon to Ramla telling me why I should stay in Ramla, how many points I'll average, how I'll play for Maccabi one day," Massiah told me. "It was actually working. Then I get there and it's like 'Whoa! This is completely different from where I was.' The apartment was ghetto. There were pigeons everywhere, pigeon droppings everywhere. The apartment was really, really small, it just didn't feel right. The next day, I just flew home."

Ramla is on an attempted upswing with recent steps to develop and beautify the city. It now has new shopping malls, public parks, and a municipal museum. Jitim Young, an African American player from Chicago, had a slightly different take on the city some six or seven years after Massiah made his hasty retreat. Young spent the second half of the 2009–10 season there, before playing the following year for Hod Hasharon, in suburban Tel Aviv. He acknowledged the many differences between the two cities, but he also noted that living in Ramla wasn't entirely negative.

"Well, Ramla is more … it's kind of country a little bit," Young said. "There is a lot of open area. Hod Hasharon is a beautiful town. A lot of wealthy people live in Hod Hasharon, and it's fifteen minutes from Tel Aviv, so it's really convenient. Ramla is more of a country area, but the fans there were great, the people there were great. Being out there for two months, I knew everyone in the city, so that was a lot of fun. When I would go to the store, I'd see some of the people I saw every time. I would just talk to them, I'd say '*Mah nishmah?*' [What's happening?], and they'd ask how I was doing and I'd say '*Beseder, tov*' [all right, good]. I just always try to be polite, always try to speak to everybody."

Ramla's Winning Women's Team

Interestingly, although Ramla is known as one of the least popular destinations for male players in Israel, it is also home to one of the country's most successful and popular female teams, which includes a number of African American players. In no way was this a random occurrence. Beginning in the mid-1990s, the mayor of Ramla, Yoel Lavi, focused on turning his city of 70,000 into a center of women's hoops, recruiting a series of local businesses to sponsor the team and also committing substantial municipal funds to the effort. Because male players command larger salaries than their female counterparts, the resources Lavi came up with would not have been enough to field a successful men's team. They were, however, enough to entice WNBA players to come to Israel. The team reportedly was willing to pay each of its Americans around $80,000 a season, tax-free, in addition to providing a car and apartment, matching or exceeding what players can make during the WNBA season.

The investment paid off in 2011, when Elitzur Ramla became the first Israeli women's team to win the European championship. Simone Edwards, a Jamaican player who spent six years in Israel, said the city's passionate fan base plays a big part in making it such an ideal destination for the best female players.

"It's a totally different feeling when you were in Ramla than anywhere else," Edwards said. "The crazier fans just make the game feel that much more real. And Ramla had the craziest fans," she said with a laugh. "You were glad when you played on the Ramla side. They're crazy, they're so intense. As soon as you walk in the gym you hear them. You just want to play well because you don't want them to leave the game bitter. And they are intense all the way to the end—sometimes even too intense. But I love that. It's great for women's basketball, the way they fill the gym and cheer for their team."

Interestingly, the quality of women's basketball in Israel compared to the WNBA is actually higher than the quality of men's game in Israel compared to the NBA. Whereas men who play in Israel often do so before or after having achieved their NBA dreams, women who play in Israel do so *while* playing in the WNBA. Because the WNBA's season is held in the summer, female players can play in the WNBA *and* play overseas in their "offseason" from fall to spring. The effect is that the quality of African American female players in Israel is comparatively higher than the quality of the male players. In fact, during the 2010–11 Israeli season, fifteen active WNBA players played in the Israeli women's league, fourteen of them African American. In addition, while the men's league has been dominated for decades by European powerhouse Maccabi Tel Aviv, the competition in the women's league has been wide open.

Overall, female African American players in Israel described similarly positive impressions of the country as their male counterparts and similar experiences overall. One teammate described Edwards as "bigger than Michael Jordan" in the Holy Land, and although the Jamaican humbly downplayed that assertion, she did not deny attaining a level of celebrity in Israel approaching if not equal to that of her male counterparts.

"The male player's experience is always a bit different," Edwards said, noting specifically that the bigger budgets of male teams entail more frequent official team functions. "But apart from that I felt the same treatment like any of the male players, except the ones that played for Maccabi (laughs). I did things for TV, I felt the same like any other player that was there, especially in the communities that I played in. I didn't feel like less of a star than any of the male players."

On the Border

Israel's southernmost city is Eilat, which is about a four-hour drive from Tel Aviv but for some players represents a whole other world. Joe Dawson, who signed to play in Israel almost thirty years ago, continues to live in the country more than a decade after he retired from the game. And yet after playing that very first season in a large suburb of Tel Aviv, he developed an impression of Israeli life so negative that he left to play the next few seasons in France, Italy, and a minor league in the United States. Dawson eventually returned to Israel, but only because he was seriously involved with an Israeli woman whom he later married. He had disliked the rushed pace, pressure, and stress he felt living in Tel Aviv, and he assumed that represented the vibe in the whole country. Then he signed with Eilat.

Though geographically and historically significant, the city of Eilat barely existed (with the exception of a solitary police station) when the modern State of Israel was founded in 1948. In the 1950s, government officials decided to develop Eilat to establish a permanent Israeli presence in the small Israeli-controlled piece of land between Jordan and Egypt. This would provide a port for shipping to destinations in Eastern Africa and Asia via the Red Sea. It took almost two decades for the tourism industry to even begin its development in the city, so the ultra-modern tourist hub of today is a far cry from the small-town vibe Dawson encountered in the 1980s.

"I had heard all the stories about the Israeli people being very warm, but in Eilat I got to feel it," Dawson told me. "It was like the whole town was one big family. And from the experience in Eilat, I became more open, and I made visits to the rest of Israel. And then I started to understand that the pressure and stress was just part of [living in Israel]. The basketball and everything else [became] just a perfect combination to keep me here."

In many respects, players' experiences living either in the northern or southern part of Israel are quite different. But there is one important reality they share: being at greater risk of attacks from Israel's enemies. In general, the African American players in Israel find that violence isn't a big concern for them because incidents take place so far from where they live. Indeed, for those living in or around Tel Aviv and Jerusalem, news about attacks in other parts of Israel is likely to come from American friends or family who watched it on television. But players who live in cities along Israel's borders carry a heavier burden, as attacks or the threat of attacks are a more frequent cause of concern.

Cory Carr may be the most important player in the history of the Ironi Ashkelon organization—the town of Ashkelon being located about fifteen minutes from the Gaza Strip, in the south of Israel. Carr has played for the team on four separate occasions, having some of his best individual seasons with them including making the single most memorable shot in the franchise's history—a 17-foot buzzer-beater that put the team into the Israeli Final Four in 2005. In addition to his time in Ashkelon, Carr also spent time playing for Galil Elyon, a team located close to Israel's border with Lebanon to the north. As we sat in his apartment in the central city of Ra'anana, the walls were adorned with *hamsas* (amulets depicting the open right hand, believed to provide defense against the evil eye) and the balcony overlooked construction of a synagogue across the street. Carr talked about basketball's particular significance in those cities.

"I'm usually more tied to the cities that have endured a lot, gone through a lot of pain and suffering—my heart goes out to those cities," Carr told me. "You think about basketball, and it's such a small, small, small thing. When you think about some of the things these people have to deal with in these cities on a daily basis—not knowing what's going to happen, if a terror attack is going to strike them on a given day. Basketball obviously is a way out for the people. They give their all, they give their heart, especially in the south in Ashkelon or in the north in Galil, these families and these communities really embrace the sport, and it takes their minds away from what's going on at least for a little while," Carr said.

"It means a lot for me personally—coming from a very small town in Arkansas, coming from tough times and hard times, being able to deal with not having, having to work for everything," Carr explained. "I'm always supportive of the underdog and can relate to their pain and suffering. Any gratification that I can give them through this game is something that I've tried to do. I've taken pride in that over my career, and that's why I think I'm respected as a player here. Not only for the sport itself and my performance but for my compassion for the people, the love, and my understanding of what they're going through."

Show Me the Money

Even more than geographic and lifestyle factors, another difference between playing for Maccabi and non-Maccabi teams stands out: the money. Not only do most non-Maccabi players earn considerably less than their Maccabi peers, there are financial factors beyond salary levels. Horror stories abound worldwide concerning basketball organizations being unable to sustain financing and failing to pay players on time, if at all. The Israeli league's reputation is much better than average in that respect, but it has hardly been perfect.

"The professionalism of the franchises varies," said Kennedy, who spent six seasons playing for Galil Elyon, in the northeast of Israel, and another six seasons for a variety of other teams around the country.

"Galil Elyon was very professional, but [elsewhere] it ran the gamut. Some were, some weren't, which is unfortunate. And that's one of the differences coming from the Western world—you expect to be paid if you play or work. Sometimes [teams] don't adhere to that. It was difficult hearing stories from other guys on other teams that weren't getting paid or they were going through difficult times. It happened, absolutely," he added disappointedly.

James Terry spent thirteen years playing in Israel, and he is one of the best big men in the league's history. He said Maccabi dominates the league financially and on the court, so he understood the drive of upstart teams to keep up. Still, he took issue with the fiscally irresponsible manner in which some organizations tried to bridge the gap. "In the end, everything comes down to this—if you don't have money, then you shouldn't promise something you can't afford," Terry said. "The problem is that you have so many good people that care for their teams but they don't know a thing about basketball. If you have a certain amount of money, bring the best players you can afford but not more than that! At least you know that you can pay the players. They will give you all that they got and feel dedicated to you. Maybe you won't get stars on your team, but at least they won't break and leave in the middle of the season."

For fans of North American professional sports, the concept of a team's failing to make its payments and going bankrupt in the middle of a season is hard to fathom, especially for a major league in a popular game like basketball. But it's not that unusual overseas, including in Israel and, as Terry pointed out, for reasons of poor management. Campbell said that when he played for Hapoel Eilat, management was so certain that the team could not beat the mighty Maccabi squad that it offered players exorbitant bonuses for each time it did so. During player contract negotiations, the team's strategy was to offer those big bonuses as concessions, never expecting to actually have to pay them. One year Eilat exceeded expectations, beating Maccabi twice during the regular season before losing to the powerhouse in the championship. The team was now in the awkward position of owing its players a variety of different bonuses, while its pockets were essentially empty. As the next season began, word got out that the team was in default on its prior obligations and that players had not received their bonus payments. The league ended up shutting down Hapoel Eilat, leaving a roster full of players unpaid and out of work not even ten games into the season.

Ironically, the financial and managerial shortcomings of some organizations led to players remembering certain Hebrew phrases years after returning to the United States. Several told me laughingly that they would never forget how to ask the question, *"Eifo ha kessef sheli?"* (Where is my money?), and how the answer was often, *"Machar, machar"* (tomorrow, tomorrow). Dawson, who bounced back and forth between Greece and Israel early in his professional career, said he had problems getting paid in both countries. In Greece he said a team actually falsified his X-rays to claim that he had ulcers which he had not disclosed to the team and thus they released him without pay. He added with a chuckle that Israeli teams were at least more direct in their financial malfeasance. "In Israel they just don't pay you," he said.

Dawson continued that he and his wife did a tally at one point about how much money he had lost over the course of his many years playing in Israel. "It's more than $200,000 that I didn't get," he said. "That's why players in Israel prefer to play for Maccabi and sit on the bench, because Maccabi is one of the only teams that pays no matter what. There are a lot of stories about players who didn't get [one payment], but there are a lot of bigger stories too." Dawson recalled how when he played in Rishon LeZion his last season in the first division, the team pulled a trick on him by signing him to a deferred payment. "I was supposed to get three [payments], and they said they had problems so instead of paying me [the last installment] in May they would pay me in October. I agreed to it, but that summertime they filed [for bankruptcy]." Dawson said he ended up with just 60 percent of what the team owed him.

Dawson continued to play in Israel despite the issues he had with some teams, but as we talked in a café in Rehovot about Israeli basketball in general and nonpayment specifically, his frustration with the situation was still palpable. I was coming from an NBA perspective, where a team failing to pay a player his rightly negotiated salary was unheard of, and I wanted a better sense of what it was like. I asked Dawson if he felt that failure to be paid carried any unique significance in Israel, as compared to anywhere else. I wondered especially about two factors: if a player's having taken a risk by playing in the volatile country in the first place might make getting shortchanged there even more difficult to swallow; and if being taken advantage of by another minority group might intensify the feeling. Dawson made it abundantly clear that issues with non-payment are a problem internationally, not just in Israel. While the feeling around failed payments is obviously strong, the anger and frustration comes from the most basic of reasons.

"As a player, you hate it," Dawson said. "The main reason is that I did the work, and I deserve the pay. That's my main focus. The fact that I'm in Israel, it's a little more risky, but everyone does what fits them. By coming to this place, I accepted that, and I'm not afraid of it. I didn't get paid in Greece, either, and I didn't think about any [other factors]. The only thing I thought about is, just pay me. Pay me, and I'll get out there."

Friends in High Places

According to Carr, not only does playing for non-Maccabi teams affect whether and how much an African American player is paid to play in Israel, it also affects the process of a player's getting to stay in Israel. Carr had lived in the country for five years when he married his Israeli girlfriend and began the process of applying to become a citizen. Given his years already spent in the country and his marriage to a *sabra* (as native Israelis are known), Carr expected a quick and easy road to citizenship. What he encountered was entirely different—a drawn-out process that took more than five years, during large parts of which he had to refrain from visiting his family in the United States because his immigration status was in limbo. When we met for lunch in the summer of 2009, only a few months had passed since his citizenship paperwork had finally come in. Carr was happy to have seen it through and proud to have become an Israeli citizen, but he wasn't all smiles. Had he been with Maccabi, like Derrick Sharp, Deon Thomas, and Jamie Arnold, he said he would not have had to go through the same wait or jump through the same hoops as he did.

"All these players got citizenship without going through the process of a normal citizen," Carr said. "They had Maccabi behind them, so they got their citizenship in one or two years. Me? Nobody supported me. I didn't have backing from some basketball team with power. I didn't have someone supporting me from the political system. No high-powered government official or something—none of that. Everything we did, we did by the book, like I was any other foreign worker."

***

Although he didn't directly address the topic of Maccabi benefits, Carr subtly but poignantly summarized the differences of playing for Maccabi and playing for any other Israeli team. Maccabi Tel Aviv's African American players live in the biggest city and make the biggest salaries; they win the vast majority of the time; and they are even alleged to earn national citizenship more simply. They sit comfortably at the top of the Israeli basketball hierarchy. But African Americans who play for Israel's other teams see the country from a different perspective, one that is more representative of everyday Israeli life.

Certainly, Maccabi Tel Aviv players have provided some of the most memorable images of African Americans working in Israel. However, a proper account of African American basketball players' experience in Israel would not be complete without images of players on the country's less publicized teams: Ramon Clemente piling six moshavnik children into the back of his car to take them with him to his game; Andrew Kennedy riding his bike to partake in dinner in a communal dining hall; Cory Carr hitting a miraculous shot to lift a team from the embattled city of Ashkelon to unprecedented heights; and Simone

Edwards drawing enthusiastic cheers from women's basketball fans in the newly revitalized town of Ramla. It's only by considering all of these images in their totality that you get a sense of the true picture of the lives of African American players in Israel.

11

BLACK AND JEWISH

AT FIRST GLANCE, SYLVEN LANDESBERG's experience looks like that of a prototypical African American basketball player in Israel. Standing 6-foot-6 and weighing 210 pounds, the New York City native was a star shooting guard in high school and college, and his hopes ran high when he declared himself eligible for the NBA draft after his sophomore season. Everything in his career to that point had gone according to plan, but the 2010 draft came and went without his name being called, forcing him to consider alternative options. Like many African American players hoping to eventually achieve their NBA dreams, he decided to play in Israel. Unlike almost every one of them, however, Landesberg was raised Jewish.

"My father comes from a Jewish background," he explained to an Israeli television show. "My [paternal] grandfather is Austrian and my [paternal] grandmother is Polish. My mother is from Trinidad. So when people ask me what I am, I just say 'confused,'" he said with a broad grin.

The percentage of African American basketball players who end up playing part of their career in Israel is relatively small. A tiny fraction of that subset ultimately convert to Judaism and/or obtain Israeli citizenship. Landesberg, as an African American with Jewish heritage, is part of an even more miniscule segment of this population. He's not alone, however, and the stories of a few members of this cohort show just how fluid and complex a seemingly simple classification of faith can be, and just how much the differences in their upbringings can impact their lives. Like Landesberg, former Israeli league stars David Blu (originally Bluthenthal) and Willie Sims and former NBA All-Star and current Israeli league star Amar'e Stoudemire are also African Americans who were raised to identify as Jewish (or Hebrew, as will be discussed later in this chapter). Despite backgrounds that may on the surface appear similar, their life stories offer contrast and insight into the complexity of the very concept of religious identity.

Born Jewish—or Not?

In Chapter 2, my focus on "Who is a Jew?" related to converts to Judaism. But the same question is also relevant to individuals born to Jewish parents. Orthodox Judaism traces Jewish identity through maternal lineage. This would mean that the twenty-seven-year-old Landesberg, whose mother is Christian, would not be considered Jewish by that strict interpretation. That's not how he views it, though. He has always identified himself as being a part of, and a believer in, both Judaism and Christianity, and he carries evidence of that dual religious identity on his body. On his left leg he bears a tattoo of a cross; on his right arm is a tattoo of a *Magen David* (six-pointed Jewish Star, or Star of David). Landesberg explained his choices in faith-based body art this way: "That kind of signifies how I grew up—a little bit of everything."

By identifying as Jewish, even if not exclusively so, Landesberg quickly became a fan favorite among Jews who were eager to debunk a long-held stereotype about their people. One of the more memorable expressions of the stereotype can be found in the movie *Airplane!*, a classic comedy from 1980. When a passenger asked a flight attendant for something to read, she specified she wanted something light. "How about this leaflet, *Famous Jewish Sports Legends*?" the flight attendant responded—a line that has provoked laughter in multiple generations of viewers. A more recent example took place on Comedy Central's edgy cartoon *South Park* when fourth-grader Eric Cartman, typecast as anti-Semitic, told a classmate, "Everybody knows Jews can't play basketball."

In spite of the multitude of decorated Jewish athletes in a variety of sports, including basketball, the common sentiment persists that Jews are simply less athletic than their non-Jewish peers. Consequently, Jewish fans take great pride in Jewish athletes who gain prominence in their respective sports and also have considerable curiosity about them. When a Jewish athlete is African American the fans' curiosity increases exponentially. Landesberg, with his omnipresent smile, gregarious nature, and unique background, developed into both a fan and media favorite as he became a McDonald's All-American at Holy Cross High School and won Atlantic Coast Conference Freshman of the Year at the University of Virginia.

Landesberg became used to the attention paid to his Judaism, being featured during his college years on websites and blogs with names such as *Jew or Not Jew*, *Jewish Journal*, *Shalom Life*, and *The Great Rabbino*. For anyone in his unusual position, the constant line of questioning on the topic might have grown tiresome, but when I called him in Haifa from my desk in Canada he gave up a beautiful afternoon in Israel to patiently address my queries. Landesberg told me he was proud of his Jewish background and identity, and he was happy to discuss it whenever the opportunity arose. He said he had added another tattoo in tribute to that part of his heritage, the Hebrew word *neevchar*, which means "chosen." Landesberg was quick to point out that it wasn't meant as a reference to *his* being chosen but rather as a tribute to his paternal grandfather, who was a major role model for him in his childhood. When Landesberg was a boy his grandfather would tell him stories of growing up Jewish in Austria and eventually having to leave the country to avoid becoming a victim of the Holocaust. The tattoo, he said, was a tribute to that grandfather, the atrocity he had escaped, and the life and family he was eventually able to build.

I was curious to know more about the practical, participatory aspect of Landesberg's Jewish identity. That he identified himself as Jewish was clear, and I knew he made a point in his first year in Israel to visit Judaism's holiest site, the Western Wall in Jerusalem. But just how significant was Judaism in his upbringing?

"It was huge!" Landesberg told me. "We weren't the most religious family growing up, but we did celebrate the holidays. My mother being a Christian, we celebrated Christmas and Hanukkah, all of the Christian and Jewish holidays. My grandparents were religious, so on Jewish holidays we would go to their house as much as possible. It was a big part of my life."

Similar to Landesberg, Blu, a California high school star and USC standout before making his basketball pilgrimage to the Holy Land, is also the product of a mixed-race, mixed-faith couple. Unlike Landesberg, Blu is the son of a Jewish mother and an African American father who converted to Judaism, so the thirty-six-year-old is considered Jewish by even the most stringent definition. Yet despite his father's conversion, Blu's religious upbringing also included observance of both Jewish and Christian customs and holidays. Although Blu's mother passed away when he was fourteen years old, she impressed upon him and his siblings the importance of their religious identity.

"We didn't celebrate every Shabbat—we weren't religious to the point that we couldn't do anything Friday night and Saturday morning, because I had basketball," Blu said. "I had games Friday night, and Saturday mornings I was at the park playing with my friends. We lit the candles on Hanukkah, but we also celebrated Christmas and Easter, so it was sort of like the best of both worlds. They never really pushed us to be religious," he said, but pointed out that he and his sisters all identified themselves as being Jewish. "We were proud of it. Our father was Black, but he wore a Jewish star."

Blu had been surprised to discover that his Jewish identity actually traces to his father's side of the family as well. In fact, Bluthenthal, the family name passed down to Blu from his African American father, is a Jewish name, believed to be derived from a nineteenth century Jewish-German slave owner. We spoke by phone as Blu sat in his car at LAX airport, waiting for his daughter's flight, a fitting context for our lengthy discussion on heritage.

"My wife has been doing some genealogy, and we couldn't get the origin of Bluthenthal," Blu told me in 2011. "Finally, she got in touch with this ninety-year-old woman in Arkansas, and she said that my great-great-great-great-grandfather was white and Jewish. His last name was Bluthenthal. He had a child with a Black woman, who was probably a slave, and the child was named Bluthenthal," he continued. "The child, who ended up being my great-great-great-grandfather, was really light, and then throughout the years, he married a Black woman, and they had a son, and he married a Black woman, and they had a son, until my father came around. He had Bluthenthal and the Jewish religion. I only found out about a week and a half ago! My wife had been doing research for the last four, five, six months, and she had reached a dead end until she somehow got a hold of this woman, and she told us the story."

When it comes to complex stories and religious identities, though, it's hard to beat that of Willie Sims. Now fifty-nine years old, Sims wore dreadlocks growing up in Queens, New York, and was more observant than Landesberg and Blu as a youngster. In addition to celebrating the Jewish holidays with his family, he also wore a kippah over those dreadlocks every day. Yet the family, all of whom were Black (Sims's complexion is considerably darker than that of the mixed-race Landesberg and Blu), did not consider themselves Jewish. Instead they identified themselves as Hebrews.

Hebrew vs. Jew

To understand the implication and meaning of Hebrew as a separate identity requires going back in biblical history. Today we use the term Jew to describe all those who are the descendants of the Old Testament's Abraham, Isaac, and Jacob. Thus the words "Jew," "Hebrew," and "Israelite" are mostly used interchangeably. But in fact each actually has a different genesis and specific connotation. The term *Hebrew* came first chronologically, and was in relation to Abraham and his brothers. Although Abraham is considered the patriarch of the Jewish people, the words Jew and Israel did not exist in his lifetime. Abraham's son Isaac had two sons: Esau and Jacob, the latter of whom had his name changed to "Israel," the first use of that word. He then had twelve sons, the fourth named Judah, which initially spawned the name Judean, and subsequently, Jew.

According to the Old Testament, Jacob's twelve sons and their descendants made up the Kingdom of Israel, which eventually split into two. The descendants of Judah and his brother Benjamin constituted the Southern Kingdom, and because they were from the Tribe of Judah and lived in Judea they went on to be referred to as the Jewish people. The descendants of the remaining ten sons constituted the Northern Kingdom, the details of whose destinies has been the subject of dispute since shortly after the Kingdom was divided—in fact, the descendants of those sons are referred to as the ten Lost Tribes of Israel. Today, there are descendants of those ten tribes who self-identify as Jewish, or as descendants of the Kingdom of Israel, who inhabit places like China, India, and Southern Africa.

With that background in mind, the subtle distinction between "Jews," like Landesberg and Blu, and "Hebrews," like Sims, is easier to understand. All Jews are Hebrews because they are all descendants of Abraham, but all Hebrews are not necessarily technically Jews, as they are not descendants of Judah or Benjamin (even if they follow substantially similar religious customs and beliefs). Of course, an entire PhD dissertation could be written on this topic, but what is important for our purposes is to understand that Sims could grow up wearing a kippah and observing the rituals of Hanukkah, without ever considering himself Jewish.

In fact, it wasn't until basketball brought the matter of religion to the forefront that Sims gave that aspect of his identity any thought. He told me he just was what he was and grew up how he grew up. Sims's high school coach, who was himself Jewish, was the first to make the connection for the player and his family, explaining to Sims and his grandmother that being a Hebrew and being Jewish were basically identical, just with different names. His grandmother was convinced, and from that time forward, Sims identified himself as Jewish. That allowed him to compete in the Maccabiah Games, essentially a Jewish Olympics held every four years in Israel, and earned himself the considerable exposure that came with it. Sims went on to represent the United States in two Maccabiah Games, one prior to beginning his college career in 1977 and another after graduating in 1981. It was at the Maccabiah Games that Israeli teams began recruiting Sims, which resulted in his playing professionally in Israel from 1981 to 1999 before retiring and remaining in the country to this day.

Interestingly, those same Maccabiah Games played a part in drawing Stoudemire to Israel as well. In the summer of 2013, following an injury-riddled season with the New York Knicks, Stoudemire went to Israel not as a tourist, but as the assistant coach of the Canadian basketball contingent in that year's Games. The public first learned of Stoudemire's connection with the country a few years earlier, when he took a well-publicized trip to Israel in 2010, which some described as a "voyage of discovery" and which Stoudemire said was for the purpose of exploring his "Hebrew roots." It was the first public indication that Stoudemire's faith and ancestry were not necessarily typical, and it came with great fanfare. Fresh off signing a maximum value contract with the New York Knicks, Stoudemire was arguably at the peak of his fame in 2010 and media and fans were captivated by the African American superstar who occasionally tweeted in Hebrew and shared pictures of himself in the Dead Sea.

That journey of self-discovery continued on Stoudemire's return to New York, where he engaged in multiple informative conversations with local rabbis and continued to strengthen his connection to his faith and to Israel in the years that followed. Stoudemire donned a yarmulke and prayer shawl at his 2012 wedding, and in 2013, prior to coaching the Canadians at the Maccabiah Games, he purchased a stake in Israeli basketball club Hapoel Jerusalem. That summer, he made a clear proclamation of his religious identity.

"I study Torah all the time," Stoudemire said. "We study the Tanach. Our family celebrates all the High Holy Days. We're definitely all in, and we're Jewish. I had a Hebraic wedding in New York, so I'm definitely Jewish."

Like Landesberg, Stoudemire does not appear stereotypically Jewish at first glance, but a closer look at the 6-foot-11, 245-pound African American basketball star (and his jewelry choices) reveals a far more complicated religious identity (one that, despite his quote above, cannot be so simply classified). Stoudemire, now thirty-four years old, sports a Star of David tattoo on his left thumb, inches from a tattoo depiction of Jesus on his left forearm. He has a "Black Jesus" tattoo on the same neck he adorns with a gold necklace sporting a diamond YHWH charm, spelling out God's unspoken name. Finally, there's his gold ring with twelve sections studded with gems, evoking the ancient Temple's priestly breastplate and the twelve tribes of Israel (a wedding gift from his wife, Alexis).

Yet even with all of his physical and emotional connections to Israel, Stoudemire was still an unlikely Israeli league free agent acquisition in the summer of 2016. This was no fringe NBA player, but rather a six-time All-Star who had once signed a contract for the league's maximum salary. Yet, after considering his options in free agency, Stoudemire opted to leave the NBA behind and sign a two-year contract with Hapoel Jerusalem. Speculation was rampant as to just how much Stoudemire would impact Hapoel Jerusalem on the court, as well as financially and in terms of media attention in Israel and abroad. For Stoudemire, though, the decision was about so much more than basketball, money, or attention. It was about his faith and his family.

"The Scripture speaks about Jerusalem as a holy place, and I can feel that whenever I'm in the city," Stoudemire wrote in a first-person essay on *The Players' Tribune*. "This is a chance for me to be a better husband and a better father, to help me lead my family into righteousness. The opportunity to play there, and grow as a player and person, is a blessing. As my father used to tell me, 'The sky's the limit.'"

It is clear that spirituality was a driving force in Stoudemire's decision-making, but the exact nature of his religious identity has been difficult to pinpoint, in part because of changing descriptions by the player himself in different interviews over the years. When he first visited Israel in 2010 the Jewish community was abuzz with the concept that Stoudemire could be one of their own. Over the years, though, a more complicated picture emerged. What's clear is that his mother told a teenage Stoudemire that she and the family were Hebrew Israelites, descendants of the ancient tribes of Israel, and that Stoudemire has studied his unique ancestry since then. According to pastor Henry Buie, the founder and leader of Israel of God, a Chicago-based Messianic Hebrew Israelite group with twenty-three outposts across the United States (and one in Zimbabwe), Stoudemire discovered one of the group's churches in Memphis through a friend of his agent's in 2013 and has been a member ever since. (To be clear, Israel of God is not a part of nor affiliated with the well-known Hebrew Israelite community in Dimona, Israel, which is discussed in Chapter 12.) Buie baptized Stoudemire, along with his wife and mother, in 2013, an act he said has transformed the player.

Initially, Stoudemire did express interest in formally converting to Judaism, but Buie dissuaded him. "You should not have to convert to something that you were born to," Buie recalled telling Stoudemire. Instead, Buie baptized Stoudemire "in the name of Jesus" and welcomed him to his flock. The question of whether Hebrew Israelites are Jewish is a sensitive one, and Stoudemire has taken different positions at different points in time. One theme that has remained consistent, though, is that Stoudemire prefers to be judged by what he does, rather than how he defines himself or others define him. Stoudemire's actions include practices from multiple faiths. His church recognizes Jesus Christ as the Messiah and he still considers himself a Christian, but Stoudemire observes the High Holidays and the Saturday Sabbath, and he and his family don't eat pork or shellfish, in accordance with Judaism's laws of kashrut.

"I'm not a religious person, I'm more of a spiritual person, so I follow the rules of the Bible that coordinate with and connect with the Hebrew culture," Stoudemire said. "You have to read the book to get an understanding. The Bible is a history book. The ultimate goal is to start to live the actual Scriptures instead of reading about [them]. It's the actions that count."

Playground Pressure

When he was young Sims did not think of himself as Jewish per se, but other kids paid a lot of attention to the role the religion's customs played in their classmate's life. His neighborhood in the borough of Queens was a diverse one; even so, an African American boy with braids and a kippah was still a rarity and provoked much curiosity from other children.

"I grew up wearing a kippah [every day], and it wasn't a small kippah, it was a bigger one," Sims said. "But the kids didn't know what that was, so I would have fights over it, and they would snatch it off my head and throw it around and it became a game of [keep-away]. A lot of kids didn't know why I was wearing it. Some of them thought I had something on my head, under my hat, because I wore it so much. They wanted to see."

Although Landesberg also grew up in New York, he told me that his diverse heritage was never a source of mockery or derision. He had a large and diverse group of friends in which no particular background stood out. Even in his years playing in opposing gyms during high school, Landesberg can remember his religion being made an issue only once. It was via a chant from an archrival school's fans which today he can't even remember.

Blu, on the other hand, had more difficulty in his adolescent years in Los Angeles. "I grew up in a Mexican and Asian neighborhood, and all of my best friends were white, Mexican, or Asian," he said. "They were good basketball players, but they weren't at the AAU level. So when I was playing with my AAU teams, which were predominantly

Black, it was a little bit of a culture shock for me." He recalled how he "always felt a little bit uncomfortable being who I was around Black kids. I wasn't trying to hide who I was, but it taught me how to talk with both sides of my tongue. At one time I felt comfortable, I don't want to say 'talking Black', but using the word *nigger* or talking Ebonics or slang and things like that when I was with the AAU guys. And then when I would go back to hanging out with my buddies on the beach, it was back to saying 'dude,' or 'what's up,' and I guess, talking like a white guy," he said.

"Maybe subconsciously I made that switch depending on where I was," Blu continued. "It was a little uncomfortable at times. I was a little bit more uncomfortable being around Blacks than I was being around whites, Asians, or Mexicans. And then when I got to college, there were times when my teammates made fun of me for being Jewish. It was weird because I really had no way to come back. If I was a white guy, I would come back by making fun of them for being Black, but I'm half Black, so I didn't really have anything to say. That was a little bit difficult," he sighs. "But now? Now, I'm grateful for all of my experiences, because I feel so comfortable with anyone I'm with."

The Controversy Continues

During the mid-1970s, undeterred by the fascination and occasional harassment his unique background elicited in others, Sims chose to attend Louisiana State University in Baton Rouge, Louisiana, right in the heart of America's Deep South (a decision he both takes pride in and laughs about today). Like Landesberg, at the University of Virginia, and Blu, at the University of Southern California, Sims had great success at a high level collegiate program. All three were courted by a variety of leagues around the world when they failed to be picked up by an NBA team. But for each, Israel offered some things that no other country could. First, there was the emotional benefit of being in a place where each felt familial ties and a spiritual connection. Second, as Jews, they could benefit from the Law of Return, the Israeli law that guarantees citizenship for anyone who is Jewish. Signing elite American players who could obtain citizenship added huge value for Israeli teams, as those players are not counted in relation to rules limiting the number of foreign players on a team's roster, or on the court at a given time. That added value to teams meant those players could demand higher salaries for their services.

Landesberg actually received a more lucrative offer from a team in Italy, but he chose Israel for the opportunity it provided to connect with his roots in addition to playing basketball. Although his is an example of financial sacrifice, the more customary financial benefit that comes with being signed as an Israeli made some fans skeptical, in particular of the legitimacy of Blu's Jewish identity.

"[Some Israelis] did question my background," Blu told me. "At first, they said, 'Oh, he's doing it for money,' and 'He's not really Jewish,' or 'He's not proud to be Jewish.' And then I changed my name [from Bluthenthal to Blu] and it got even worse," he said. "But then I played for the Israeli national team [representing the country in 2010 and 2011] and all of that disappeared. They really welcomed me as Israeli. I think that was the biggest difference, playing on the national team. Up until then, people had questioned me or hecklers in the stands would say things to me about not really being Jewish or this and that. But once I played for the national team and wore the Israeli jersey, it was like finally they welcomed me as Israeli."

Although Blu's participation with the national team changed some cynics' views of his Judaism, it is questionable that such cynicism had any validity in the first place. I discussed this with Rabbi Yaakov Gloiberman from Israel, whose relationships with former Maccabi Tel Aviv coach Pini Gershon and other Israeli basketball VIPs earned him the nickname "Hoops Rabbi." During our conversation, I asked Gloiberman about questions like the ones Blu faced, regarding how "real" or "legitimate" his Judaism was. The rabbi dismissed the questions out of hand, saying there is something inherent in being Jewish that forges a bond between God and all Jews, regardless of their respective levels of day-to-day observance. That connection, according to the rabbi, is especially apparent in Israel.

"The land of Israel has a special holiness to it, and because of that holiness everyone becomes connected to it," Rabbi Gloiberman told me, in Hebrew. "Every Jew in the world goes to the Western Wall. What does the Jew have to do with the Western Wall? The soul of the Jew speaks. Do you understand? A Jew doesn't necessarily have to be a religious person. Just by virtue of being called '*Yehudi*' (Jew), [that word] includes the letters of the name of God. That means it is the soul that is speaking. Not being religious means that you're not Jewish? Who has a monopoly on Judaism? Nobody."

Unlike Blu, Stoudemire never had to deal with cynicism or questions from native Israelis. On the contrary, he was embraced immediately, becoming an immensely popular figure in Israel even before he arrived. ESPN broadcaster Jeremy Schaap visited the former All Star in October 2016 and chronicled one scene after another of Israeli fans mobbing Stoudemire wherever he went, the locals mesmerized by his size, fame, and personality. Schaap spoke to Gabriel Haydu, a broadcaster with Israel Sports Channel, to summarize the public's response to news of Stoudemire's decision to move to Jerusalem to play.

"First, astonishment—'How can it be?'" Haydu said. "Then, 'Really, is it happening?' Then he arrived at the airport, and it was 'He's here!' When he's going to play [for the first time], it's going to be 'Wow, all our dreams have come true.' It's that big a deal."

Changing Observance

Gloiberman's sentiments about religion and faith gave rise to a further question—if every Jew, no matter how observant (or non-observant, as the case may be), is specially connected to Israel, would living in Israel affect that level of observance? Research conducted on North American tour groups suggests that visiting the country can have a lasting impact on the religious identities of Jewish youth. Although the circumstances leading Landesberg to Israel differed considerably from those of the teens and twenty-somethings customarily participating in such trips, the impact on his identity was no exception to that general rule. For example, he told me that toward the end of his first season in Israel he started kissing the mezuzah whenever he walked through doorways and that it became an instinctive habit. When he returned home to New York the summer after his first season he saw that his family did not have a mezuzah. He said he started giving his father a hard time about it and vows he will continue until the mezuzah goes up. In addition, although he was used to going to his grandparent's home as a child to participate in Judaism's celebratory holidays, in particular Hanukkah and Passover, he had no history of partaking in the religion's more contemplative or somber customs. But after a season of talking to his Israeli teammates about the reasons and traditions related to *all* of the holidays on the Jewish calendar, that changed.

"I had never really celebrated Yom Kippur, but last year I actually fasted for the whole twenty-four hours," Landesberg said in 2012. "That was probably the toughest thing I've ever done in my life, but I was happy with myself when I accomplished it. It was an experience, and I'm actually planning on doing it again this year. [An Israeli teammate] was telling me, 'All the Israelis are getting ready for the fast,' and I was like, 'I think I'm going to do it with you guys.' He didn't believe me, because he said it's really tough. I think we had a day off after, but I came back to practice the next time and I told him I did it, and he was very happy for me. It being my second year, learning all the traditions and stuff, picking up the holidays, made me want to do that," Landesberg explained. He added that his father was very surprised by his fast. "Growing up, he was Bar Mitzvah'd and he was pretty religious, but I don't know if he ever fasted. He was pretty surprised and pretty happy too, that I went through it. Even my mother, she's Christian and doesn't know too much about Yom Kippur, but just the fact that I sacrificed for that whole day, she was really happy for me."

Interestingly, although Sims's childhood included celebrating all of the holidays on the Jewish calendar, he said that in Israel he has become *less* religious over the years. In that sense Sims's experience is much like that of others who live in Israel permanently. According to an article in the *Washington Post*, the attitude of Israelis in general is that "religion is an Orthodox-or-nothing affair." To the country's secular Jews—estimated by pundits to run a wide range, anything from as little as 20 percent of the population to as much as 80 percent—being Jewish has less to do with faith and ritual than with cultural identification and national commitment. In that vein, I found it particularly interesting that when I asked Sims about his level of religious observance, his answer took an unexpected turn: he pointed out that he votes in every election and even served in the Israeli army. He said he did go to synagogue from time to time, but he no longer fasts on Yom Kippur. In fact, he admits that he more often finds himself milling about outside the service, exchanging pleasantries with old friends and acquaintances that are fasting and "trying to hold out until they get to eat their honey cake."

Even though Sims's personal observance of Judaism's rituals has decreased over time, he was proud to take part in the most important religious rite of passage in his children's lives—their Bar and Bat Mitzvahs. Sims's youngest son had his Bar Mitzvah in 2010, and Sims played an active role in all aspects of the ceremony. But even in describing that religious custom, Sims's nationalistic focus on being Israeli still came through.

"I took part in everything, and it was touching, you know?" Sims told me. "I just don't like the long [ceremony]. I'm not a person with ADD, but I'm standing there looking all around and then the rabbi is telling me to repeat this and this and this. It goes on and on and on. I'm just happy about [the fact that] he becomes a man. This is his country, and that's it. And then [eventually] he fights for the country, becomes a part of the country. That's why I don't believe you understand Bar Mitzvah until you're doing it here. You know that you're putting everything into becoming a man for your country. You do everything for your country," he added proudly.

Now the Exception

From a practical perspective, neither Israeli basketball teams nor the Israeli government made much of an issue of the players' day-to-day religious observation. Their respective teams advised Sims, Blu, and Landesberg of the procedural requirements for obtaining citizenship and moving to Israel (described for Jews as making "*Aliyah*," in Hebrew, literally meaning "the ascent"), and the players set about digging up the information and documentation required to prove that they were each, in fact, Jewish. All of them met the governmental requirements for citizenship so the process went smoothly. But when Sims later became engaged to his Israeli girlfriend, the question of "Who is a Jew?" popped up again and in a much more difficult way.

"When I wanted to get married, it was like, 'Wow!'" Sims said, describing his difficulty in obtaining an Israeli marriage license, as opposed to the relative ease with which he obtained Israeli citizenship. "Going into the *moatzah* (city hall), and trying to apply, you're standing in front of all of these rabbis, and you know something? A lot of those guys are Americans! Those rabbis, sitting up there and saying, 'So you want to marry one of our women...'" Sims said, laughing. "I was like, 'Oh my God, here we go.' They wanted all kinds of information on why I wanted to get married, my mother's background, my grandmother's background. I gave them all of that stuff, but still they said we had to wait and see and this and that. My wife said, 'Look, we don't have to do this. We can go to Cyprus.' I was like, 'OK.' I never knew about Cyprus. I didn't even know [where it was]. They told me about it, and that's where we went. We came back, had a wedding party, and went from there."

Their experience was not uncommon for a couple with varied backgrounds who wish to get married in Israel. Like Landesberg's and Blu's, Sims's religious bona fides stood up to government scrutiny when the result of that evaluation was another gifted hoopster being added to an Israeli league roster. But when the result was to be an officially sanctioned marriage, the level of that scrutiny ratcheted up considerably. In

Israel, marriage falls under the jurisdiction of the applicable religious authorities, and no religious intermarriages can be performed legally in the country. The determination of whether an individual is Jewish for the purposes of receiving a marriage license is made by the chief rabbinate and the country's rabbinical courts. However, the government does accept the legitimacy of all marriages legally entered into in other countries. Accordingly, many couples in which one person's Judaism is certain and the other's may be in question opt to get married abroad, often in nearby Cyprus, rather than wait for an official, and sometimes unpredictable, decision.

Landesberg, who is not married, has not faced the thorough marriage-license examination, but not from a lack of (lighthearted) trying. On *Inside Israeli Basketball*, a half-hour television show produced by the Maccabi Haifa organization, Landesberg spent a day working various jobs on Haifa's public transit system, the *karmelit*. While tasked with checking passengers for tickets, he came across an attractive young woman and went on to ask her not only to go out with him, but to marry him. She rebuffed his advances, but Landesberg was not disheartened and continued to engage various other passengers with humorous exchanges. One interaction Landesberg particularly liked was telling the Israelis that he was, in fact, one of them, an Israeli Jew. Their reactions, Landesberg said, were par for the course.

"Aw, man, I wish I had pictures I could show you," Landesberg told me, when I asked how Israelis responded to being told he is Jewish. "I wish I could take a snapshot every time I tell somebody [in Israel]—it's like they're on a roller coaster ride and it's just right on the dip and their face opens and they're like, 'What?!' Every time I see it, it never gets old," he said with a laugh. Landesberg's name did cause him some grief while tasked by the television producers with checking passengers for tickets. At one point he encountered an elderly white male passenger who expressed the usual disbelief when told that Landesberg was Jewish. When the passenger shook his head and wore the exact shocked expression of so many others before him, Landesberg did what he always did in those circumstances.

"I bring out the *Teudat Zehut*," Landesberg said, showing the interviewer his Israeli identity card, which every citizen over sixteen years of age is required to carry. "When I first got this, I showed it to my Israeli teammates, and they told me it had me down as a female [because of Sylven, his gender-ambiguous given name]. So I had to go back and switch it! Now it says Yehoshua [Landesberg's Hebrew name] Shuki— Shuki's what they call me," he said, clearly pleased with his card and new nickname.

The name issue was of a more serious nature for Blu. He told me people found his previous family name of Bluthenthal difficult to say, and he just never grew fully comfortable with it. In 2010, after much thought about the benefit for him and his family he decided to change the name, from Bluthenthal to Blu. "For me, growing up with Bluthenthal [as a name] was tough," he told me. "Nobody could pronounce it. I was always self-conscious about every time I would go somewhere, I knew I would have to spell it out, and it would take them four times until they got it right. Kids would make fun of me, because they thought [the name] was funny. And that's just not something I wanted my daughters to grow up with."

The diversity of Israel is reflected with citizens from more than seventy different nationalities, a diversity that also applies to American Jews. Nearly 7 percent (roughly 435,000 people) of the approximately six million Jews in the United States say they are African American, Asian, Latino/Hispanic, Native American, or of mixed race, according to a study by the Institute for Jewish and Community Research. And anecdotally, at least, the concept of an African American Jew is becoming somewhat better known. In 2011, the comedy website *Funny or Die* released a parody of the popular rap song "Black and Yellow" with the chorus changed to "Black and Jewish," rapped by two African American Jewish actresses. Revised lyrics included lines such as, "Black dad, Jewish mom, eating gefilte fish while pouring Dom." In addition, popular rapper Drake from Toronto is Black and Jewish, and he even set an entire music video around the scene of his "re-Bar Mitzvah." I asked Landesberg if his being both Black and Jewish should be less surprising at this point.

"I'm still going to say my mix is very different," Landesberg said, laughing. "Drake has it too, but I haven't really found too many other people like that. I hope it's a growing race, we need more of us out there!" he adds with his usual good humor. "It does get tough sometimes, just hearing the same questions over and over. But I'm also proud to discuss my culture. My Jewish side is so surprising to some, but I'm happy to talk about it."

When I spoke to Landesberg during his third season in Israel (with Maccabi Haifa), he was settling in to Israeli life. He said he had gotten used to the little differences, and he had seen the sites with the notable exception of Yad Vashem, the Israeli Holocaust museum. He said he wanted to visit but others had warned him to time it accordingly, since he will likely be "depressed for a week." But he said he still had a ways to go to catch up with Blu, whom he would eventually team up with on Maccabi Tel Aviv.

"I haven't really spoken to Blu too much, but I do remember he was speaking a little Hebrew, so I guess he's one step up on me, and I've got to catch up," Landesberg said, laughing once again. "I can't let him beat me! I've got to be the best African American Jewish player in every area—I've got to be the best Hebrew-speaking one, but he's killing me right now! He was putting whole sentences together and stuff. I was a little jealous, but I didn't say anything. I kept it on the low."

Landesberg's Jewish grandfather passed away before his grandson signed up to play in Israel, so he never knew that there would be a renewed Israeli connection in the family. But Landesberg said his grandmother and the rest of his relatives are incredibly supportive and "love" that he is in Israel (where he recently completed his seventh season). Most of his family had been to visit him there, and the few family members that hadn't were planning to very soon. After all those years, the son, grandson, or cousin they are coming to see will no longer be an African American, Jewish visitor to Israel, but an Israeli.

"Every day I learn something new, whether it's Israeli traditions or just little things," he said. "I can get around now, if I need to. I feel a lot more comfortable. I feel like I'm home."

12

RACISM

ONE QUESTION THAT IS INEVITABLY posed about and to African American players who have spent time in Israel relates to racism—namely, did they experience it while they were there? The vast majority of players I spoke to said they had never personally experienced racism in the country, and many said they would be surprised if I met any players who had. But the issue of racism in Israel, and its impact on the experience of African American players there, is hardly that simple.

Before delving into the issue more deeply, it is important to contextualize the prevalence of African American players in Israel. Basketball today is very much an international game. With the explosion of its popularity worldwide, specifically since the 1992 Olympics and the spellbinding performance of the one and only Dream Team, basketball talent has emerged from every corner of the globe. The NBA, universally recognized as the best basketball league in the world, boasts players from more than forty countries. And yet, the foreign players in Israel's top professional league are comprised almost exclusively of African Americans. In a non-scientific review of Israeli Super League rosters in January 2017, 82 percent of foreign players were African American (62 out of 76). Factor in the handful of African American players who obtained citizenship and play as Israelis, and it's clear that professional basketball players in Israel are either Israeli, or African American, or both, with very few exceptions.

I asked a number of players and insiders why this might be and received a variety of responses. Former Israeli league coach and current broadcaster Simmy Reguer proposed simply that most American college basketball players are African American and that college basketball offers the best talent pool from which to recruit. However, it does not appear that the proportion of African Americans in other leagues around the world is comparable. For example, African Americans comprise only 63 out of 110 foreigners playing in the top league in Italy (57 percent). In Greece, only 60 out of 98 foreign players are African American (61 percent).

Cory Carr, a long-time player in Israel, told me that the breakdown of nationalities of a country's foreign players depends largely on the quality and style of play of the country's domestic players. "I think all of the European countries have their own unique style and way of playing, and you have to bring the right type of player to fit the local ones," Carr said. "The European style is a bit different, a little bit more structured. The Israeli league is a lot more open court, players like to get the ball up and down, play a lot of one and one, and this is similar to a lot of the African American players and their style of play. There isn't the traditional big man, like the European countries have, that you can play the two-man game with, go inside, and play more of a structured game. The point is it depends on the type of player that's already in the country."

Something More?

The question that persisted in my mind was whether the paucity of European basketball players in the Jewish state could be related to the checkered history between the European continent and the Jewish people. The Jews have been expelled from anywhere between 80 to 109 countries since the year 250 AD, and the Jews of Europe have been victims of nationally organized atrocities including the Spanish

Inquisition and the Holocaust. Today, anti-Semitism is again on the rise in Europe. It was reported in 2013 that one-third of European Jews admitted to refraining from wearing religious garb or Jewish symbols out of fear, with a further 23 percent avoiding attending Jewish events or going to Jewish venues. According to another report, anti-Semitic incidents in London increased by more than 60 percent in 2015 and such incidents increased by more than 84 percent in France in the first quarter of that year. Were Jewish team owners simply reluctant to bring over a player from a country with an anti-Semitic past or present?

I posed my question to a few African American players: Could the prevalence of African American players in Israel be the result of Jewish management's reluctance to sign players from countries with histories of anti-Semitism, a reluctance that would not be felt about signing African American players? The response I received was mixed. Carr, for one, laughed and advised me that I'd have to ask management about that. But Mark Brisker, an African American from Detroit who spent 13 years playing in Israel and lives there now in his retirement, acknowledged that the legacy of anti-Semitism could definitely play a role. He actually took my theory a step further, saying that not only could it affect a Jewish owner's willingness to bring in a European player, but that it could also impact a European player's willingness to sign in a Jewish state. Jitim Young, a Northwestern graduate and veteran of three seasons of Israeli basketball, in addition to playing in Greece, Belgium, Hungary, and Poland, agreed that the theory had merit.

"That's really, really interesting," he said, thoughtfully. "The Holocaust was not that long ago and you had Germany and all these countries that were trying to destroy the Jewish people and countries like Spain or Italy that probably weren't involved and just stayed neutral and stayed away but didn't allow for any type of aid," Young said. "And you kind of feel like, is that one of the reasons why a lot of those European countries don't have players playing over here [in Israel]? One thing I've learned about being overseas since graduating college is that kids, players, everybody—they really know their history and everything [their countries] stand for. They have so much pride about where they're from and what that means. That definitely has to play a role, because you've got good players from Europe who might be like, 'No, I'm not going to go to Israel to play in a Jewish league,' based on their history or whatever. And you've got [Israeli] owners that probably feel like, 'No, I'm not going to sign guys from certain parts of the world.' That makes a lot of sense," he concluded, actually joining Brisker in expanding my hypothesis (which was based solely on possible reluctance from the Israeli perspective) to include a possible reluctance on the part of the European players as well. A more fulsome consideration of that perspective would require further analysis and the input of European hoopsters as well, but the possibility of there being aspects of reluctance from both sides is an interesting one.

A Shocking Display

Although there are a variety of possible reasons to explain it, no one would or could dispute that, year after year, decade after decade, foreign roster spots in Israeli basketball have been filled almost exclusively by African Americans. In 2001, few would have been in a better position to understand the quantity and impact of African American players in Israel than Pini Gershon, then the coach of Maccabi Tel Aviv. By that point, Gershon had been coaching Israeli basketball and African American players for twenty-five years with great success and without any known racist comments or conduct to speak of. Yet, while delivering a lecture to a group of officers from the Israeli military—a lecture that was supposed to be about leadership—he veered off topic with dramatic and deeply disturbing words.

"Even among Blacks there are different colors," Gershon started off on his infamous ramble. "There is dark Black, and there is mocha. The mocha type are more clever, usually the darker color come from the street. You could see the standing of those with a bit more mixture in their color. The darker Black are stupid, they will do whatever you tell them, like slaves," he added.

When the controversial speech was reported by the newspaper *Yedioth Ahronoth*, Israel's culture and sports minister Matan Vilnai responded, "If the quotes are correct, I condemn each and every word Pini said, and I expect him to explain himself." Gershon was, in fact, called to address the incident before the *Knesset* (the Israeli legislature), where he apologized and said his comments were made in jest and taken out of context. The coach assured the assembled officials that he was speaking from the heart in telling them that he had never chosen players according to their race or their religion and that he treated them each as if they were his own children. His remorse notwithstanding, Gershon was asked to step down by Maccabi's board of directors, and he resigned his post a few days after the speech came to light.

In the course of his full comments, Gershon referenced a former player, Andrew Kennedy, as an example of a lighter-skinned, more "clever," African American. Kennedy had been a member of Gershon's 1993 Galil Elyon squad, the only team to take the Israeli championship from Maccabi over a thirty-eight year span. Kennedy took Gershon's words with a small grain of salt, attributing it to the coach's affinity for attention, but in no way was he willing to let the coach entirely off the hook. Although the remark about Kennedy was intended to be complimentary toward him, albeit in a woefully misguided manner, the sting was no less severe.

"I didn't hear [the comments] exactly, but I knew he had made some reference to me and my skin color, and that was really unfortunate," Kennedy said. "It's so weird, because I played for him for two years without issue. If he said it, he meant it, that's the only conclusion I can draw. But he never gave the impression or said anything to indicate that those were his views," Kennedy continued. "Pini goes for the laugh. He's an entertainer. He says some outrageous things. Sometimes people say things to get a chuckle. He does like to command a room and take charge, and sometimes people go too far. Again, if he believes that, that's really sad, but I find it hard to believe those are really his feelings, that he honestly feels that way, considering I've had many meals with him, we've talked about a lot of different things, and I never once got any hint that these were his feelings. I was really surprised and taken aback when I heard that."

Despite the maelstrom of negative attention Gershon's speech brought to himself and Israeli basketball, it did not preclude him from securing subsequent employment in the game. He was rehired by Maccabi Tel Aviv two and a half years after resigning, coaching the club from 2003 to 2006 and again from 2008 to 2010, then held various other roles in Israeli basketball before eventually moving into broadcasting. Although some pundits derided Maccabi's decision to bring Gershon back, the criticism was minimal and the results drowned them out—Gershon ended up leading Maccabi to unprecedented success. Gershon's second stint with Maccabi, his first after resigning following the remarks, resulted in two Euroleague Championships and another runner-up finish. In leading those teams, he was able to forge strong relationships with a variety of African American players who continue to support Gershon to this day.

Derrick Sharp, an African American from Orlando, Florida, played for Gershon for all of the controversial coach's eight seasons with the team, getting the chance to know him both before and after the incident. I was curious to hear how Sharp felt, as an African American playing for a coach who had made such inflammatory statements, and I asked him about it following a Euroleague contest in 2011. While he did not necessarily forgive the comments, he did provide some additional context about Gershon, comparing him to one of North American sports' most eccentric characters.

"Obviously there are no facts behind [Gershon's words]," Sharp told me. "That's probably just something he got caught up in saying, and I'm sure he regrets it. I'm sure if he had to do it all over again, he wouldn't make those comments, [but] I don't read into it too much—I know he's a good person, he has a good heart. That time is over, it's in the past," Sharp continued with emphasis. "We have a good relationship—I don't think he's a racist or anything. It's just Pini being Pini. In the States there's Manny being Manny [referring to the idiosyncratic and sometimes unpredictable Manny Ramirez, of baseball fame], well this is Pini being Pini. He likes to talk a lot, and sometimes his words are controversial or misread."

Deon Thomas, a forty-six-year-old from Chicago who played two seasons for Gershon at Maccabi, called the comments "dumb" but told me unequivocally that "Pini's not a racist." I asked Thomas whether he had experienced any racism in Israel, from Gershon or anyone else. He said not only had he never experienced any racism there, he didn't know of anyone that had. "I know a lot of players that have gone there to play, that have eventually married Israeli women and are still in the country—I have never heard of any of them having any type of issues at all."

Discrimination Abroad

The relative paucity of racism has been part of the narrative of the African American basketball player's experience in Israel since Aulcie Perry, who told *Ebony* magazine in 1978 that in Israel, "For the first time in my life, I felt free!" According to a number of the players I interviewed, the same can't necessarily be said for other countries they encountered in their international basketball travels.

"Woo, yeah, I've definitely felt [racism] in other places!" Young told me. "It's not even things that were said—you know how you can walk into a place and feel, 'What am I doing here?' That energy, that vibe is just [brutal]. Hungary, Poland, they're good leagues, but the environment? There were people I had encounters or interactions with, people that were stuck in 1902, 1840, or something like that. You walk around and can't believe how ignorant people are, even today."

Long-time Israeli league player Mark Brisker recalled being called a monkey and various other racist names while playing in Europe, but never in Israel. Pooh Jeter, an African American from Los Angeles who has spent time in the Ukraine and Spain in addition to Israel, said he had issues with locals in other countries calling him "nigger." He made it clear, however, that the word was not used out of anger or hate. Rather, he said, Europeans often knew the term from hearing it in rap music and movies; they were not familiar with many actual African Americans and frankly had no idea how offensive they would find people using that word.

The homogenous makeup of some countries was also an issue for African Americans when they signed to play there. Current NBA player Gerald Green has never played in Israel, but his experience in Russia speaks volumes. "I've never been to a whole country and not seen one Black person," he said. "Just never seen it. And then when you're Black, they look at you crazy because they've never seen it either. You're just as shocked as they are. A lot of times, people touch you like, 'What is this?' They'll touch you and look at your skin to see if it's paint. I'm not playing. All Russia is not like that. You've got your big cities like Moscow, Saint Petersburg. Some cities understand that there are Black people. They do exist. But the smaller cities, the little villages, they've never seen it."

Israel's Surprisingly Diverse Inhabitants

Although more than 75 percent of the population of Israel is Jewish, that figure belies the variety of ethnicities and races that make up the nation's inhabitants. Historically, Jews have been classified by two major groups, each named for its distinct region of origin: the *Ashkenazim* (*Ashkenaz* meaning "Germany" in Medieval Hebrew, denoting their Central European base) and the *Sephardim* (*Sefarad* meaning "Hispania" or "Iberia" in Hebrew, denoting their Spanish and Portuguese base). Even those designations tend to understate the diversity of the Jewish population in Israel, whose origins span the globe (including Jews from China, India, North Africa, and other places).

Perhaps most notably, in the context of the present discussion, Israel has a population of more than 120,000 Ethiopian Jews who came to Israel under the Law of Return. The majority arrived in the country during government-organized rescue operations, including Operation Moses (1984), Operation Sheba (1985), and Operation Solomon (1991). As of 2013, approximately 135,000 Israelis of Ethiopian origin were living in the country, about 50,000 of whom were born in Israel.

The players I spoke to were nearly unanimous in pointing out that Ethiopian Jews in Israel were the ones who suffered from discrimination in attitude and jobs available to them. New York native Ramon Clemente spent three seasons in Israel, but in that amount of time he met only a handful of Ethiopians. Nevertheless, he paid close attention to their circumstances.

"[They are treated] way different," Clemente said. "From my experience, Ethiopians are treated like a lower class for sure. Just from seeing where they work, you know? I've never seen an Ethiopian with a high-class job. They're always cleaning stuff," he continued. "And I've mentioned that to Israelis! We kind of joke about it—like, 'Yo, I haven't seen one yet have a good job.' They'll be like, 'Nah, nah, nah' like that. But I see it. They don't really notice it, but I notice it."

While Ethiopian Jews face discrimination and had a difficult time integrating into Israeli society, things are improving. In part due to compulsory military service, they are becoming more and more a part of Israeli society and many now speak Hebrew rather than the language of their parents. Fifty-seven-year-old Joe Dawson is no stranger to race and racism having grown up near Selma, Alabama, the town made famous by Dr. King's symbolic march across a bridge that had been blocked for civil rights workers by state troopers and local sheriff's deputies. So in his nearly thirty years in Israel he has paid particular attention to the circumstances of Ethiopian Jews. Dawson observed that the Ethiopians were dealt a difficult hand by arriving in Israel about the same time as many Russian immigrants (due to their differences in background and demeanor), but noted a positive trend in recent years.

"The Ethiopians are very quiet people, the Russians are aggressive," Dawson said. "The Ethiopians have nothing, and the Russians have nice houses and everything. They put all the Ethiopians in little projects. [The Ethiopians] didn't know anything—they came from farms and sleeping in the dirt. But the generation that grew up here—they're starting to change everything. The parents are still second-class citizens, but the kids? Some of them have fallen away, they're into drugs and alcohol and crime, but there are a lot of them who are really educated, and they're religious, and they're going to college. And you can see, half of them are moving up."

Another small part of the Israeli population is made up of Black Israelites, also known as Black Hebrews or Hebrew Israelites (discussed in some detail in Chapter 11 as well). Black Israelites believe they are descendants of the ancient Israelites and adhere in varying degrees to the religious beliefs and practices of mainstream Judaism. Ben Ammi Ben-Israel established the African Hebrew Israelites of Jerusalem in Chicago, Illinois, in 1966, and moved to Israel with about thirty Hebrew Israelites in 1969. Most Black Israelites continue to reside in the United States—mainly in cities such as Chicago, St. Louis, and Washington, DC—but more than 5,000 presently live in Dimona and two other towns in the Negev region in the south of Israel. Although there are Black Israelites who say they experience discrimination, there are others who dispute their claims. In addition, after decades of debate, Black Hebrews were granted permanent residency status by the Israeli government in 2004. Dawson noted that Black Israelites are in a much better situation than are Ethiopian Jews for two reasons: they speak and write perfect Hebrew and they are from America, which Israelis view positively.

Finally, there is another community in Israel that merits inclusion at this point in the discussion of race in the country: the tens of thousands of Africans who have recently illegally migrated to Israel, most frequently from Eritrea or the Sudan. Seeking asylum from alleged human rights violations, these migrants navigate a perilous smuggling route through Egypt and into Israel, facing a multitude of threats in order to cross the Sinai border and enter the Jewish state. But of the thousands of African migrants in Israel, only about 150 have been granted official status as refugees through the United Nations High Commission of Refugees. According to the UNHCR, the vast majority of those trekking toward Israel are doing so in a form of "mixed migration," meaning they are doing so both to avoid political repression and also for economic gain.

The integration of the migrants into Israeli society has not been a smooth one. Most of them settled in south Tel Aviv, and longtime residents came to derogatorily refer to their neighborhood as "South Sudan" and complain about the lawlessness of the new residents. Aware of the potential racial undertones of those concerns, they assert that their position is not based upon race, but rather behavior. They note that Jews had lived peacefully for decades in south Tel Aviv with foreigners of various races, including other Africans, and that Israeli police did find that the arrival of the migrants coincided with a spike in crime in the area (including a 53 percent increase in felonies committed by the migrants in 2012). After years of general inaction to the influx of migrants, Israel constructed a fence along its border with Egypt in 2013, a move that stemmed the flow of migrants to a mere trickle. The move came a few months after the passing of an anti-infiltration law, which encourages migrants to self-deport and allows the government to detain infiltrators for up to one year.

In May 2012 I had coffee with Willie Sims, who played for almost twenty years in Israel and stayed in the country following his retirement. It was the day after a large protest had been held in Tel Aviv, supporting the migrants and objecting to their purported mistreatment at the hand of Israeli citizens and authorities. We met in Caesarea, where Sims now teaches fitness classes at a posh country club and where the migrants and their circumstances were a hot topic of conversation. Sims told me that his daughter had attended the protest the day before, and he bemoaned a series of myths that were being spread about the migrants, which he said were ridiculous since many of them had lived in the country for years without incident. By coincidence, my brother, while waiting for me at a nearby restaurant, noted overhearing diners complaining about Sudanese migrants getting jobs as dishwashers at local establishments, since they supposedly "spread their HIV into the water." What I couldn't realize at the time was that Sims, who in these circumstances identified *with* the Sudanese migrants and derided their treatment by Israeli officials, would one day be incorrectly identified *as* a Sudanese migrant and be treated unjustly as a result.

Sims, who has lived in Israel for more than thirty years, had been invited with his family to attend a December 2012 dinner marking the completion of one year of mourning since the death of beloved Israeli singer Yafa Yarkoni, a close friend of the Sims family. After dinner Sims accidentally locked his keys in his car, and despite their best efforts, he and a friend were unable to get the door opened. While his friend went inside to call a locksmith, Sims was using the friend's knife in a further attempt to get the door unlocked when he and his thirteen-year-old son (standing by his side holding a flashlight) were jumped by three plainclothes police officers. According to Sims, they held him and his son against the car, handcuffed them, and pushed them to the ground. Sims said the officers accused him of trying to steal the car and were undeterred by his repeated attempts to tell them that he was a guest at a dinner party, the car was his, and a locksmith was being called. Rather, Sims said the police were convinced that he and his son were among the Sudanese migrants who had been responsible for a rash of thefts of electric bikes in the city. Eventually, the rest of the dinner party guests spilled out into the street to see what was happening, among them two lawyers who helped defuse the situation and got Sims and his son released. If it were up to Sims that would have been the end of the issue, but his son had been significantly affected by the experience and Sims's wife convinced him to sue.

"My son was terrified—every time he saw a policeman in blue he was freaking out a little bit," Sims told me. "He had to go see a psychiatrist. [The police] knew this, they knew about all of this, but it didn't help. He was thirteen at the time, and they put handcuffs on him, even though they're not supposed to put handcuffs on a youth. Then they took them off real quick. He was tall, so they thought he was an older guy. It was ridiculous."

Although a formal apology was issued, the lawsuit was unsuccessful and the court ultimately held that the officers were justified in their actions. Sims, perhaps not surprisingly, was less than satisfied with the result. "I said, 'Now, if this was a blonde white guy and his son, would this have happened?' And then everyone got quiet. No one could answer that," he said.

I wondered whether the incident might negatively impact Sims's view of Israel or lead him to seek a return to the United States. On the contrary, he actually used the incident to draw a positive distinction between living in Israel and the United States, comparing what happened to him and his son to the tragic and highly publicized series of shootings of African Americans by police officers in recent years. According to Sims, the mandatory military conscription in Israel ensures that all police officers are well-trained and confident with their weapons, an important factor in ensuring that situations like the one involving him and his son are not escalated dangerously.

"Most importantly, we're alive," Sims said. "Things happen here, but [the police] don't go to the point of pulling a gun out! Do you know what I mean? They talk to you and do whatever they have to do without pulling a gun—they don't shoot you. [American police] have no army experience, no training, no nothing. And I went to the [Israeli] army for a year and a half—I see how these guys work, the [training], the things they have to go through. I was amazed—they're ready, not jumpy like the in the States. There's too much going on over there! Everyone's gun happy, and I don't want to be a part of that. I miss the States, I talk to my friends and everything, but they tell me about what's going on over there, and I don't want to be a part of it."

Looking Deeper

Multiple players cited the ability to blend in physically with Israel's diverse population as a possible reason for what they perceived as an absence of racial discrimination in the country. But when I spoke to Young about the subject, he pointed to a different, and interesting, factor. "It's kind of ironic—you know, as an African American, we've been slaves, and we had to come to another country and get our freedom," Young said. "The Jewish people, they've been slaves in Egypt, and they went through the Holocaust. It would be weird to experience racism from people that have been through the same things you've been through—it wouldn't make sense. I'm glad that since I've been here I haven't experienced anything like that. How could you act a certain way, when me and you, with our cultures and our histories, our people have encountered pretty much similar circumstances, you know? That's probably the reason a lot of the [African American] guys that come out here and play feel so comfortable."

It was with great interest that I asked Dawson how and why the Israeli basketball scene had remained racism-free. He didn't totally agree that it had. Dawson certainly knows what racism feels like, having grown up in America's Deep South. After college and before pursuing his basketball career overseas, he worked as a computer programmer for a hospital in Hattiesburg, Mississippi, where he said he was the "first Black to wear a tie" (as opposed to a janitorial or, at best, nurse's uniform). But when the white manager for whom he had worked for more than a year left for another job, Dawson was passed over for the promotion in favor of an applicant with less education and no knowledge of the program they were using to modernize the hospital's operations. The sting of this event led Dawson back to basketball, and eventually to Israel, which he made clear he doesn't consider a racist country or one with a major racism problem. He applauded the warmth of the Israeli people and proudly considers himself one of them. However, he does find it strange that the very existence of any racism in Israeli basketball is denied entirely.

"There has been [racism] in basketball, it just doesn't get publicized," Dawson said. "I've been asked this question by every reporter—'Do I feel racism here?' And I tell them, 'Of course.' And I think there will always be racism, because there's a difference [between people]. Some people, if they don't know anything bad to say to you and they want to hurt you, they're going to use [racism]. When I was playing—I don't take offense to getting called *Cushi* at all—but there have been fans that called me nigger and other things when I was on the court. But I'm used to it, and I think the players are. We just don't pay attention to it."

Dawson mentioned not taking offense to being called Cushi, a biblical Hebrew word that has become the subject of much debate. *Cush* (or *Kush*) is an ancient ethnic group from a land known by the same name (in northeast Africa) who are considered descendants of Noah. According to Yaacov Lozowick, the chief archivist of the State of Israel and former director of Yad Vashem, Cushi was a perfectly innocuous Hebrew word, generally used to refer to a dark-skinned person of African descent as recently as the 1970s. Once Americans began updating their racial terminology, however, from Negro to Black to African American, a rising sentiment took hold that the Hebrew terminology should change as well, tying Cushi to now-outdated and offensive English terms. The word was famously used to refer to African American basketball players in Israel in the summer of 2013, when David Lau, Israel's newly elected chief rabbi (one of the two men who serve as spiritual authorities for Israelis) was speaking to orthodox Yeshiva students, one of the few sub-groups in Israel who are exempt from compulsory military service. Lau was concerned with the growing number of orthodox students watching Israeli basketball in public places, instead of studying Torah, and with the possibility that it could ultimately lead to the elimination of the military exemption. To underscore his point about the significance of Torah study and the insignificance of basketball, he uttered the stinging statement: "Why do you care whether these Cushim who are paid in Tel Aviv beat the Cushim who are paid in Greece?"

Sims echoed Dawson's views of the existence of racism in Israeli basketball. He told me that in his early days in Israel tension developed when some locals questioned what he, as an African American, was doing in what they considered "their" country. In addition to the offensive looks and comments, he too was referred to as Cushi, which hardly bothered Sims until Israelis explained the word's apparent—but according to him, inaccurate—translation. Although a 2007 Israeli court decision deemed the term to be a pejorative one, Sims doesn't see it that way.

"If you don't know the language, and they start saying Cushi, you don't understand what they're talking about," Sims said. "And then some idiot tries to translate it for you, and he's like, 'You know, Cushi means nigger.' [Now] you're like, 'Wait a minute, did he just say that?' And there've been a lot of fights [over that]. When I started understanding it, when I understood what the people were [really] saying, I had to explain it to some of the new players coming in, because they heard from another idiot, ignorant person, 'It means nigger.' But it doesn't, you know?! Cushi is what it is. Cush—it's in the Bible, he was one of Noah's sons. That's what it means, really. Hopefully these other basketball players can come and hear it and Israeli people won't put a negative meaning behind it. That's the problem, when they put that negative meaning behind it. That's when everything flares up."

Discrimination in the Workplace

Name-calling is one thing, but there are other, more subtle, means of racial discrimination that can have a more significant impact. New York native Carlton Neverson, now fifty-nine years old, spent 14 seasons playing in Israel's first league and two in the second division. He chose to remain in Israel after his retirement from playing, but unfortunately feels that his race has been a factor in his inability to find work in his next chosen vocation. And he's not the only one.

"I would say there is a bit of a prejudice in this country," Neverson told me when we first spoke on the phone in 2011. "I'm not going to say there isn't, because there is. Have I personally experienced a lot of it? I would say a minimum amount. But yes, it does exist. As a Black American, you don't get the total anti-Black thing right away—it rears its ugly head from time to time. As far as me coaching, as an example, I've been trying to coach here in the first league for the last eight years, and for some reason they won't give me a job in the first league. Now, I can coach in the second league, or the third league, or work with the kids, no problem," he noted, "but when it comes to getting a job in the first league, it seems like everyone is giving me a pass. 'No, no, no.

We'll be in touch, we'll be in touch, we'll be in touch.' And I've done great work here with all the kids, coached here for six or seven years, won championships with the kids' teams and the younger teams in the second league and the third league, but they will not give me a job in the first league. My friend, Willie Sims, is in the same situation. We've been going through this for like forever. I can't think of any other reason why they wouldn't give me a job, because my qualifications are great. So there is a bit of a prejudice situation when it comes to that," he said.

When I last spoke to Neverson in November 2016, he was the head coach of each of the Hapoel Lud men's team (in the third division) and women's team (in the second division). Although he enjoys both roles, he continues to knock on the doors of first-division men's teams, still to no avail. Dawson has also attempted to get a job coaching in the Israeli Super League, but with no success. And like Neverson, Dawson sees his struggles as part of a bigger issue.

"Most of the places I've played in Europe [France, Italy, Greece] accepted players who come from wherever they come, and they try to integrate [their styles] into the system," he said. "But here it's a little bit slower. [The native Israelis] want to keep it more along the lines of how they want it, they want to have more control over it. It's like an unwritten rule that nobody talks about, but from the players that you've talked to, players like Fred [Campbell], and Cory [Carr], and Stanley [Brundy], these are all players who are getting older in their years, who've played a lot of years in Israel and decided to stay. But there's more, all the way back to Aulcie [Perry], and Willie [Sims], and Carlton Neverson. There are many players who've stayed here, and we thought that with all of our wealth of experience we could find a career in basketball, but it doesn't work like that. It's sort of closed to outsiders."

By and large, the head coaches and assistant coaches of first-division Israeli teams are Israelis who were born in the country. During the 2016–17 season, ten of the twelve Super League teams were coached by native Israelis, the exceptions being Hapoel Jerusalem (coached by Simone Pianigiani, an Italian) and Maccabi Tel Aviv (coached by Ainars Bagatskis, a Latvian, though the team started the season coached by a native Israeli who was fired). Other foreign coaches have come and gone over the years, and Jewish American head coach David Blatt actually brought Charles Barton, an African American from Columbus, Ohio, to be his associate head coach with Maccabi Tel Aviv from 2001 to 2003. Yet, while Israeli coaches often depend on veteran African American players for team leadership, the seemingly natural progression to a first-division coaching position very seldom happens for those players.

To date, of all of the retired African American players Neverson and Dawson mentioned only Sims spent time on the coaching staff of a first-division Israeli team, and that was for one season as a second assistant with a focus on conditioning. Since Dawson and I spoke, Sharp was added as an assistant coach for Maccabi Tel Aviv, but he lasted only two seasons before returning to the United States, again leaving the Super League without an African American head coach or assistant coach. However, Dawson did not draw a direct line between his race and his inability to find coaching work—instead he highlighted the Israeli basketball's community's general resistance to change as the major issue.

"There's one set of rules, and nobody wants to stray away from that," Dawson said. "If you want to coach here, you have to go to one of their schools. They want to put their own brand on it, and in effect they're telling you how they want to keep basketball [in Israel]. I think it's more about status quo. If I had to throw something else in, it would be that with the history of the Israeli and Jewish people, it becomes like you can trust only so much. You depend on and trust yourself and your people more. That's part of it too, but I think it's more just the status quo, and you just have to find a way in," he concluded.

Ironically, Israeli entrepreneurs are lauded in the business world for their penchant for thinking outside the box and for questioning standard operating procedure. In basketball, though, as Dawson pointed out, status quo is king. All prospective coaches, regardless of their level of experience, are required to pass a certification course at the Wingate

Institute, Israel's National Centre for Physical Education and Sport. The result is entire generations of young Israeli coaches who were taught to coach the same plays on offense and implement the same type of defense. Israeli basketball teams are also notoriously quick on the trigger to make coaching changes but select from only the small pool of qualified native Israelis. This ends up cycling and recycling the same coaches with the same strategies time and time again.

"What did Einstein say?" Deon Thomas asked me over lunch. "Doing the same thing and expecting a different result is the definition of insanity. So it's crazy for them to continue to do the same things, rotate through the same coaches, and think they're going to get a different result."

I spoke at length with Dawson, Sims, and Neverson about their attempts to break into the Israeli coaching ranks. Each completed the mandatory courses required of all prospective coaches at Wingate, and each expected that his certification, combined with decades of high level basketball experience and years as an Israeli citizen, would be enough to land him a coaching job in the Israeli Super League. Yet neither Dawson nor Neverson ever received an opportunity. This is in sharp contrast to the experiences of some native Israelis, who were able to secure first-division coaching positions immediately upon retiring from playing. Sims did crack the coaching circle, but only for a limited time. He was working as a personal trainer when he was offered a position as a second assistant and trainer/conditioning coach with Barak Netanya in 2009. The team had a great season with Sims on the bench, even qualifying for the Israeli Final Four, and Dawson said he was optimistic that his friend's success might open the doors for other African American coaches in the Israeli league.

According to Dawson, though, Sims might have done *too* good a job, as players gravitated toward him instead of the head coach at times, a reality often caught by the cameras televising the game. Sims said he and the head coach worked well together and without incident, so he was more than a little bit surprised to find out that he was not being retained.

"A lot of people said it was jealousy, because this coach wasn't known," Sims said. "It was his first year in the first league, and when the cameras were on, the American players were constantly saying, 'Wait, wait, who's the coach here? We always see you, Willie, the camera's always on you.' When you're in a locker room watching your film, and the guys are tossing little jokes around, the [head] coach is taking that seriously, like, 'Wow, who is the coach here?' And we would laugh about it, but I guess at the end, he got the last laugh."

A number of the veteran or retired African American players I spoke with were reluctant to point definitively to race as the limiting factor in their coaching opportunities. Some suggested the inner circle of coaching may want to keep the profession largely Israeli, making it an issue of nationality, not skin color. Others wondered whether Israeli coaches preferred to keep their professional circle Jewish, making it an issue of religion instead of race. A recent academic article examined the perception of Jewish-Israeli nationality and the boundaries of the Israeli collective. It concluded that even naturalized foreign athletes are never fully accepted into the Israeli collective. The authors do state that the players' vital contribution to the success of Israeli clubs in the European arena makes them, in the eyes of many in the Israeli media and public, part of the "us." However, the authors submit that this inclusion is provisional and contingent on various factors and even deficient or incomplete in some ways. Sims's inability to land a sustainable coaching position would arguably be an example of that deficiency.

"Look, I'm accepted to a point. Up until a point, it's 'Villie! Eizeh ben adam' (What a human being)!'" Sims told me, accentuating the "V" sound with which Israelis pronounce his name. "But when it comes to professional things, they'd rather do it themselves, they don't want you involved in it. You'd think, you say all these good things about me and how professional I am and this and that, but to get a job? Wow—they won't let you in the door. It makes you wonder. And believe me, I've seen coaches that are coaching that," as he paused and exhaled deeply, "they really didn't know basketball. I mean, they've gone to Wingate, but really don't know the game. It's tough, but I just leave it alone. I don't want to make it a big issue. Carl Neverson, his Hebrew is better than mine. His Hebrew is really great, and they wouldn't even look at him. And he knows basketball, and Joe [Dawson] knows basketball. These guys, you talk to them, and they really know basketball. And they've done everything the people asked to get in [to the coaching circle]. But to no avail. They keep you out."

Change Ahead?

To Dawson, Neverson, Sims, and others, the idea of having an African American former player on the coaching staff is a no-brainer for Israeli teams. They argue that, having been high school and college stars in the United States and elite performers in the Israeli league and elsewhere around the world, they would have valuable insight to share with all of their players. And with so many roster spots taken up by African Americans, they would be uniquely qualified to assist with the coaching of those players in particular. As Dawson succinctly put it, "If you've got six Americans, six Black guys, it just makes sense to have one Black guy on the sideline." Sims noted that Europe is starting to make progress in embracing diversity in coaching, and he is optimistic that change will follow in Israel as well. When we spoke in 2012, Sims said he hoped Sharp would get a more legitimate chance than he had been given and that more wide-reaching change would follow.

"I'm not giving up on coaching—hopefully one day I'll get a call, 'Villie [pronouncing it as Israelis do], can we talk?'" Sims told me. "I'm happy for Derrick, happy that he was put there. I hope that they will keep him in the league, he'll continue on, and one day become a head coach in the league. That will open a door."

Unfortunately, as of the completion of this book, that door has remained closed and not without consequence. Sharp was an assistant coach for Maccabi for two years, but things didn't work out and the Israeli icon responsible for the Zalgiris Miracle and countless other memorable moments ended up leaving the country and returning to his home state of Florida. Stanley Brundy—an African American who played for decades in Israel, married an Israeli woman and earned his citizenship—told me he is trying to talk his wife into moving their family back to the United States. Although he loves the country, he simply sees more opportunity to make a better life for his family in the States than what they have in Israel. Chris Watson, an African American from White Plains, New York, played more than 15 years in Israel, earned his citizenship, and represented the country twice as a member of its national team. Yet he chose to return to his American hometown upon hanging up his sneakers, in large part because of the struggles he saw his predecessors go through in trying to build a coaching career in Israel after their respective retirements.

"Of course [I considered staying]. Israel is where I grew up, Israel is where I became a man," Watson told me by phone from his new job, working as an account manager selling memberships at Life Time Athletic fitness center. "I just didn't see the opportunity, unfortunately, looking at the guys who came before me. Everybody said I should coach and do this or do that, but there just hasn't been a person who did it before me. I've seen guys that played on bigger levels than me, guys that played for Maccabi Tel Aviv or Hapoel Jerusalem, guys who were really, really famous and tried to do it and it just didn't work out. I'm a pretty big name in the country, but I just didn't see a lot of opportunity to continue, so I had to do what I had to do. I think it's unfortunate—there's guys out there with a lot of knowledge, guys that broke their backs and gave their blood, sweat, and tears to play the game at a very high level and help a lot of clubs achieve success. Whether it's race or that type of stuff I stay away from because I don't know what's in another person's head, but I just know that it's really unfortunate that you've got some guys who've dedicated their lives to the country and unfortunately they haven't been able to become head coaches. It's a shame."

The issue of race is always a complex one in basketball as it is in other spheres, and it is likely that biases—conscious and willful or otherwise—impact the sport wherever it is played. The acceptance and generally stellar treatment of African American players in Israel is commendable and the frequency with which those players choose to retire and stay in the country speaks highly to their level of comfort there. Nonetheless, the fact that those same players have been almost entirely unable to land coaching jobs on first-division teams in Israel is a clear shortcoming to be addressed in the future. In 2012, Israeli Prime Minister Benjamin Netanyahu gave a speech in which he said, "In the State of Israel, there is no room for racism." Until the likes of Stanley Brundy, Joe Dawson, Carlton Neverson, Willie Sims, and others are given an equal opportunity to coach in Israel at the game's highest level, the country's basketball community will still have work to do to fully realize that pronouncement's implicit promise.

13

LIFE AFTER BASKETBALL

MORE OFTEN THAN NOT, FRED Campbell fit right in with his fellow employees when he worked at the northern Tel Aviv offices of BMC Software, one of the most successful companies in Israel's thriving high-tech industry. They commiserated over long hours at the office, took coffee breaks together, and chatted about topics such as their favorite television shows. But standing 6-foot-7, weighing a fit 231 pounds, and still an active professional basketball player into his fifties, Campbell couldn't help but get noticed.

"One day I was working out on my lunch break," Campbell said. "When I came back [my colleagues] were like, 'Damn man, you look like you're in pretty good shape!' And I was telling them, 'Yeah, I play a little basketball.' They're like, 'Are you still playing?!' and I'm like, 'Yeah, I play a little bit.' But I don't get too much into it with them," he said.

Campbell, of course, has played much more than a little bit. He has been a pro in Israel since the early 1990s, spending time in the first, second, and third divisions. To start the transition into his post-playing career, Campbell decided to get a second job while still competing on a third-division team. Playing on a lower league team carries fewer time commitments, which enabled him to balance his office job with his basketball job.

Campbell is one of a number of African Americans who spent years playing in Israel and ended up staying in the country after hanging up their sneakers. Among the country's biggest celebrities at one time, these retired players each made the decision to turn Israel from a home away from home into just plain home.

The Earliest Roads to Change

Among the first and best-known players to live in Israel after retiring from playing was Aulcie Perry, who had led Maccabi Tel Aviv to its historic first European Cup championship in 1977 and subsequently converted to Judaism. He initially signed on with Maccabi for only a two-month contract, hoping to facilitate a quick return to the NBA, but it didn't quite work out that way. Perry ended up playing nine seasons in Tel Aviv before troubles with drugs and with the law, as detailed in Chapter 9, derailed his promising career. Surprisingly, though, once Perry was in a position to put those difficult experiences behind him, he chose not to stay in the United States. Instead, Perry returned to Israel and has remained there ever since.

Since his return, Perry has had several careers in Israel. He managed a Burger Ranch, a once-popular Israeli fast-food restaurant chain, and he worked for a time as a sports agent. Recently, he has been delivering seminars to the management of major Israeli companies. Perry called the seminars "Winning Team," using basketball as a tool to show the correlation between building a winning team in sports and a winning team in corporate management. At the same time, throughout his various career changes, Perry has been working to develop the next generation of Israeli basketball players. Soon after returning to the country he started a summer camp for Israeli youth called Sal Stars (Basketball for Stars) with Greg Cornelius, another former player. The camp runs annually for three weeks each summer at the Wingate Sports Institute near Netanya, and it is open to Jewish youngsters from around the world.

Carlton Neverson is a retired African American player who coaches at Sal Stars, but unlike Perry, he's followed a career journey which has always kept him near the basketball court. Neverson, a New York native and third-round pick in the 1981 NBA Draft, came to Israel in 1984 and was a star in the first division for more than a decade. He continued playing into his forties, including two years for a second-division team, while preparing to transition into a non-playing career in the sport. Although first-division coaching jobs have been out of reach for retired African American players in Israel, Neverson and others have had some success with finding coaching work in other capacities. During the last few years of his playing career and in the dozen years since he retired, Neverson has coached kids from the peewee league all the way up to seventeen-year-olds, and he has held both assistant and head coaching positions in Israel's lower leagues.

For Neverson and other African Americans who stayed in Israel after their stardom faded, working with youth scratched a coaching itch as well as serving a more practical function. Joe Dawson recalled to me how once he turned forty, offers to play in the first division, and the lucrative salaries that accompanied them, no longer came his way. This left him in a bind. Wanting to stay in Israel and in basketball, he had only two options immediately available. He could continue playing in the lower leagues or he could take part-time jobs teaching the game to youth. Neither of these, though, would provide him with anything more than a modest income. However, Dawson was able to make ends meet by doing what Neverson did—taking on a hybrid player/part-time instructor role. Their playing salaries, while considerably reduced, when combined with payments for coaching kids, and with bonuses they often earned for helping elevate their second-division teams into the first league, allowed Dawson, Neverson, and some other players to piece together enough money to justify their decision to stay in Israel.

The Fitness World

By having to keep themselves in prime condition well into their middle-age years, some players become so skilled about developing and maintaining their bodies that they are able to make their post-playing livings in the fitness industry. When I met with Dawson to discuss his life in Israel, we scheduled it in between exercise classes he was teaching. For a man with a degree in computer science and a master's in business, he lives a nomadic professional existence today, which has admittedly been a source of some frustration. But a change in his personal circumstances made his job situation much more tolerable, even if his typical day is more of a patchwork than he would like.

"Well, everything changed for me two years ago, when I got my sons to live with me," Dawson told me in 2011 about being granted primary custody of his two children from his first marriage. The boys were teenagers at the time (and have gone on to build successful basketball careers in their own right, as discussed further in Chapter 7). "I'm living my dream now, because I'm with my kids and I'm involved in everything. My [second] wife's family has a bakery," Dawson said, before describing a typical work day for him at the time. "Every once in a while I change it up and work there—do drive-in, do delivery, anything that can get me into Israel, so I can get more of a feeling of the real life here, how the real people live. But most of the time, I work in the afternoon. I work three hours a day most days, doing basketball schools, from three to six or four to seven. And then after that, four nights a week I go to different clubs and teach kickboxing or body-shaping. And the other hours I fill out with my personal training, basketball training, or body-shaping."

Willie Sims's post-playing career has included both basketball and fitness-related roles. He spent one season as an assistant coach of Barak Netanya in the first division and another season acting as a league official, attending games to oversee the work of the local referees and mediate and resolve any disputes that arose on game night. He also runs an instructional basketball camp for Israeli youth every summer. Like Dawson, he also went into the personal fitness and training industry. Sims developed his passion for working out early in his playing career; in fact, during his time in the Israeli army he trained high-ranking officers, a role he greatly enjoyed.

Today, Sims works in a variety of fitness capacities—he teaches three group classes a week at the Caesaria country club for about thirty-five people each, alternating between shape classes, aerobics, and what he calls aero-boxing, which is similar to Tae Bo (a total body fitness system that incorporates martial arts techniques). He also has four to eight individual clients that he personally trains twice a week. He works with Wingate, training physical education teachers in recent advancements in the fitness world and new ways to engage and encourage their students. Finally, he also has his own business, called Simsport, which runs classes twice a week for about fifty clients at a time. His facility and client-base was bigger in years past, so big that it became a serious competitor to some of the more established fitness facilities. This triggered a price war when the other facilities dropped their prices in an effort to entice Sims's clients to switch over.

"If I was charging $200, they put theirs down to $100," Sims said about the circumstances. "It was unbelievable. A lot of people kind of jumped ship because of that—I wouldn't say they were loyal," he added with a wry laugh. "If the price was right, they were gone, in a heartbeat. They're getting a great workout, but they hear the price and it's 'Oh, got to go. Sorry Willie. Love you!' I had a big place, and I made it smaller—it's better to be in a small place."

Sims said some of his clients were well aware of his basketball success, but he finds that many people come to him because of the advertising and networking he's done in the years since he retired from playing. He keeps his focus on providing clients with the most intense and entertaining workout possible, utilizing all kinds of music—Romanian to Russian, Ashkenazi to Sephardic. This approach has garnered him an incredibly diverse clientele, in terms of ethnicity and also in age, with clients ranging from sixteen to sixty-six years old. "They come to work out," Sims said. "Women in their sixties, and they don't even look it. They are working out! I glance over at some of those twenty-three or twenty-four-year-olds, and I point to these three ladies in their sixties and say, 'You all have got to start doing something, because these ladies are working out! And they're working out at a high level, they're not just messing around.'"

Adapting to the Office

Campbell's post-basketball career path has been unusual, in that his first job did not leverage his sport or physical fitness acumen. As he transitioned away from scoring and rebounding, he took a job that had him editing and processing. Companies that work with BMC send the corporate giant various software programs for their consideration. Campbell's daily task was to go through those programs, approving or deleting them based on different criteria. Approximately 1,000 programs are inputted into BMC's system every day, and Campbell said he worked "crazy hours," although the independent nature of the work meant he had considerable control over when he had to be in the office. Some days he started in the afternoon and worked into the wee hours, and other days he came in to work in the middle of the night and left in the early afternoon.

Campbell, who had unsuccessfully applied for a number of high-tech jobs before breaking through with BMC, said that the interview process was nerve-wracking for him. He had to take written and computer exams and even a polygraph test over the course of six weeks, and admitted that as days passed in between each stage of the process, he assumed the company had rejected his application. Upon being hired, he was the only African American among the 116 employees at BMC, but he stressed that he was treated no differently than any of the others. The company is filled with American and Canadian employees, making English the primary language of the office, and Campbell's Hebrew (which is passable, but not fluent) was not an issue. He said he worked hard on the transition from court to cubicle, with excellent results.

There is a wise adage, "Choose a job you love, and you will never work another day in your life." As much as Campbell enjoyed the office job, computer software wasn't a passion of his. Basketball was, of course, but so too was something not quite as obvious, which is why Campbell left BMC after three years for a more entrepreneurial venture. "I've always been crazy about [motorized] dirt bikes," Campbell said. "My best friend, he had a company in the bike business and he wanted to pull me in with him. He said, 'Fred, why don't you come in with me?' I thought about it for a while, and I thought it was a great idea, so I left. And it just took off."

Campbell said he went from riding recreationally to helping his friend sell a small number of bikes to local kids and then to negotiating with the Israeli Minister of Sport for licenses to import bikes from England and Italy. He and his business partner also organize large-scale dirt-biking shows, featuring stunts, tricks, and performances by top riders they bring in from the United States. In the twilight of one career he's been so passionate about, Campbell is thrilled to have found another. "[The bikes] did it for me," Campbell told me by phone in 2017. "It's something that I've always loved, and to again have the opportunity to do something that I love, other than basketball? That's what I want to do. I'm actually on my way to the track right now!"

Making the Return

Mark Brisker is a retired African American basketball player in Israel who initially chose to leave the country after he finished playing. He returned to the United States after completing his thirteenth season in Israel in 2006, bringing his Israeli wife and two kids with him. Unfortunately, things didn't go as planned for the Brisker family—he and his wife divorced, and she took the children back to Israel with her. He spent the next six years in Winter Haven, Florida, never even visiting Israel in that time. He explained that it wasn't a voluntary absence—he had made some "crazy investments" in the United States, the consequences of which were multiplied when the financial markets crashed. It simply wasn't financially feasible for him to fly to Israel at all, let alone to move there.

Brisker maintained contact with his kids through video chats, but he wasn't able to see them for five years, a circumstance he refers to as "disgusting." But things would eventually turn around for him. He focused on getting his financial affairs in order, spurred on by his desire to get back to Israel and be part of his children's lives again. He worked, he saved, and he even reconnected with an old friend from Israel, who would become his girlfriend. In 2011 he was finally able to move back, returning as a more mature man. In the years when he was playing, Brisker's favorite cities were lively Tel Aviv and nearby Ra'anana, but on his return to Israel he and his girlfriend chose Neot Mordechai, a kibbutz in the northern part of Israel, as their home base. So how does his new lifestyle in the Galil compare to his old one in the center of the country?

"It doesn't compare," Brisker said. "It's one word—quiet. I grew up in a city, Detroit, where on Friday night at ten o'clock there's traffic, there are people outside. Here, on weekends, every day at eight or nine o'clock at night, it's quiet, it's *very* quiet. But at my age, I'm not looking for the party or the excitement. And my kids love it, so I love it."

Indeed, Brisker took his return to Israel very seriously. He made his first order of business completing his ulpan—immersive Hebrew language and Israeli culture study for immigrants, students, travelers, and tourists from around the world. Brisker said he picked up some of the language as a player, but to earn a living in Israel he needed to learn to speak, read, and write it properly. Every day from 8:30 a.m. to 1 p.m. Brisker joined other ulpan students, predominantly from Russia but also from places like Yugoslavia and Spain, to study. As a member of Maccabi Tel Aviv for three years he was a star in Israel, but what impressed his classmates was his already vast knowledge of the country, not his dazzling displays on the court.

"I like [ulpan] a lot because most people there don't know me from playing basketball, they know me from ulpan," Brisker told me in 2012. "There are a couple of guys older than me, a couple of guys my age, but the rest are twenty-four or twenty-five. We learn about all the major holidays and Israeli traditions, but this is stuff I've known for years. For me, it's a little different, because a lot of people in my class have just come to Israel now, but I have been in Israel for thirteen years."

Most of the ulpan classes focus on the nitty-gritty of Hebrew grammar and punctuation. When he and I spoke, Brisker was working to master *zman avar* (past tense) and *zman atid* (future tense), and his Facebook wall showed a post from his instructor giving an example of the same verb being conjugated in *pa'al* (active), *hit'pael* (reflexive), and *nif'al* (passive). More broadly, ulpan is meant as a tool to help integrate newcomers into Israeli society. Brisker, however, said he felt integrated as soon as he arrived back in 1993. The people embraced him immediately and treated him with nothing but warmth, making Israel feel like home in his very first season. Still, he said in his mannerisms and behavior he remains more American than Israeli. As he told me, "I was there [Detroit] more years than I was here [Israel], so it's kind of hard to change my ways." Certainly one of the greatest examples of his unchanged ways is his lack of interest in politics, unlike many Israelis who have intense regular debates about the local and international issues of the day.

"I've never done it in my life in the States and definitely not here," Brisker said about his lack of political involvement. "I've never voted in my life, and I probably never will. It's just not me."

The Israeli Way

Some players who stay in Israel do pay particularly close attention to the country's political issues. Over coffee in Tel Aviv in 2011, Campbell sounded every bit the prototypical Israeli when talking about his reflections on the nation's politics. He spoke passionately of his fondness for the late Prime Minister Yitzhak Rabin, and he told me in vivid detail about where he and his wife were when they found out about Rabin's assassination. He also made it clear that, although he was born and raised in America, he keeps himself completely up to date on Israeli political affairs.

"I've always voted," Campbell said. "Benjamin Netanyahu was my man for a while, but then again, in politics, they change so much, and there are so many different influences. But I like the fact that Netanyahu realized that [Mahmoud] Ahmadinejad [Iran's president at the time] is very close to having a nuclear weapon, and if America can't stand by Israel, Israel is going to have to do something alone. He opened the gates to it when he went to Capitol Hill and told them, 'If you're not going to stand by me, I'm going to have to protect Israel.' You've got to do what you've got to do to protect Israel."

Campbell said that people tend to assume he doesn't pay attention to politics because he seldom brings it up in conversation. However, once others start on the topic he is quick to weigh in. He said he constantly watches the news, to the point of driving his wife and son crazy, and he often gets into heated political debates with his neighbor, a religious Jew. His outspokenness got him into some hot water when he was playing for a third-division team in the Arab village of Kafr Qara in 2016. The team is owned by and predominantly composed of Arab Israelis, and tensions arose when Arab Israeli journalists asked Campbell about the recent spate of stabbings of Israeli civilians by Palestinian assailants. Campbell told me that he referred to the killings as "senseless" and that the media subsequently wrote that they could feel his hatred of Arabs through his words.

"I got a lot of backlash from some of the Arab coaches and whatever, but I didn't care—I defended myself," Campbell said. "That's the way I feel. I said, 'I don't hate Arabs. But I love Jews.' There's no hatred there. I have nothing against non-violent Muslims. These are innocent people being killed—just innocent people being killed going to work, kids being killed in the street. That's how it all started."

A Rite of Passage, for Parents and Kids

Whether political or apolitical, all former players who have children in Israel must accept that those children will join Tzahal (Israel's armed forces) when they turn eighteen. Mandatory conscription has been a reality of Israeli life since the country's founding in 1948, and no matter the level of stardom they may have achieved on the hardwood, African American players must go through the same difficult experience as all parents in the country. I asked Brisker whether that reality made him feel even more Israeli, but he said it simply made him feel like more of a father who worries. "I think ahead, of course—for an American, it's a challenge because we don't have to go to the army, you know?" Brisker said. "But I understand this is how it is in the country, and my son will serve in the army and my daughter will serve in the army, like everybody else. No problem. I'm not trying to get them out of it. They have to do it—they're Israeli citizens."

Even so, accommodations can be made for especially talented basketball players. Brisker's son Michael, for example, played well enough with his youth teams and on Israeli junior national teams that he was recruited by major American college basketball programs. Accordingly, the Briskers considered seeking a deferral of his service until the completion of his college career, an accommodation that has been granted to multiple Israeli basketball prospects over the years, including eventual NBA player Gal Mekel, who attended Wichita State prior to enlisting.

When I spoke to Dawson in 2012 he said his sons, Shawn and Tyler, had chosen not to pursue the American college route. However, he hoped that both of them, then seventeen and fourteen, would be considered good enough basketball prospects to earn military classification as a *sportaee*—an elite athlete whose service is steered away from combat duty. I spoke on the phone with Dawson just months before Shawn was set to enlist, and his tone conveyed a mix of admiration and worry. "He wants to do the army, but no one wants to go on the front line, fighting, I would think," Dawson told me. "We're just going to go through the process and see what happens. I told him, 'If you have to do it [fight on the front lines], then it's supposed to happen.' Since they were little, they both wanted to do the army. If you're going to live in Israel as an Israeli, you will do the army. So I wouldn't even try to talk him out of that. The bottom line is, hope for the best. It's out of my hands—I have no control," he admitted with a sigh.

In the end, Shawn Dawson didn't receive any special sports-related status or serve in the Israel Defense Forces. Rather, a routine pre-enlistment physical showed he had a high level of protein, and although subsequent follow-up exams were inconclusive, the IDF did not want to take a chance on the potential medical risk and released him. And although his younger brother Tyler did serve, the IDF accommodated his basketball career and he was able to complete his military service while playing for Maccabi Rishon LeZion.

Sims's eldest child Danyelle, now twenty-seven years old, completed her mandatory two-year service in the Israeli Navy. Sims expressed amazement at the speed with which Israeli youth grow up during their time in the military, a transformation he's reminded of whenever he asks his daughter for detailed accounts of her experiences. "She was in a special unit, the *Shayetet*, it's like the SEALs," Sims said. "This is all I can say before she kills me! (laughs). She's always saying, 'I can't tell you anything.' I say, 'I'm your father. Don't worry, I'm not going to tell anybody. I put diapers on you!' She's like, 'I can't tell you *Aba* [Dad].'"

Thankfully for Sims, one thing he did know is that his daughter's role was administrative and not on the front lines. Israeli women can serve in combat roles, but not those who are in special forces units such as the Shayetet. His second child, twenty-five-year-old son Ittai, wanted to join but has a kidney problem that kept him out of the army entirely. In lieu of army service, Ittai spent three years doing *Sherut Leumi*, essentially community service for those unable to serve. When we spoke on the topic, Sims's youngest son Guy was only twelve years old (he is now seventeen). Although Sims advocates mandatory service for all Israeli citizens, he admitted to being happy that his middle child didn't have to join and hoped that his youngest would have an administrative job. More than 95 perrcent of the country's combat soldiers are male, so parents are always particularly concerned about the roles their sons are assigned.

"The young ones here today, they want to be fighters, and it's no joke," Sims told me in 2012. "There's no war [presently] like Vietnam, but anything can happen … I saw things that happen in the army, even by accident [during training exercises]. And then, when their group is called, they end up going to Lebanon, or Gaza, things happen, man. These guys are fighters, they're not afraid of anything at that age. They're not afraid, but their parents are scared. When you asked me about my daughter, I wasn't so worried about her. It's the boys you worry about. All the parents worry about the boys."

**

Years removed from the peak of their celebrity, retired African American players describe their lives in Israel as decidedly normal. They fret over the rising cost of living, work hard at their respective jobs, and value their time with family and friends (including one another: many of the players I spoke to have become quite close over the years). Their experiences may not be perfect, but their lives tend to be, on balance, happy ones. Dawson told me he knew in advance that staying in Israel would be to his detriment from a career perspective, but he chose to stay anyway, for his children. Even with his inability to find professional fulfillment, it's a choice he is more than satisfied with.

"I hit the lottery," Dawson said. "I have two great sons that are good people, and it was worth everything [to stay in Israel]. I love this country. I found my family and my wife's family here. I have good friends. [Israel has] been good to me. Everybody's got problems, but I love the country. There are good parts and bad parts, just like anywhere, but I have no complaints. I hope that Israel feels as good about me as I do about it."

The affection for Israel that Dawson and others express so warmly, Campbell literally wears proudly. When I met him for the first time, I was intrigued by Campbell's necklace. It was a chain with two pendants, one a gold basketball and the other a *hamsa*, the palm-shaped amulet that is said to to ward off the evil eye according to Jewish and other cultures. I asked him how he came to wear such interesting pieces.

"This is my basketball I've had since college and [the hamsa represents] my love of Israel, right there," Campbell told me. "That's my protection on the court—that's what it symbolizes to me and I've been wearing it for twenty-five years," he said. "This one [pointing to the hamsa], my wife's mother gave me this in '95."

I was struck by the symbolism of these two pendants. Campbell was a basketball player first, but after the game brought him to Israel, he fell in love with the country and with one of its citizens, and he (like Neverson, Dawson, Sims, Brisker, Stanley Brundy, and others) ended up staying. Now, as surprising as it may be to him and to people he meets, the hamsa has become as much a part of his identity as the basketball.

"Even in the States, people are always coming up to me, wanting to know about [the pendants]," he said. "Sometimes Jewish people come up and say, 'Where'd you get this from?!' And I tell them, 'I live in Israel. I'm Israeli.'"

APPENDIX:
PROFILES OF SIGNIFICANT
INDIVIDUALS

David Blu, thirty-seven, was born in Los Angeles to a Jewish mother and an African American father who converted to Judaism. The 6-foot-7, 240-pound Blu played collegiately at the University of Southern California and for Maccabi Tel Aviv four separate times between 2002 and 2014, winning two Euroleague championships. Born David Bluthenthal, he changed his name to Blu, for reasons described in Chapter 11. Blu is a naturalized citizen of Israel, and he represented Israel twice on its national team. He is currently a commercial real estate specialist in and around Los Angeles.

Mark Brisker, forty-eight, was born in Detroit, Michigan. The 6-foot-5, 180-pound Brisker played collegiately at Central Michigan and at Stetson. He first came to Israel in 1993 and played for five different Israeli teams, including Maccabi Tel Aviv, before retiring in 2006. After living in the United States for a few years, Brisker, a naturalized citizen, returned to Israel in 2011. He currently lives in Neot Morde-chai, a kibbutz in the northern part of Israel, with his girlfriend and his son and daughter from his first marriage. Brisker's son Michael is an up-and-coming basketball prospect who recently represented Israel at the under-18 European Championship and currently plays for Maccabi Ra'anana in Israel's second division.

Tal Brody, seventy-four, was born to a Jewish family in Trenton, New Jersey. He played collegiately at the University of Illinois and was picked 12th overall in the 1965 NBA Draft by the Baltimore Bullets. Brody passed up the opportunity to play in the NBA in favor of signing with Maccabi Tel Aviv, leading the team to the 1977 European Cup championship. After Maccabi defeated CSKA Moscow in the semi-finals, Brody uttered his iconic Hebrew quote, "We are on the map, and we are staying on the map. Not only in sports, but in everything." Brody became the first sportsman to be awarded the Israel Prize, Israel's highest civilian honor, in 1979. Since 2010 Brody has served as the first international Goodwill Ambassador for Israel, assisting with Israel's international diplomacy efforts. He lives in Netanya, Israel, with his wife, Tirtza.

Stanley Brundy, fifty, was born in New Orleans, Louisiana. The 6-foot-6, 210-pound Brundy played collegiately at DePaul before being taken in the second round of the 1989 NBA Draft (32nd overall). He played one year in the NBA before taking his career overseas, and he has primarily played in Israel since 1999. He eventually earned his citizenship and now lives in Nes Ziona with his wife, Limor, and their two sons, Nadav and Dorian.

Will Bynum, thirty-four, was born in Chicago, Illinois. He played for Crane High School in Chicago before attending the University of Arizona and Georgia Tech University. Bynum spent the 2006–07 and 2007–08 seasons with Maccabi Tel Aviv, playing with, among others, eventual NBA player Omri Casspi. Bynum leveraged his success with the club to return to the NBA, and he has since bounced between the NBA and teams in China. He is currently playing in the NBA G League, hoping for a return to the NBA.

Fred Campbell, fifty-five, was born in Macon, Georgia, and played collegiately at Fort Hays State University, an NAIA school in Kansas. He first came to Israel in 1992 and has stayed in the country since, with stints playing in the first, second, and third divisions. During his time in Israel, Campbell got married, converted to Judaism, and served in the Israel Defense Forces. For more than three years, he held a job in Israel's thriving high-tech industry, which he left to partner with his best friend and run a motorbike company. He and his partner import bikes from all over the world and host motorbike shows and exhibitions. All the while he has continued to play in the third division. Campbell lives in Netanya with his wife, Liat, and their son, Toi, himself an aspiring basketball player.

Cory Carr, forty-one, was born in Fordyce, Arkansas. He played collegiately at Texas Tech and represented the United States on the under-20 and under-21 national teams. The 6-foot-4, 220-pound Carr was a second-round pick in the 1998 NBA Draft, being selected 49th overall by the Atlanta Hawks. After playing one lockout-shortened NBA season for the Chicago Bulls, he took his career overseas, signing in France. He first played in Israel in 2000, representing Maccabi Ra'anana. He has played for more than a dozen teams in Israel since then, in the first, second, and third divisions, and he obtained his Israeli citizenship in 2009. He currently plays in the third division, in addition to coaching youth basketball and working in player development. He lives in Ra'anana with his wife, Ilana, and their daughter.

Omri Casspi, twenty-nine, was born in Holon, Israel. The 6-foot-9, 225-pound Casspi made his professional debut for Maccabi Tel Aviv at only seventeen years old, and he ended up playing three seasons for the club and one for Hapoel Galil Elyon. Casspi was selected 23rd overall in the 2009 NBA Draft by the Sacramento Kings, for whom he became the first ever Israeli born player in the NBA. Casspi has been in the NBA since, playing eight seasons for five different teams. He married his Israeli girlfriend, Shani Ruderman, in June 2016, and he runs the Omri Casspi Foundation, which works with the National Basketball Players Association to organize annual goodwill trips for NBA players, WNBA players, and other celebrities to visit Israel.

Ramon Clemente, thirty-one, was born in Queens, New York. The 6-foot-7, 225-pound Clemente played collegiately at Wichita State before spending four seasons in Israel, from 2009 to 2013. He now plays professionally in Argentina.

Joe Dawson, fifty-seven, was born in Tuscaloosa, Alabama. The 6-foot-6, 222-pound Dawson played collegiately for Southern Mississippi before taking his career overseas, beginning in France. His first stint in Israel was with Hapoel Holon in suburban Tel Aviv in 1987. He subsequently left the country to play in Europe but returned and ended up playing more than 14 years in Israel, eventually becoming a citizen. Dawson presently lives in Rehovot with his second wife, Orna, and his two sons from his first marriage, Shawn and Tyler. Tyler plays for Maccabi Rishon LeZion, while Shawn recently left the team to sign with Bnei Herzliya and is widely considered the most likely Israeli to next make the jump to the NBA.

Marcus Fizer, thirty-nine, was born in Inkster, Michigan. The 6-foot-8, 265-pound Fizer was a consensus All-American at Iowa State University and was selected fourth overall in the 2000 NBA Draft by the Chicago Bulls. He played more than five seasons in the NBA before taking his career overseas, eventually signing with Maccabi Tel Aviv for the 2007–08 and 2008–09 seasons. He tried to return to Israel with Maccabi Ashdod in 2010 but failed his physical and wasn't signed. He is currently an entrepreneur, motivational speaker, and youth minister based out of Las Vegas, Nevada.

Pini Gershon, sixty-six, was born in Tel Aviv. He played professionally until an injury ended his career prematurely at the age of twenty-four. Gershon began coaching in the Israeli league in 1976, and in 1993 he lead Hapoel Galil Elyon to the Israeli championship, the first time in thirty-six years the title was won by a team other than Maccabi Tel Aviv. A long-time critic of Maccabi, Gershon surprised everyone when he signed with the club in 1998, coaching the team until 2001. His controversial remarks about African Americans, discussed in detail in Chapter 12, led him to resign in 2001, though he returned to coach the team from 2003 to 2006 and 2008 to 2010, and he served as an assistant coach with the club in 2014–15. In all, Gershon won three Euroleague championships with the team.

Brandon Hunter, thirty-seven, was born in Cincinnati, Ohio. The 6-foot-7, 260-pound Hunter played collegiately at Ohio University. The Boston Celtics selected him in the second round of the 2003 NBA Draft (56th overall), and Hunter played one season for Boston and one for the Orlando Magic before heading overseas. He spent the 2009–10 season with Hapoel Jerusalem and returned to Israel in 2012–13 to play for Hapoel Gilboa Galil. He is currently living in Cincinnati, working as a real estate broker and basketball agent.

Andrew Kennedy, fifty-one, was born in Kingston, Jamaica. The 6-foot-7, 228-pound Kennedy played collegiately at Virginia and was a second-round pick (43rd overall) in the 1987 NBA Draft. He played 12 seasons in Israel, the most ever by a foreign player, living as far north as Galil Elyon, as far south as Eilat, and in suburban Tel Aviv and other cities in between. He returned to the United States upon his retirement, holding a variety of different positions, including scouting for the Houston Rockets.

Sylven Landesberg, twenty-seven, was born in Brooklyn, New York, to a Jewish father and a Christian, Trinidadian mother. The 6-foot-6, 210-pound Landesberg was a McDonald's All-American in high school and played two years at the University of Virginia before declaring himself eligible for the 2010 NBA Draft. Upon going undrafted, Landesberg signed with Maccabi Haifa and played for the club from 2010 to 2012 before moving to Maccabi Tel Aviv, the club that he has played for since. Landesberg is a naturalized Israeli citizen and has served in the Israel Defense Forces.

Shimon Mizrahi, seventy-eight, has been chairman of Maccabi Tel Aviv since 1969. Also a lawyer who specializes in motor vehicle accident cases, Mizrahi was named one of *Time* magazine's 50 best sports managers in 2007, and he was awarded the Israel Prize for Sport in 2011.

Carlton Neverson, fifty-nine, was born in New York and played collegiately at the University of Pittsburgh. He converted to Judaism in 1984, prior to arriving in Israel. The 6-foot-5 Neverson played 16 seasons of Israeli basketball, 14 in the first division and two in the second. He has stayed in the country since his retirement, working in coaching and player development in a variety of capacities and roles. Most recently, he was the head coach of each of the Hapoel Lud men's team (in the third division) and women's team (in the second division), and he instructs at Sal Stars, a basketball camp run by Aulcie Perry.

Anthony Parker, forty-two, was born in Naperville, Illinois. The 6-foot-6, 221-pound Parker played collegiately at Bradley. He was a first-round pick (21st overall) in the 1997 NBA Draft and played three seasons in the NBA before going overseas. He played for Maccabi Tel Aviv from 2000–02 and then again from 2003–06, winning three Euroleague Championships, two Euroleague Most Valuable Player Awards, and five Israeli championships in that time. Upon returning to the NBA, Parker wore the number 18 for both the Toronto Raptors and Cleveland Cavaliers, a tribute to his time in Israel and his fans there (the number 18 being a symbol of life and good fortune in Judaism). He is currently a scout for the Orlando Magic.

Aulcie Perry, sixty-seven, was born in Newark, New Jersey, and played collegiately at historically Black Bethune–Cookman University in Daytona Beach, Florida. Discovered by Maccabi Tel Aviv manager Shmuel Maharovsky while playing at New York's famed Rucker Park, the 6-foot-10, 215-pound Perry signed with the club in 1976. A few months later Perry helped Maccabi defeat CSKA Moscow in the semi-finals and then Mobilgirgi Varese in the finals to win the club's first European Championship. Prior to his third season in Israel, Perry converted to Judaism and was given the Hebrew name Elisha Ben-Avraham. A few years later, a worsening drug problem led to legal problems for Perry in both Israel and back in the United States, and he ended up serving eight years in prison. He subsequently chose to return to Israel, specifically Tel Aviv, where he has lived since 1995.

Simmy Reguer, seventy-one, was born in New York, the son and grandson of rabbis. He played professionally in Israel for seven years, then coached in the country for 18 years before resigning in 1992. Except for a brief coaching comeback in 2004, Reguer has been a popular basketball broadcaster since his retirement from coaching, covering the Israeli league as well as the NBA on Sport 5 (Israel's equivalent of ESPN). His autobiography, *Rak Reshet* (Hebrew for Nothing but Net), was released in 2017.

Jeron Roberts, forty-one, was born in Covina, California. The 6-foot-6, 210-pound Roberts played collegiately at the University of Wyoming before heading overseas. He began playing professionally in Israel in 2000, became a naturalized citizen in 2006, played for the Israeli national team in 2007, and played his final season in Israel in 2012. He returned to the United States upon his retirement and has since held roles as a college coach and athletic director.

Derrick Sharp, forty-six, was born in Orlando, Florida. The 6-foot, 185-pound Sharp played collegiately at South Florida before beginning his professional career in the Israeli second division in 1993. He was eventually picked up by Maccabi Tel Aviv, for which he played from 1996 to 2011. In that time he became an Israeli citizen, served in the Israel Defense Forces, and played for the Israeli national team. After retiring, he served as an assistant coach for Maccabi for two seasons. He also partnered with an Israeli restauranteur to open Shine and Sharp, a high-end steakhouse near Maccabi's Nokia (now known as Menora Mivtachim) Arena. He eventually left Israel, and currently lives in Florida. His eldest son from his first marriage, DJ, was born in Israel and currently plays professionally there for Bnei Herzliya.

Willie Sims, fifty-nine, was born in New York. His African American grandmother converted to Judaism to marry his Jewish grandfather, and the Sims family considered itself Hebrew (discussed in detail in Chapter 11). The 6-foot-3, 195-pound Sims played collegiately at Louisiana State University, and he was selected by the Denver Nuggets in the fifth round of the 1981 NBA Draft (101st overall). Sims represented the United States in two Maccabiah Games, hitting the game-winning shot in the gold medal game in 1977. He played professionally for six different Israeli teams, including Maccabi Tel Aviv, during a career that spanned from 1981 to 1999. Sims and his wife, Ariela, live in Tel Aviv with their youngest son, Guy. Their middle child, son Ittai, lives in Herzliya, and their eldest child, daughter Danyelle, married Israeli basketball star Gal Mekel in 2016.

Amar'e Stoudemire, thirty-five, was born in Lake Wales, Florida. He declared for the 2002 NBA Draft straight out of high school and was selected by the Phoenix Suns with the ninth overall pick. Stoudemire played 14 seasons in the NBA, being chosen as an All-Star six times. He visited Israel for the first time in 2010, and in 2013 he was an assistant coach for the Canadian basketball team at the Maccabiah Games. That same year he purchased a minority ownership stake in the Israeli basketball club Hapoel Jerusalem. In 2016, Stoudemire relinquished his shares and signed a two-year contract to play for the club, moving to Jerusalem with his wife, Alexis, and their four children.

Deon Thomas, forty-six, was born in Chicago, Illinois. He played at legendary Simeon High School in Chicago and then collegiately at the University of Illinois. The 6-foot-9, 231-pound Thomas was a second-round pick in the 1994 NBA Draft, taken 28th by the Dallas Mavericks. He played in the preseason for the Mavs but never appeared in a regular season NBA game before taking his career overseas. Thomas first played in Israel in 1998, representing Maccabi Rishon LeZion. He played two seasons for Maccabi Tel Aviv, winning the Euroleague Championship both years, and subsequently he played two more seasons in the Israeli first division for Maccabi Givat Shmuel and Maccabi Haifa. He became an Israeli citizen in 2003, and he currently lives with his wife, Dafna (who is Israeli), and their daughters, Gabrielle and Liel, in Naperville, Illinois.

Chris Watson, forty-two, was born in White Plains, New York. The 6-foot-7 Watson played collegiately at Niagara University. He began playing in Israel in 1999 and competed for a number of teams in the first, second, and third divisions until his retirement in 2016. Watson became an Israeli citizen in 2003 and played for the Israeli national team twice. He returned to White Plains upon his retirement, and he is currently an account manager at Life Time Athletic fitness centers.

Jitim Young, thirty-five, was born in Chicago, Illinois. The 6-foot-2, 190-pound Young played at the renowned Gordon Tech High School in Chicago and then collegiately at Northwestern University. He played in Israel for three seasons, from 2009 to 2012. He has since moved back to Chicago, where he does color commentary, runs basketball camps, and lives with his girlfriend Neohrah, a Black Hebrew Israelite he met in his time in Israel.

SOURCE NOTES

1. In the Beginning

2 "Israel ... is a monotheistic melting pot": Dan Senor and Saul Singer, *Start-up Nation* (Toronto: McClelland & Stewart, 2011), 17.

3 "almost manic self-confidence": Ze'Ev Chafets, *Heroes and Hustlers* (New York: William Morrow and Co., 1986), 45.

4 "I felt completely at home as soon as I landed in Israel": *Jerusalem Post*, September 8, 2010.

4 "The prototype for a Kevin Garnett" and "We used to go over to Amsterdam for a preseason tournament": *Heeb*, December 16, 2008.

5-8 Israeli newspaper headlines, quotes from Ralph Klein, details of the postgame celebrations, and quote from Jarvie Grant all from Bar-Eli, Michael and Yair Galily, "From Tal Brody to European Champions: Early Americanization and the 'Golden Age' of Israeli Basketball, 1965-1979." *Journal of Sports History* 32, no. 3 (Fall 2005): 401-422.

8 "Those were the best nine months of my life," "Maybe it's because I play ball," and "Aulcie Perry for Prime Minister": *Ebony Magazine*, February 1978.

9 "Bringing honor to the people of Israel": *New York Times*, September 10, 1980.

2. The Path to Israel

12-13 "Every other team in the Israeli league had to find foreign players": *Houston Chronicle*, April 21, 1985.

13 "The new country would "open wide the gates of the homeland to every Jew" from "The Declaration of the Establishment of the State of Israel": *Official Gazette*: Number 1; Tel Aviv, 5 Iyar 5708, 14.5.1948.

16-17 Details regarding the situations of Dailey, Rankin, and Irving from *Sports Illustrated*, April 29, 1985.

16 "It was a big lie in basketball": *Boston Globe*, March 22, 1987.

16 "circumstantial circumcisions": *Baltimore Sun*, February 13, 1996.

16 Reference to the editorial cartoon from Yair Galily and Ken Sheard, "Cultural Imperialism and Sport: The Americanization of Israeli Basketball" *Sport in Society*, 5, no. 2 (Summer 2002): 55–78.

16 "Orthodox Globetrotters": *Boston Globe*, March 22, 1987.

17 "I knew a girl who got married three different times, with three basketball players": *Los Angeles Times*, April 1, 1985.

17-18 "In the beginning, I wasn't 100 percent sure" and "After a decade in Israel, though, he admitted that his wife": *Miami Sun-Sentinel*, April 17, 1992.

18 "I want to join the fold": *New York Times*, September 10, 1980.

20 "The Midrash says, 'G-d loves proselytes dearly'": www.jewishvirtuallibrary.org/conversion-to-judaism.

3. Why Israel?

25 "Mostly everybody [85 percent] speaks English": http://www.draftexpress.com/blog/Pooh-Jeter/.

26 Video about "Zalman the Man": https://www.youtube.com/watch?
v=nS3IqV3skQQ&feature=em-subs_digest&list=TLeRd-
spN40Dhk.

26 "Outsiders customarily perceive Israel in grandiose terms" and other
Chafets quotes, Chafets, *Heroes and Hustlers.*

32-33 Information about Jeremy Tyler's difficult year in Israel from
New York Times, November 8, 2009.

36 "You're going to heaven" : *Tablet*, June 13, 2004.

4. They're Not in Kansas Anymore

43 The record for largest plate of hummus was set in May 2010: http://
www.guinnessworldrecords.com/world-records/largest-serving-
of-hummus.

5. Violence

51 "Jerusalem has been destroyed at least twice, besieged 23 times,
attacked an additional 52 times, and captured and recaptured 44
times": https://www.archaeological.org/lectures/abstracts/9873.

52-53 The story of Donald Royal's witnessing (and narrowly avoiding)
a bombing at a Tel Aviv mall, including quotes relating to the incident, from *Orlando Sentinel*, May 11, 1995.

53 The story of Donald Royal and Maccabi Tel Aviv continuing to
play during the Gulf War from *Sports Illustrated*, March 11, 1991.

57 "After a while you develop a thick skin", "You know, in the States
we might have somebody," and "In the midst of war": all from "Go
Israel—In times of war and peace, one constant in Israel is unrelent-
ing passion for basketball," *SLAM Magazine*, May 2010.

59 "You learn to watch out for things that don't look right": *The Tavis
Smiley Show*. PBS. December 10, 2004.

60 "The army was definitely an experience": http://amirbogen.blog-spot.ca/2007_02_01_archive.html.

61 "You can only start eating when your commander": *Israeli Yellow Nation*, Season One Episode One: https://www.youtube.com/watch?v=LMVs8edpi-8.

63 "In troubled times, you realize two things": *Chicago Sun-Times*, August 6, 2006.

64 Gilad Shalit's comments about sports providing a common denominator with his captors quoting Shalit's Hebrew *Yedioth Ahronoth* newspaper column: *New York Times*, June 15, 2012.

65 "We *want* to keep playing," "Of all the bad things," and "Some Israelis serve in the military": *Sports Illustrated*, March 11, 1991.

67 "They knew where Israel was": http://www.celticslife.com/2013/06/what-hell-happened-toearl-williams.html.

6. Religion

75 "It was a very important and emotional event for me": http://amir-bogen.blogspot.ca/2007_02_01_archive.html.

79-80 "All I could do was laugh," "I had never even considered," and "Billy certainly was not shy": *Jerusalem Post*, August 2, 2006.

80-82 Details of and quotes regarding the "Zalgiris Miracle": http://www.espn.com/insider/story?id=1794483.

7. On-Court Impact

86 "It's much cheaper to buy a ready-made player": *Financial Times UK*, June 23, 1987.

86 "To call a team that is 80 percent foreign": http://www.ynetnews.com/articles/0,7340,L-3203622,00.html.

87 "Hell, if I was in America": *Jerusalem Post*, November 5, 2003.

87 "The Americans take it more seriously": *Baltimore Sun*, February 13, 2006.

8. Love and Basketball

103 "She saw how handsome a guy I was" and "We used to do a lot of sneaking around" from a February 2007 episode of *Chamishiot* (Hebrew for "the Fives"), a basketball show on Channel 5, Israel's equivalent of ESPN.

105 The 2016 University of Washington study: Skinner, Allison L. and Hudac, Caitlin M. "'Yuck, you disgust me!' Affective bias against interracial couples," *Journal of Experimental Social Psychology* 68 (January 2017): 68–77.

106 "I have nothing against Saras" and "The greatest danger to our people is assimilation": http://www.ynetnews.com/articles/0,7340,L-3223268,00.html.

9. The Israeli Yankees

116 "It's 2010, and I'm with Cleveland": Anthony Parker about Lebron. Retrieved from https://www.youtube.com/watch?v=Mu_1D-kVUm3I.

117 "This is my third consecutive Euroleague Final Four": http://www.espn.com/nba/news/insider/story?id=2163611.

120 "The same Maccabi is not good enough anymore": *Jerusalem Post*, February 23, 1995.

119 "The number 18, it means 'chai'": https://web.archive.org/web/20100208201959/http://theclevelandfan.com/article_detail.php?blgId=5669.

123 "Yesterday night there was a party attended by a number of basketball players": from a statement police spokesman Micky Rosenfeld gave *Agence France Presse* on January 5, 2008.

124 "All that Will was trying to do was to escape the danger": *Jerusalem Post*, January 7, 2008.

126 "Nothing short of a miracle": *Jerusalem Post*, April 30, 2008.

127-128 Details of Aulcie Perry's issues with drugs and the law from *Jerusalem Post*, September 8, 2008, and Alexander Wolff, *Big Game, Small World.* (New York: Warner Books, 2002), 210-216.

129 "He came out, the son of a bitch" and "It was a big hall with hundreds of people": *Heeb*, December 16, 2008.

10. How the Other Half Lives

137-138 "Bigger than Michael Jordan": *Seattle Times*, May 28, 2002.

141 "In the end, everything comes down to this": http://amirbogen. blogspot.ca/2007_02_01_archive.html.

11. Black and Jewish

151-152 The description of the terms "Jew", "Hebrew", and "Israelite" is a high level summary of content from a variety of sources, including: http://www.jewfaq.org/whoisjew.htm; http://www.forward. com/articles/11238/#ixzz1m7EVavdV; and https://www.britannica. com/topic/Jew-people.

154 "I study Torah all the time" and the description of Stoudemire's religious tattoos and jewelry: from *Washington Jewish Week*, August 1, 2013.

154 "The Scripture speaks about Jerusalem as a holy place": http:// www.theplayerstribune.com/amare-stoudemire-knicks-suns-israel/.

158-159 Details and background of Amar'e Stoudemire's faith and quotes: from *The Forword*, August 1, 2016.

158 "I'm not a religious person": *Washington Jewish Week*, August 1, 2013.

159 "First, astonishment—'How can it be?'": http://www.espn.com/video/clip?id=17781588.

161 "Religion is an Orthodox-or-nothing affair": *Washington Post*, July 11, 2004.

162-163 "In Israel, marriage falls under the jurisdiction of the applicable religious authorities": Hanna Lerner, *Making Constitutions in Deeply Divided Societies* (New York: Cambridge University Press, 2011), 73.

164 "Nearly 7 percent (roughly 435,000 people) of the United States' approximately six million Jews": http://www.aish.com/jw/s/48923742.html.

164 "Black and Jewish" rap video performed by Kali Hawk and Katerina Graham. Retrieved from http://www.funnyordie.com/videos/d056b3dd60/black-and-jewish-black-and-yellow-parody.

12. Racism

169 Statistics about recent rise in anti-Semitism in Europe from *Jerusalem Post*, January 24, 2016.

170 Gershon's speech retrieved from https://www.youtube.com/watch?v=E2iZO5gz_Xw.

171 "If the quotes are correct, I condemn each and every word Pini said": *Jerusalem Post*, July 2, 2001.

173 "For the first time in my life, I felt free!": *Ebony Magazine*, February 1978.

174 "I've never been to a whole country and not seen one Black person": http://grantland.com/features/the-improbable-return-nba-new-jersey-nets-gerald-green/.

174 More than 75 percent of the Israeli population is Jewish: http://www.jewishvirtuallibrary.org/latest-population-statistics-for-israel.

174 Historically, Jews have been from one of two major groups: http://www.myjewishlearning.com/article/sephardic-ashkenazic-mizrahi-jews-jewish-ethnic-diversity/.

174 Israel has a population of more than 120,000 Ethiopian Jews: http://www.cbs.gov.il/reader/newhodaot/hodaa_template.html?hodaa=201211307.

176 Background information on the Black Israelite community from a variety of sources, including *San Francisco Chronicle*, November 15, 2002. and http://www.jta.org/2015/01/04/news-opinion/the-telegraph/from-the-archive-black-hebrews-from-chicago-to-dimona.

176 "These migrants navigate a perilous smuggling route through Egypt and into Israel" and references to south Tel Aviv becoming "South Sudan": *Times of Israel*, December 2, 2013.

181 "According to Yaacov Lozowick": *Tablet*, August 2, 2013.

181 "Why do you care whether these Cushim who are paid in Tel Aviv beat the Cushim who are paid in Greece?": *Jerusalem Post*, July 30, 2013.

181 The court case involving the term "cushi" being Avi Tzaguy vs. Inga Avi Avshalom, January 11, 2007.

186 The academic article analyzing media reports in an attempt to examine the perception of Jewish-Israeli nationality and the boundaries of the Israeli collective was Eran Shor and Yuval Yonay, "Sport, National Identity, and Media Discourse over Foreign Athletes in Israel," *Nationalism and Ethnic Politics* 16, no. 3 (2010): 483-503.

189 "In the State of Israel, there is no room for racism": *Jerusalem Post*, May 20, 2012.